1993

Democracy
and Human Rights
in Developing Countries

Democracy and Human Rights in Developing Countries

Zehra F. Arat

Lynne Rienner Publishers ■ Boulder & London

Some sections of this volume have been adapted from previously published articles. Although the data and the substance of each have been updated and extensively modified for the purposes of the book, a list of the original publications by Arat is as follows:
"Democracy and Economic Development: Modernization Theory Revisited," *Comparative Politics* 21, 1 (October 1988): 21–36.
"Can Democracy Survive Where There Is a Gap Between Political and Economic Rights ?" in David Cingranelli, ed., *Human Rights: Theory and Measurement* (London: Macmillan Press, 1988): 221–235.
"Human Rights and Democratic Instability in Developing Countries," *Policy Studies Journal,* Special Symposium on Human Rights Policies (September 1986): 158–172.

Published in the United States of America in 1991 by Lynne Rienner Publishers, Inc.
1800 30th Street, Boulder, Colorado 80301

and in the United Kingdom by Lynne Rienner Publishers, Inc.
3 Henrietta Street, Covent Garden, London WC2E 8LU

Library of Congress Cataloging-in-Publication Data
Arat, Zehra F.
    Democracy and human rights in developing countries / by Zehra Arat.
    p.   cm.
    Includes bibliographical references and index.
    ISBN 1-55587-500-9 (pb : alk. paper)
1. Human rights—Developing countries. 2. Civil rights—Developing countries. 3. Developing countries—Politics and government. 4. Democracy. I. Title
JC599.D44A73 1991
321.8'09172'4—dc20   91-11280
                                                                                          CIP

British Cataloguing in Publication Data
A Cataloguing in Publication record for this book is available from the British Library.

Printed and bound in the United States of America

The paper used in this publication meets the requirements of the American National Standard for Permanence of Paper for Printed Library Materials Z39.48-1984. ♾

To my parents,
who taught me that everyone is entitled to live in dignity,
and to those who have struggled to establish this entitlement

Contents

Tables and Figures

TABLES

FIGURES

Acknowledgments

Although this study is a product of eight years of research and analysis, my search for an explanation for the decline of democracies began much earlier. The process of democratization in Turkey started in 1946, but has been subject to three military interruptions, which occurred approximately every ten years (1960, 1971, and 1980) and which suppressed civil and political rights. As a citizen of Turkey, I have found the viability of democracy and human rights a natural and continuous concern to me. But my interest in the subject could not have become an intellectual challenge and academic pursuit without the encouragement and support that I received from many.

I am most indebted to Richard Hofferbert and William O'Neill, who not only helped me to clarify my ideas, read several versions of the work, and provided invaluable comments, but also persuaded me that the research deserved to be developed into a book. I deeply appreciate Semih Fırıncıoğlu, who created time in his busy schedule and meticulously produced the graphic art work included in the book. Jacci Rosa, although only a sophomore, accomplished the work of a graduate assistant and, with her wonderful personality and friendship, brought sanity to my lonely work days. Art Weisenseel demonstrated his patience in converting the incompatible data tapes from one filing system to another. I am also very appreciative of the people whose studies are referred to in this book. Without their accomplishments, my work would be much harder, if at all possible. I am also grateful for the meticulous and skillful editing of Ida May Norton. Of course, whatever errors remain are my contribution, and I am solely responsible.

Last, but not least, I would like to acknowledge the contribution of my husband, who took over my share of family responsibilities and provided me with time to concentrate on my studies; and of my son, who settled for a single parent for many days during the past two years, including an entire summer.

Z. F. A.

1

Introduction:
Social and Economic Rights
as a Condition for Democracy

*There is nothing mysterious about the foundations of a healthy and strong
democracy. The basic things expected by our people of their political and
economic systems are simple. They are: equality of opportunity for youth and
for others; jobs for those who can work; security for those who need it; the
ending of special privilege for the few; the preservation of civil liberties for all;
the enjoyment of the fruits of scientific progress in a wider and constantly rising
standard of living.*—Franklin D. Roosevelt

The 1980s were exciting years for advocates and students of democracy. The
military rule in many Latin American countries, in Turkey, and in Pakistan gave
way to civilian, multiparty electoral systems. The Eastern Bloc countries
moved away from one-party "communist" rule one after the other, illustrating
the process of the domino effect. Authoritarianism in Senegal and the
Philippines was replaced with democratic systems. Major steps toward competitive elections were taken in Jordan, Nepal, and the Soviet Union.

What has been the response to this wave of democratization? Some, especially those who focused on the changes that were taking place in Eastern
Europe, called it "the end of ideology," or "the crisis of authoritarianism."
Others interpreted these simultaneous developments as the triumph of an "ideology"—that of democracy. But is it? In a quite comprehensive discussion of
this trend of democratization demonstrated in the 1980s, Rustow lists differing
underlying reasons for each case without being able to identify a single common denominator, but concludes that due to the "end of the cold war" the world
would be safer for democracy.[1]

Recalling the occurrence of similar events in the past, however, calls for
caution in reaching hasty conclusions. Some other periods in recent history
were also characterized by a process of democratization taking place simultaneously in various parts of the world. What happened to the democratic systems
that were established in the 1950s, or to the democratic institutions founded by
the newly independent states of Africa in the 1960s? Within a few years after
their establishment, many of these regimes were subject to military takeover,
and others were maintained as democracies only in name. Contrary to earlier
expectation, democracy failed to establish itself as the political system that is

1

necessarily approached by all (or even most) countries with increasing levels of socioeconomic development. Some countries that established democratic structures failed to maintain them and shifted back and forth between highly authoritarian and democratic systems. Their numbers are too many to be treated as exceptions to the norm, but only a restricted number of studies have dealt with the question.

Even though democracy has been a popular topic for social scientists in general, and for political scientists in particular, the output has been mostly theoretical, emphasizing what a democratic system should be. Empirical research has appeared in the form of case studies focusing on the democratic experiences of individual countries. The number of systematic comparative studies of democratic systems has been small, and those that exist are limited in scope. Some studies, such as Bingham Powell's *Contemporary Democracies* and Arend Lijphart's *Democracies: Patterns of Majoritarian and Consensus Governments in Twenty-One Countries*, are confined to so-called Western Democracies. Others, which do include non-Western societies, were prompted by the waves of democratization in developing countries in the 1960s or in the 1980s and emphasize the process of transition to democracy and its determinants (e.g., Lipset's *Political Man*; or the series *Democracy in Developing Countries*, edited by Larry Diamond, Juan Linz, and Seymour Martin Lipset). The causes of instability and the decline of democracy, however, have hardly been the focus of studies.

Robert Dahl's famous work, *Polyarchy*, stands out because of its attempt to identify conditions that are pertinent for polyarchy to prevail "for a considerable period of time."[2] Dahl's work, however, does not provide an analysis of the interactions among these conditions or explain how the decline of the regime ultimately occurs, even if favorable conditions lead to the establishment of a polyarchy and sustain it for a time. A recent study that attempts to explain relative stability or instability of democracy in Latin America identifies the characteristics of the founding process as the determinant of the future of democracy. According to Terry Lynn Karl, Latin American democracies that endured for a considerable length have been the ones founded through "pacts" among several elite groups that recognize each other, compromise, and "define the rules of governance on the basis of mutual guarantees for the 'vital interests' of those involved."[3] She does not examine, however, the factors that destabilize a democratic regime that was originally based on such a pact. *The Breakdown of Democratic Regimes*, edited by Juan Linz and Alfred Stepan, which focuses on the instability of democracy and offers an insight to the process of decline, appears as an important volume attempting to fill the void.

This study is concerned with the social, economic, and political conditions that lead to reversals in the efforts of developing countries to maintain democratic institutions and practices. Linz's analysis of breakdown in "Crisis, Breakdown and Reequilibration," which emphasises the effectiveness and efficiency of the regime—issues also raised by Lipset and Dahl—has established the starting point in the research. But the effort to explain the relevance and determinants of regime performance required further elaboration and led to the development of a more comprehensive model that includes a historical perspective on development and democracy. Aware of the changes in the world economic and political structures since the beginning of Western modernization, in this book I focus on the development of the concept of human rights as parallel to the concept of democracy and study the impact of human rights trade-offs on the stability of democracy.

HUMAN RIGHTS AND POLITICAL DEMOCRACY

Although the concept of human rights is old, its content and scope are still debated. Liberalists limit the scope to the traditional civil liberties and political freedoms,[4] whereas others extend it to a broader concept that includes social and economic rights.[5] *The Universal Declaration of Human Rights,* officially recognized by most countries, is broad and includes individual rights that can be classified into T. H. Marshall's threefold typology as follows:

1. *Civil Rights:* freedom from slavery and servitude, torture and inhuman punishment, and arbitrary arrest and imprisonment; freedom of speech, faith, opinion, and expression; right to life, security, justice, ownership, and assembly;
2. *Political Rights:* right to vote and nominate for public office; right to form and join political parties;
3. *Social and Economic Rights:* right to education, work, food, clothing, housing, and medical care.

The rights in the third group, social and economic rights, establish the "new" rights summarized by Marshall as ranging from "the right to a modicum of economic welfare and security to the right to share to the full in the social heritage and to live the life of a civilized being according to the standards prevailing in the society."[6]

This new set of rights, however, is often rejected, particularly by the followers of classical liberalism. The resistance of the liberalists to extend the definition of human rights to include economic and social well-being stems partly from their perception of these two groups of rights as "positive" in the one case and "negative" in the other case. Civil and political rights are considered negative rights in the sense that they forbid action by governments. Governments should not torture citizens; should not conduct arbitrary arrests; should not prevent meetings, political participation, and freedom of speech. Social and economic rights, on the contrary, are positive rights requiring action by governments. Governments should maintain a certain quality of life; should prevent unemployment; assume responsibility in providing food, shelter, and medical care. Moreover, socioeconomic rights are often considered as group rights that can be maintained only at the expense of individual rights (civil-political rights), or vice versa.

The inevitability of a trade-off between individual liberty, reflected in civil-political rights, and social equality, reflected in socioeconomic rights, is argued both by the liberalists and by those who try to justify the need for authoritarian rule at least during the period of transition to a society of equals. The liberalist arguments about the incompatibility of the two groups of rights are criticized by several students of political philosophy.[7] Okin has developed three arguments in defense of social and economic rights:

> First, liberty rights, too, involve expensive and far-reaching activity as well as restraint on the part of the state; . . . Second, it is clear that the criterion of their importance for human well-being does not separate all liberty rights from all economic and social rights. This is reinforced by the fact that the enjoyment of certain basic rights of both types is the necessary condition for the enjoyment of many other rights of both types. Third, no human rights can be regarded as absolute and exceptionless in all circumstances, and the problem of immediate practicability, which can affect both types of rights, need not preclude the admission of a right to the status of a human right.[8]

Insisting that social and economic rights are also individual rights,[9] I present a fourth argument that observes the experience of young states with a democratic form of government: Contrary to the liberal theory, civil and political rights cannot prevail if socioeconomic rights are ignored, and the stability of political democracy (liberal democracy) depends on the extent of balance between the two groups of human rights.

POLITICAL DEMOCRACY AND HUMAN RIGHTS

An examination of civil and political rights shows that they include some major ingredients of a democratic political system. As discussed in the next chapter in detail, democracy is not a have/have not attribute of political systems, and where a political system falls on the scale of democracy largely depends on the extent to which it recognizes and enforces civil and political rights. Thus, in the presence of democratic structures, the more strongly civil and political rights are reinforced in a society, the more democratic it becomes. But what causes governments that already rank high on the scale of democracy to move away from democratic principles and suppress the civil and political rights of their citizens?

One common argument advanced to explain the breakdown of highly democratic systems holds that disintegration takes place because of loss of legitimacy.[10] Legitimacy is defined as the "degree to which institutions are valued for themselves and considered right and proper."[11] Or, more pessimistically, a legitimate political system is considered as the one regarded to be the "least evil" of the systems of government.[12] Lipset identifies legitimacy, in addition to economic development, as a necessary condition for democracy.[13] What constitutes legitimacy, however, not only varies from one type of system to another but also changes over time. For example, feudalism was a legitimate political and social system even though it was based on dominance and inequality. In modern times, however, individual freedom and equality appear to be essential and make systems like feudalism illegitimate and unacceptable. Thus, it is citizens' perception of the role of government that determines the criteria for legitimacy of a political system.

POLITICAL AND SOCIAL DEVELOPMENTS IN THE WEST

The emergence of the nation-state was, in many respects, a turning point in history. The most significant change for purposes of this study is that the individual, not God's command or custom, has appeared as the source of law, sovereignty, and legitimacy. In a secular and emancipated society, members are not under the protection of cultural, spiritual, and religious forces. Social struggle and development in Europe throughout the nineteenth century led to the consensus that individuals have some rights and that these should be guaranteed by governments and constitutions and invoked whenever individuals needed protection against the arbitrariness of either state or society.

Breaking human rights into three elements of citizenship, T. H. Marshall states that "it is possible without doing much violence to historical accuracy, to assign the formative period in the life of each to a different century—civil rights to the eighteenth, political to the nineteenth and social to the twentieth. These periods must, of course, be treated with reasonable elasticity, and there is some evident overlap, especially between the last two."[14] Similarly, Lipset lists the major issues of modern times as the place of religious institutions in the society, extension of "citizenship" to the lower strata, and the distribution of national wealth.[15] He argues that the religious issue "was fought through and solved in most of the Protestant nations in the Eighteenth and Nineteenth Centuries," the "citizenship" or "political rights" issue has also been resolved "in various ways around the Twentieth Century," and the "only key domestic issue today is collective bargaining over differences in the division of the total product within the framework of a Keynesian welfare state."[16]

Though the process of change was slow and not without resistance, the twentieth century has witnessed a major addition to the role of government. It formerly consisted of ruling, maintaining peace and order, and protecting the society from foreign offenders, but the new list of government obligations includes contributing to the "material security" of the members of society.[17] As Moore clearly states, "The Nineteenth-Century notion that society bore no responsibility for the welfare of the population, that it was both especially futile and quite immoral to expect the chief of state to take effective action countering threats to popular welfare, now looks like a minor historical aberration."[18] After such historical changes in their role, governments today are expected to respond to the needs of their citizens rather than simply to rule them—a role that gains importance, especially in highly democratic systems.

LEGITIMACY OF A MODERN DEMOCRATIC SYSTEM

The accountability introduced by elections in a more democratic system makes it necessary for the government to give the impression that it is pursuing collective goals that the majority agrees upon. Legitimacy is based on the belief that in a particular social setting no alternative regime could be more successful in the pursuit of those goals.[19] Therefore, the responsiveness and effectiveness of governments can reinforce or weaken the legitimacy of political systems. A governmental action is responsive if it addresses the public demand, but can be considered effective only if it accomplishes its specific desired end. Responsiveness is the capacity of a regime to find solutions to the major problems facing the political system. Therefore, responsiveness (termed "efficacy" by Linz) is likely to be judged by policy outputs. The extent to which "policy approaches the collective goal" is the main criterion of responsiveness.[20] Effectiveness, on the other hand, involves the actual capacity of government to implement policies formulated to attain the desired results. Thus, it is the achievement of the desired policy impact that influences the perception of effectiveness. Lack of responsiveness or effectiveness weakens the authority of the state and, as a result, the legitimacy of the regime.

In a way, responsiveness is associated with leadership: Leaders are expected to perceive the expectations of citizens and formulate policies to meet their demands. The administrative capability for successful implementation of responsive policies determines the effectiveness of a government. The crucial factor is whether most of the major policies implemented are considered to be responsive and effective by most of the "aware" citizens. A modern democracy, then, to sustain its legitimacy, should pursue policies that respect and protect the civil and political rights of its citizens and provide effective responses to their social and economic needs. A balance in the government's performance in these two areas is crucial to the destiny of democratic political systems.

If we assume that both groups of rights are measured by the same scale, a political system would approach a balance and stability when the ratio (RT) of civil and political rights (CIVIPOL) to social and economic rights (SOCIECO) approaches 1.

$$RT = CIVIPOL / SOCIECO = 1$$

An imbalance between the two groups of rights would be observed if a system ranks high on one and low on the other, and the ratio is greater or less than 1.

$$RT = CIVIPOL / SOCIECO < 1$$
or
$$RT = CIVIPOL / SOCIECO > 1$$

The imbalance in favor of social and economic rights (RT < 1) refers to a condition in which the political system is highly authoritarian but social and economic policies are effective. We would expect the regime to be relatively stable, though not completely immune to challenge or change. If the imbalance is in favor of civil and political rights (RT > 1), however, the regime reflects the characteristics of a democracy doomed to decline. Young democracies of our time tend to appear in this group.

HUMAN RIGHTS TRADE-OFFS

The process of economic and political change in Europe that started in the late medieval era—referred to as "modernization"—displayed a particular pattern that established itself as a model of development. This Western model has been treated as a natural, inevitable process or as an example to be followed by the late developers. The sequence of changes and their universality were observed by Lerner:

> The Western model of modernization exhibits certain components and sequences whose relevance is global. Everywhere, for example, increasing urbanization has tended to raise literacy; rising literacy has tended to increase media exposure; increasing media exposure has "gone with" wider economic participation (per capita income) and political participation (voting). The model evolved in the West is an historical fact. That the same basic model reappears in virtually all modernizing societies on all continents of the world, regardless of variations in race, color, creed will be shown.[21]

The limitations of this analysis were addressed by many, especially by the dependency theorists, and the implied evolutionary thesis was challenged by the ebb and flow of democratization in developing countries during the last half century.[22]

Although the Western experience has had a demonstration effect on the new states, it fails to serve as a viable model that the developing countries can replicate. First, the economic breakthrough of the West was not an isolated phenomenon. It was a process that involved the rest of the world—mostly at the disadvantage of other regions. Its impacts were global, restructuring the world economic and political order. As a result, both the external and internal structures of the contemporary developing countries have reflected some characteristics completely different from those of the premodern Western societies.

Second, as a consequence of the intensive and hegemonic global interactions, compared to the Western experience, the process of change in developing countries has been faster, more compact, simultaneous, and less autonomous. Furthermore, although Western accomplishments in the areas of economic affluence, human rights, and democracy set the goals and standards to be attained for many developing countries, the past Western dominance—and its current repercussions—set major obstacles for the fulfillment of such aspirations.

Do these structural differences mean that democracy is not a viable political system for developing countries? Those who emphasize the lack of economic development and the continuing of economic dependence of former colonies on Western financial institutions and governments tend to see a grim future for democracy in developing countries. Moreover, disappointed by the problems and limitations of democratic practices in the West, they find the system less than desirable. But as for the probability of the system, the considerable success of a few developing countries in adopting and maintaining democracy implies that although they are restrictive factors, structural barriers can be worked around—if the national political elite is committed to the democratic principles, has the visionary capacity to go beyond the Western model, and select development policies accordingly.

However, the Western model has been so overwhelming, with outcomes so desirable, that ignored have been the enormous global transformation of the past five hundred years and the subsequent differences of the historical junctures at which democratization processes were initiated by the old and new developers. The inegalitarian development strategy of the West adopted by the governing elite in young democracies was expected to work in societies where mobility is higher, communication means are more advanced and accessible, and governments are held responsible and accountable.

Although the first democracies emerged under the capitalist system, there is an irreconcilable tension between capitalism and democracy: The first exhibits economic and social inequalities, the latter promotes political equality.[23] European countries handled this paradox, first, by keeping the political process closed to the lower classes, and then, when universal suffrage was granted, by taking some redistributive measures within the context of the welfare state. Masses in developing countries today, however, are not only enfranchised, but also politically more alert and demanding than their European counterparts were a few centuries ago.

Stability of democracy in the West was attributed to the evolution of so-called modern values and a civic culture, including a sense of political efficacy among the people and a high level of trust in their governments. The infrequent presence of such feelings among the citizens of newly emerging states was presented as the reason for the absence or instability of democracy. In a survey conducted forty years ago, Daniel Lerner asked a Turkish shepherd what he would have done were he president of the country. When the shepherd failed to put himself in the president's shoes and was unable to provide an answer, Lerner detected lack of modernity and political efficacy in this observed "traditional way of handling 'projective questions' which require people to imagine themselves or things to be different from what they 'really are.'"[24] Considering the unlikelihood of the shepherd's being the president, however, one can interpret the response as "realistic." Rephrasing the question as "What would you like your government to do for you," on the other hand, would yield a more complete response.

As with the sense of political inefficacy, the lack of trust in government and political cynicism were also interpreted as an impediment for political modernization, which in turn crippled democracy.[25] Given large gaps in the standard of living and income levels in developing countries, however, one can question if cynicism and distrust among the disadvantaged represent "traditionalism" or are evidence of "political awareness."

Access to education, social mobilization, and increasing levels of communication are factors that have important political repercussions. Instead of leading to blind trust in government, however, these factors, which are more likely to be facilitated in democratic polities, tend to result in increasing political awareness and participation. Combined with poor government performance and perceived social injustice, political participation takes the form of protests that are consequential for democratic regimes. Thus, the decline of democracy and the transition to authoritarian rule in developing countries are attributable to policies that create an imbalance between the two groups of human rights, civil-political rights and socioeconomic rights, by ignoring the latter group. The increasing gap between the two groups of rights (resembling the gap between the aspirations and actual achievement observed in the relative deprivation theory) causes frustration and social unrest, which in turn is suppressed by coercive policies. Thus, democratic experiments suffer reversals principally as a function of rather complex linkages between

- Repressive civil and political rights policies, encouraged by
- Social and political unrest, stimulated by
- Ineffective economic performance that ignores social and economic rights of citizens.

Although it may be an oversimplification of the real process, we can develop a scenario for the decline of democracy when the governments fail to pursue balanced human rights policies (see Figure 1.1). In the first phase, the process of democratization is initiated, and civil and political rights follow an increasing trend. Social and economic rights either maintain their previous level or display only slight increases. Although there may be an increasing gap between the two groups of human rights, political equality and liberties serve as sources of legitimacy. In the second phase, the country is highly democratic with stable civil and political rights practices. Social and economic rights, however, maintain their lower level or even start to take a declining course. This is the stage when the perception of injustice intensifies: The former excitement about the political democracy and participation starts to fade, and the legitimacy of the system is questioned. In the third phase, the gap between the two

Figure 1.1 Unbalanced Human Rights Policies and the Decline of Democracy

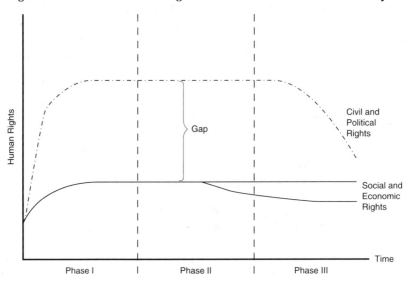

groups of rights increases, and the discontent among the disadvantaged segments is displayed in the form of social unrest. The government tries to suppress the social unrest by imposing restrictions and pursuing coercive policies.
The result is a decline in the level of civil and political rights as well as the
decline of democracy. At the end of this stage, we observe the two groups of
human rights converging, reducing the gap, and establishing more balanced
levels.

This is, of course, only an illustrative scenario. Neither civil and political
rights nor social and economic rights follow such smooth patterns, and there are
infinite interactive patterns that countries may display. Moreover, the length of
each phase would vary from one society to another. Depending on circumstances, people may be more optimistic and patient in some societies than in
others. Variations occur even for the same society. In Turkey, for example,
where such regime transformations have occurred repeatedly, the time for the
completion of the full process (all three phases) has varied between seven and
twelve years. In some developing countries, including the stable democracies
that I prefer to call "fragile democracies," the cycle may take a longer period,
with a prolonged third phase.

Figure 1.2 refers to the interaction between these two groups of
rights and their relation to the level of economic development and to
policy preferences. According to the argument just presented, the independent nation-states that fall into the first three cells are expected to

have fairly stable regimes (RT = 1 or RT < 1), but the ones in the fourth cell are expected to experience significant levels of democratic instability (RT > 1). We may classify in the first cell the socialist dictatorships that are economically developed or rank relatively higher on the scale of social and economic rights. These countries tend to be relatively stable.[26] The second cell includes industrialized capitalist societies that have highly democratic systems. Because of their overall national affluence and welfare policies, social and economic rights are recognized to a large extent. Although a gap exists between the two groups of rights, it is relatively smaller in these countries, which allows them to maintain stable democracies. The third cell consists of the developing countries under authoritarian rule where both groups of rights are largely ignored. Finally, the fourth cell refers to the middle-range developed countries (MDCs) that have failed to improve social and economic rights to the level of their civil and political rights. These countries appear to be unstable political democracies; they lean toward the second cell, but often move back to the third cell.

The increasing popularity of democracy as a political system and the development of civil and political movements as an ideological force lead some of these MDCs to restore their democratic institutions shortly after the decline. But because these democracies experience a high degree of tension between their policy goals,[27] they continue to

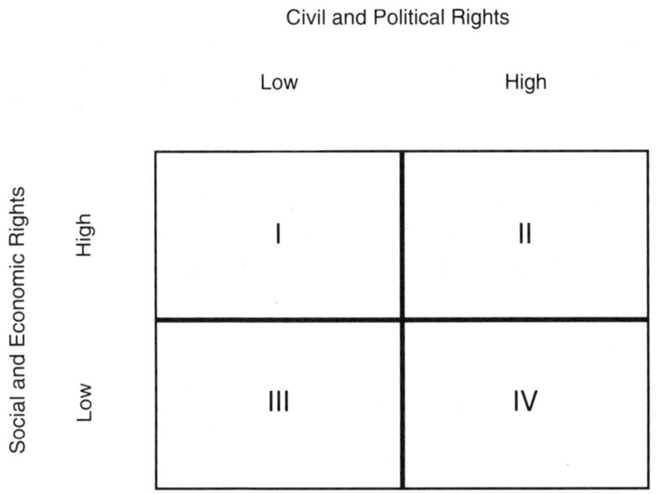

Civil and Political Rights

Low　　　　　　　High

	Low	High
High	I	II
Low	III	IV

Social and Economic Rights

Figure 1.2 Balance and Imbalance Between the Two Groups of Human Rights

stay fragile and are likely to face multiple authoritarian interruptions. The causes of these tensions as well as the policy alternatives that would avoid human rights trade-offs are addressed in later chapters.

STRUCTURE OF THE BOOK

Although this study is designed to assess the factors that determine the failure of developing countries in maintaining democratic systems, it includes a reexamination of democratic political structures and provides a critical review of the existing research on the determinants of democracy.

Explored in Chapter 2 are the meaning of the term "democracy," the change of the definition from "self-government" to "control of government," and the efforts to quantify the new "procedural-structural" definition of democracy. An alternative and new annual measure of democracy for 152 countries for the period from 1948 through 1982 is introduced here. Focusing on the developmentalist approach to the study of democracy, especially the modernization theory, Chapter 3 questions the relevance (or irrelevance) of the approach to the democratic experience of the developing countries today. The validity of modernization theory and its evolutionary thesis for the independent countries of the post–World War II era are tested empirically by using the new measure of democracy. Chapter 4 discusses the explanations of instability presented by several authors from different schools of thought. Taken together, these three chapters offer a critical review of the current literature and present the analytical tools necessary for the reorientation of the research question.

The last two chapters provide the theoretical discussion and the empirical support for the policy model of democracy that focuses on human rights trade-offs. Factors that determine the extent to which social and economic rights are recognized in a society, as well as policy choices of the democratic elite, and the structural constraints (e.g., dependency) are examined in Chapter 5. Finally, Chapter 6 presents policy guidelines for the democratic elite in developing countries. The experiences of three countries—Costa Rica, India, and Turkey—are discussed as case studies to illustrate how policy choices can result in different levels of success in preserving democratic systems. The policy implications presented here, however, are far from being a blueprint for democratic stability, nor do they offer concrete policy prescriptions. The objective is to highlight the conditions that stimulate the decline of democracy and to identify policy alternatives that would eliminate or minimize such conditions.

NOTES

1. Rustow, 1990.
2. Dahl, 1971. See especially pp. 202–203.
3. Karl, p. 9.
4. Bernard Mayo; Cranston; and "Human Rights: A Reply to Professor Raphael,"

Downie.

5. Marshall; Raphael, "Human Rights, Old and New" and "The Rights of Man and the Rights of the Citizens," in Raphael, ed.; Schneider; Peffer; Charvet; Bergmann; Okin; MacMillan; Shue.

6. Marshall, p. 72.

7. See the works by Schneider, Okin, Shue, and MacMillan.

8. Okin, p. 248.

9. Group rights would refer to rights accruing to collectivities such as labor unions; examples are the right to collective bargaining or the right to strike. These rights are quite different from the rights listed in our classification of social and economic rights (e.g., rights to shelter and food), which refer to individual needs and demands.

10. Lipset, 1959, 1960, 1981; Linz, "Crisis, Breakdown, Reequilibration," in Linz and Stepan.

11. Lipset, 1959, p. 71.

12. Linz, 1978.

13. Lipset, 1959 and 1960.

14. Marshall, p. 74.

15. Lipset, 1959, p. 92.

16. Ibid., pp. 92–100.

17. Moore, 1978.

18. Ibid., p. 22.

19. Linz, p. 16.

20. Ibid.

21. Lerner, p. 46.

22. For a brief summary of the major premises of the development and dependency theories and their controversies, see Binder, 1986; and Tony Smith. For some regional applications of these theories, see Klarén and Bossert; and Nyang'oro.

23. Hearn; Cameron.

24. Lerner, p. 24.

25. Almond and Verba, 1963.

26. Recent developments in these countries imply that the imbalance in favor of either group of rights may be a destabilizing factor. In fact, civil and political rights can be the goals around which people organize. However, it is logical to expect the authoritarian political systems to be more stable because they are more likely to prevent communication, articulation, and organization of public demands and to increase the cost of participation through coercive measures.

27. Nagel, p. 96.

2

Defining and
Measuring Political Democracy

*A democracy is a government in the hands of men of low birth,
no property, and vulgar employments.*—Aristotle

*My notion of democracy is that under it the weakest should have the same
opportunity as the strongest.*—Mahatma Gandhi

*Discussions about democracy, arguments for and against it, are intellectually
worthless because we do not know what we are talking about.*
—Bertrand de Jouvenel

POPULARITY OF DEMOCRACY

"Democracy" is a popular and even honorific term. However, words usually
have more than one meaning and meanings change through time. The meanings
attributed to the word "democracy" vary from "a way of life" to "a form of
government." For the purpose of this study, "democracy" is used to cover a narrow concept: the formal decisionmaking methods of political systems.

The common dictionary meaning of "democracy" appears to be "self-government" or "rule by the people," a definition implicit in several usages. But it
provides few guidelines to distinguish a democratic government from others.
James Burnham in the early 1940s pointed out the ambiguity of the definition
with a rather cynical statement: "If we examine not the verbal definitions that
most people, including dictionary-makers, give for 'democracy,' but the ways
in which they use the word in political application to affairs of our time, we will
discover that it does not have anything to do with self-government."[1]

Nevertheless, the implication of "self-government"—or the notion that
power is derived from the authority of the people—has promoted democracy as
a legitimizing source for governments and increased the popularity of the term.
Today one rarely encounters an argument against democracy. One may criticize
this or that aspect of a "democratic" system—even question if it is really a
democracy—but one can hardly claim to be antidemocratic himself. An inquiry

15

conducted by the United Nations Educational, Scientific, and Cultural Organization (UNESCO) after World War II, with the cooperation of more than a hundred scholars from both East and West, concludes:

> For the first time in the history of the world no doctrines are advanced as anti-democratic. The accusation of anti-democratic action or attitude is frequently directed against others, but practical politicians and political theorists agree in stressing the democratic element in the institutions they defend and theories they advocate.[2]

Mayo, in *An Introduction to Democratic Theory,* argues that "tidal wave of popularity for democracy swept around the world during and after the First World War," which was the beginning of "the century of the common man, of popular influence upon government, and of the self-determination of nations."[3] Surprisingly enough, we see the same argument several decades earlier when Viscount Bryce noted "the universal acceptance of democracy as the normal and natural form of government" as the most significant change of the nineteenth century:

> Seventy years ago . . . the approaching *rise of the masses to power* was regarded by the educated classes of Europe as a menace to order and prosperity. Then the word Democracy awakened dislike or fear. Now it is a word of praise. Popular power is welcomed, extolled, worshipped. The few whom it repels or alarms rarely avow their sentiments.[4]

Of course, the attitudinal change toward democracy was a result of the altered meaning of the word. Democracy, in its classical sense, was interpreted to mean rule by the masses—poor, ignorant, and unqualified—who would use the power for their economic interest against the propertied class, which would cause concern among that elite. Such concern is most evident in the writings of the founders of the United States, which is often referred to as the "oldest" democracy. Even at a time when property ownership was sought as a qualification for political participation, these early US leaders introduced several measures to restrain majority rule and protect minority rights because if political rights were extended, the ignorant poor would be the ruling majority.

The Western elite, however, realized that if property rights were protected by the law and through other structural arrangements, the extension of political rights would not pose a threat. On the contrary, opening the political procedure would legitimize the system. Thus, only after at least a century of experimentation with gradual extension of suffrage, democracy was found safe, and political leaders started to declare their systems democracies either to mobilize the masses or to gain their support.

Thus, various regimes that hardly resembled each other claimed to be "the democratic one." Hitler described his system as "real" democracy, and Mussolini claimed fascism to be "an organized, centralized and authoritarian democracy."[5] The ready acceptance of democracy, by practically everyone, as the highest form of political organization caused disagreements about its substance; consequently, people developed their own interpretations of democracy. The proliferation of definitions led to the development of a series of new terms all referring to democracy, but pointing to essentially different political systems. "Liberal democracy," "direct democracy," "representative democracy," "guided democracy," and "people's democracy" are some of the expressions advanced to define political systems that claim to have some democratic elements. Proponents of each have argued their system to be "real" and the rest to be "false" democracies or undemocratic systems. This problem stems partly from the vagueness of the term itself and partly from the tendency to consider democracy as a have/have-not attribute. Political systems, however, overlap and are never found as mutually exclusive pure types. It is necessary to switch from categorical definitions to a continuum where political systems can be described as "more" or "less" democratic rather than as "democratic" or "undemocratic."

SELF-GOVERNMENT VERSUS THE CONTROL OF GOVERNMENT

The term "democracy" was inherited from ancient Greece, where the city-state of Athens established the earliest known form of democracy. *Demokratia* in Athens involved periodic meetings held by citizenry to discuss the problems of the polis and decide on a solution by voting directly on alternatives. In addition to the one-man-one-vote principle, the public jury system, selection to public office by lot, short terms at public office, and holding public office according to a system of rotation allowed the Athenians to practice a direct rule that required the intensive participation of the citizen.[6]

Although all called by the same name, the city-state democracy of ancient Greece was as different from its nineteenth-century European counterpart as was the latter from the contemporary version. The crucial differences, however, are not of type but of degree—specifically, between the intensity and extension of self-government in each system. Sartori states that "*the* intensity *of self-government attainable is in inverse proportion to the* extension [both spatial and temporal] *of self-government demanded*."[7] He explains that "self-government in the strict and literal sense of the term" refers "either to inner self-government (self-determination), or to the despot."[8] In case of maximum intensity (maximum self-government possible), the extension is zero. An increase in extension inevitably will lead to a decline in intensity. A relatively small extension of land or population—as in the ancient Greek city-states—enables citizens to exercise power directly and create a society in which all governed also govern, but a larger extension, of the magnitude of a modern nation-state, makes it impossible for the citizens "to govern themselves in any meaningful sense of expression."[9] Direct participation of the entire citizenry in the decisionmaking process becomes impossible; some form of representative system becomes inevitable.[10] Thus, the modern solution to the problem has been moving away from the ideal of "direct democracy" toward a realizable one, "representative democracy."[11]

The titular right to power, on the other hand, is less effective as a guarantee of popular sovereignty. The reality of the representative system involves the emergence of a minority group of rulers that perpetuates itself as the "ruling class," according to "elite theorists" such as Mosca, Pareto, Michels, and Bachrach.[12]

Presumably, this is why Sartori asserts that the "Athenian *demos* [people] had more *kratos* (power) than any other people since."[13] It should be noted, however, that although Athenians could enjoy direct rule partially because of the small size of the land and the population living on it, they made it possible through some measures that further shrank the size of the eligible population. By excluding women, foreigners, and slaves from participation, the celebrated Athenian democracy was limited to only a small group of privileged Athenian-born male citizens, who comprised no more than one-seventh of its total population. Moreover, it was the exclusive nature of the system and its slave economy that provided the Athenian man with the leisure time to participate directly in the political process, just as it allowed him to enjoy the other activities of the polis as a participant and not as a mere spectator.

Introducing intermediary representatives into the process would of course diminish, if not eliminate, people's control over the public decisions that influence their lives. Moreover, representation may be claimed without any formal mechanisms of transmission of power and without the consent of the represented group.

Rulers have usually claimed power as representatives of popular sovereignty. Sartori notes that the absolute monarchies of medieval Europe emphasized *omnis potestas a populo,* as opposed to *omnis potestas a Deo,* in their struggle with the Church.

> The medieval doctrine aimed at bridging the gap between nominal power and the exercise of the power by *fictio* of representation, i.e., by having the titular holder of power delegate the exercise of his power to somebody else. It was indeed a fiction, since the medieval doctrine was not concerned with the fact that the representative had few or no electors. And representation without election became simply a device which legitimized monarchical absolutism in a position of permanent irrevocable representation.[14]

Thus, a true representation, as opposed to a fictitious one claimed by self-appointed rulers, requires a selection mechanism involving the represented. The nature of the mechanism employed to identify the representatives is also important in transforming the titular power into a meaningful transmission of power. Elections are crucial mechanisms of selection, but they create representatives only if the elected individuals are responsible and accountable to those who elected them, and if this is agreed by both parties. Sartori further adds that "unless elections take place in conditions that assure freedom, they cannot produce leaders who are responsive to the will of the voters . . . [and] voting without free choice cannot result in representative government, and becomes nothing more than the people's periodic renunciation of their sovereignty."[15]

In modern times the extension is large, and democracy as a political system moves away from the ideal of self-rule—the direct *exercise of power*—and becomes the *control of power*. Sartori specifies:

> A democracy, then, is a political system in which the people exercise power to the extent that they are able to change their governors, but not to the extent of governing themselves. The only way the sovereign people can maintain the degree of power they need and are capable of wielding is not to give their governors unlimited power.[16]

The argument that people in modern democracies do not and cannot govern, but rather that they control their government, predates Sartori's well-known *Democratic Theory*. MacIver wrote in 1947: "Democracy is not a way of governing, whether by majority or otherwise, but primarily a way of determining who shall govern and, broadly, to what ends."[17] The same point is emphasized by Schumpeter: "Democracy does not mean and cannot mean that the people actually rule in any obvious sense of the terms 'people' and 'rule.' Democracy means that the people have the opportunity of accepting or refusing the men who are to rule them."[18]

Furthermore, Schumpeter reminds us that people may decide on their ruler in entirely undemocratic ways. He finds it necessary to narrow his definition by "adding a further criterion identified [as] the democratic method," which is "free competition among the would-be leaders for the vote of the electorate."[19] Thus, conditions in large modern societies force us to move from an ideal political system, which permits self-rule, to a polity where leaders are determined through a *democratic procedure* and which function within the limits of *democratic institutional* arrangements. Therefore, it is no accident that the modern literature on democracy offers what Sartori calls "procedural-structural" definitions of the term. The emphasis is on identifying the procedures and institutional arrangements that increase the extent to which decisionmakers are under effective popular control.

PROCEDURAL-STRUCTURAL DEFINITIONS

Lipset was one of the first commentators to provide a definition of democracy giving a special emphasis to procedure. He defines it as a procedure guaranteeing majority rule and minority rights.

> Democracy (in a complex society) is defined as a political system which supplies regular constitutional opportunities for changing the governing officials. It is a social mechanism for the resolution of the problems of societal decision-making among conflicting interest groups which permits the largest possible part of the population to influence these decisions through their ability to choose among alternative contenders for political office. . . . This definition implies a number of specific conditions: (a) a "political formula," a system of beliefs, legitimizing the democratic system and specifying the units—parties, a free press, and so forth—which are legitimized, i.e., accepted as proper by all; (b) one set of political leaders in office; and (c) one or more sets of leaders, out of office, which act as a

legitimate opposition attempting to gain office.[20]

Definitions by other authors refer to similar conditions or principles. Lineberry defines democracy as a "means of selecting policy makers and of organizing government to ensure that policy represents and responds to the public's preferences." He identifies the principles of democratic theory as political equality, full and fair information, widespread participation, majority rule and representation.[21] Similarly, Coulter states:

> Liberal democracy is the political organization of a nation-state characterized by comparatively greater levels of competitiveness, participation and liberties; that is, a liberal democracy is pluralistic with regard to competitiveness, inclusive with regard to participation, and libertarian with regard to liberties. On the opposite end of each of these three continua are polities which are coercive with comparison to competitiveness, participation, and liberties.[22]

Mayo identifies four principles for a system to be democratic: (1) popular control of policymakers, (2) political equality, (3) effectiveness of political control or political freedoms, and (4) majority rule.[23] He constructs a working definition on the basis of these principles and defines a democratic polity as "one in which public policies are made, on a majority basis, by representatives subject to effective popular control at periodic elections which are conducted on the principle of political equality and under conditions of political freedom."[24]

Analysts who follow the Aristotelian definition of democracy do not treat "freedoms" as a necessary component of democracy. MacPhearson, in his *Real World of Democracy,* defines democracy in the classical tradition as "the rule by the oppressed class" and identifies three working systems as different models of democracy: liberal democracy and the communist and Third World versions of one-party democracy.[25] He argues that societies that followed the liberal model established liberties first, especially in the capitalist market economy, and democratized the regime later. The one-party versions, on the other hand, were designed to put the formerly oppressed class into power—the proletariat in the communist version and the native population of former colonies in the Third World version. Because most members of the oppressed class would lack political consciousness, MacPhearson continues, a vanguard group would have to rule on behalf of the entire class. But he adds three criteria a vanguard state must meet to be referred to as democratic in a narrow sense: (1) Although there is only one party, intraparty democracy should prevail—there must be effective means for those at the bottom to control those at the top; (2) membership in the party must be open to all; and (3) the price of participation in the party cannot be a greater degree of activity than the average person can reasonably be expected to contribute.[26] We should note, however, that in these nonliberal models, MacPhearson's conditions have hardly been met in reality and cannot be met at all in the absence of any political freedoms.

Thus, we must define democracy as a political setting that provides means for the effective popular control of decisionmakers by the masses—in

MacPhearson's terms, "a system of government . . . in which the majority actually controls the rulers, actually controls those who make and enforce political decisions." But if the emphasis is on the extent of effective control, then the existence of democracy in any system becomes a matter of degree, and we can classify political systems as more or less democratic on the basis of a number of criteria referring to effective popular control.

From this point of view, the works by two scholars, Anthony Downs and Robert Dahl, manifest an improvement in defining the conditions that lead to increasing levels of popular control in modern political systems. The value of their descriptions lies in their nearly operationalized character that enables us to develop a measurement sensitive to the degree of "democraticness" (popular control of government) of a political system.[27]

Criteria given by Downs are

1. A single party (or coalition of parties) is chosen by popular election to run the governing apparatus.
2. Such elections are held within periodic intervals, the duration of which cannot be altered by the party in power acting alone.
3. All adults who are permanent residents of the society, are sane, and abide by the laws of the land are eligible to vote in each such election.
4. Each voter may cast one and only one vote in each election.
5. Any party (or coalition) receiving the support of a majority of those voting is entitled to take over the powers of government until the next election.
6. The losing parties in an election never try by force or any illegal means to prevent the winning party (or parties) from taking office.
7. The party in power never attempts to restrict the political activities of any citizens or other parties as long as they make no attempt to overthrow the government by force.
8. There are two or more parties competing for control of the governing apparatus in every election.[28]

Dahl, on the other hand, prefers the term "polyarchy" to "democracy" when referring to contemporary political systems that allow effective popular control of government but not self-rule. According to him, a political system is not entitled to be classified as a polyarchy unless the conditions he sets "exist to a relatively high degree." The conditions refer to specific stages in the electoral process that he treats as the main drive of the representative democracy, or polyarchy:

During the voting period:
1. Every member of the organization performs the acts we assume to constitute an expression of preference among the scheduled alternatives, e.g., voting.
2. In tabulating these expressions (votes), the weight assigned to the choice of each individual is identical.
3. The alternative with the greatest number of votes is declared the winning choice.
During the prevoting period:
4. Any member who perceives a set of alternatives, at least one of which he regards as preferable to any of the alternatives presently scheduled, can insert his

preferred alternative(s) among those scheduled for voting.

5. All individuals possess identical information about the alternatives.

During the postvoting period:

6. Alternatives (leaders or policies) with the greatest number of votes displace any alternatives (leaders or policies) with fewer votes.

7. The orders of elected officials are executed.

During the interelection stage:

8.1. Either all interelection decisions are subordinate or executory to those arrived at during the election stage, i.e., elections are in a sense controlling[;]

8.2. Or new decisions during the interelection period are governed by the preceding seven conditions, operating, however, under rather different institutional circumstances[;]

8.3. Or both.[29]

Thus, as Lipset has stated, "Democracy is not a quality of a social system which either does or does not exist, but rather a complex of characteristics which may be ranked in many different ways."[30]

PRESENT MEASURES OF DEMOCRACY

With democracy defined as the popular control of government—sovereign citizens' titular power is converted into real power only as a power to control rulers—a scale measurement may be developed that is more refined than the common dichotomous measure of democracy. A review of the literature on democracy reveals the efforts by several authors to establish a measure of democracy that can rank countries according to the extent of popular control of their governments. These authors have developed rank-ordered measures or interval scales of democracy.[31] These measures, including an earlier measure I developed,[32] however, reflect the following considerable limitations that restrict their utility for advanced analysis of stability or instability of political systems:

1. They are cumulative in nature. That is, they mostly measure the democratic performance of political systems over a time period (one or more decades) or around one time point (e.g., circa 1960, circa 1965), which smooths disparities within the time periods and prevents any meaningful analysis of change.

2. Usually there is no distinction between national governments and colonial administrations, and the impact of this significant historical transformation and change is neglected.

3. Most of the studies limit themselves to specific regions or to certain categories of development levels and economic systems, thus excluding a considerable number of countries.

4. Ambiguous measures of popular control, such as voter turnout, are used in indices. Popular participation is clearly essential to a democratic system, but the percentage of the adult population voting in an election has complex implications. The rate of participation in an election is usually

considered as an indicator of citizens' attitudes toward the system or government, rather than an indicator of democratization. The interpretation of participation in elections, even as an indicator of the citizens' attitudes, is a matter of dispute among the students of political behavior: Some scholars interpret low levels of participation as evidence of alienation from the system, others consider it an implication of citizens' satisfaction.[33] Coulter himself points this out.[34] The ambiguous character of this variable and problems that stem from its inclusion as a component in a measure of political democracy are discussed also by Bollen. He suggests that "a measure of the percentage of the population eligible to vote (the franchise) is a much better indicator of political democracy."[35]

5. In an effort to keep an adequate number of cases in the sample, data for missing values for some countries (typically the countries that are less developed or have centrally planned economies) are generated through the employment of strategies that rely heavily upon presumed high correlations among the components. Evidence shows that although they are highly correlated, the scores for all components do not go hand in hand for all cases. In fact, this is the very reason for including several components in such measures.

6. Most of the studies rely on data drawn from the 1960s, a few being circa 1969. Because many countries gained their independence in the late 1960s and 1970s, excluding these cases of "young states" leaves biased samples.

7. Although highly competitive political procedures can be established in a society, they may not be open to the entire adult population. Women, the illiterate, and certain races or ethnic groups have been excluded from the political process in many societies. None of the measures, however, has taken the extent of inclusiveness of the regime into consideration.

In view of these problems, a new measure of political democracy appears essential to the purposes of this study.

A NEW MEASURE OF DEMOCRACY

A measurement of democracy sensitive to the extent of popular control and emphasizing the extent of available means of control must be based on principles that lead to higher levels of popular control. Popular sovereignty, or public control of government, then, is perceived to have four components. They are not, of course, mutually exclusive, but include large overlaps and reinforce each other. These can be identified as participation, inclusiveness, competitiveness, and civil liberties.

Participation

The component of participation includes measures of the extent to which the popular consent is sought in selecting people for the decisionmaking offices, which are, for the most part, in the legislative and executive branches of government.[36] It is composed of the elements of executive selection, legislative selection, legislative effectiveness, and the competitiveness of the nomination procedure.

If the effective executive—"the individual who exercises primary influence in the shaping of major decisions affecting the nation's internal and external affairs" (e.g., monarch, president, premier)—is elected (directly or indirectly), the country is assigned one point.[37] If the effective executive did not obtain the position through popular elections, the country is assigned no points for that year.

If the legislative body of the government is elected—that is, "legislators or members of the lower house in a bicameral system are selected by means of either direct or indirect popular election"—two points are assigned. If instead the "legislators were selected by the effective executive, or by means of heredity or ascription," only one point is assigned. No point is assigned if there is no legislature.

Moreover, the effectiveness of the legislature is taken into consideration in the development of the legislature component of the measure. One point is assigned if the legislature is largely ineffective, two points are assigned if it is partially effective, and three points are assigned if it is effective. No points are assigned for the cases of no legislature. In situations where the "legislative activity is essentially of a 'rubber stamp' character," or "domestic turmoil may make the implementation of legislation impossible," or the "effective executive may prevent the legislature from meeting, or otherwise substantially impede the exercise of its functions," the legislature is considered to be ineffective. If the "effective executive's power substantially outweighs, but does not completely dominate that of the legislature," the legislature is considered to be partially effective. The legislative process is defined as effective if there is "significant governmental autonomy by the legislature, including, typically, substantial authority in regard to taxation and disbursement, and the power to override executive vetoes of legislation."

No points are assigned for the competitiveness of the nomination procedure in the absence of a legislature. One point is assigned if the nomination procedure for the legislature is essentially noncompetitive, two points are assigned if the nomination procedure is competitive. The two categories of nomination procedure reflect the difference between the degrees to which nominations are determined in a public arena: The competitive category refers to a more or less open process; the essentially noncompetitive category refers to a process in which the public does not have an opportunity to influence the options. Even if competition is allowed, the options in countries with an essentially noncompetitive nomination procedure are mostly predefined, and the choices are dictated by a dominant organ that ultimately provides a single slate of nominees. The scores on these four items are added to generate the participation score.

Inclusiveness of the Process

Even when popular consent is sought in selecting representatives, the process of selection may still be closed to segments of the population.[38] Restrictions may be imposed according to gender, race, ethnicity, age, education levels, and property ownership. Theoretically, the range of scores for this component can vary between zero and one: No points are assigned if there is no suffrage, and a full point is assigned if all citizens aged 18 (age of majority) or over are allowed to participate in the elections without any further qualifications. If any restrictions are employed in a country, the estimated percentage of the population under restriction is subtracted from one. For example, in a country where literacy is required for voting and the literacy rate is 40 percent, the score for that county would be .40. Although in reality there may be more women than men (except for a few countries, e.g., India), for this study each gender group is estimated to comprise 50 percent of the population in all countries. Thus, if suffrage is granted to only men, the score would be .50. Each year above age 18 is estimated to include about 2 percent of the adult population. Thus, if universal suffrage at age 21 is established, that country's score would be .94, indicating that approximately 6 percent of the population (3 yrs x 2%) is denied participation. If there are multiple restrictions in a given year, the restricted population sizes are multiplied to account for the overlaps. Some adjustments are made for countries that extended suffrage to those younger than 18; thus, the ultimate inclusiveness score may be higher than 1 for these countries.

Competitiveness

The competitiveness of the political system refers to the extent to which the electorate is provided with choice. Data on two characteristics of the system are used for this component: party legitimacy and party competitiveness.

If there are no political parties, or all but a dominant party and satellites are excluded, the country is assigned zero for party legitimacy. If some parties are allowed but there is significant exclusion of parties, one point is assigned. If only some "extremist" parties are excluded, two points are assigned, and if no parties are excluded from the system, three points are assigned. If the largest party held less than 70 percent of the total votes in the latest national elections, two points are assigned to the country for party competitiveness. In case of no elections, or obtaining 70 percent or more of the votes, only one point is assigned. The sum of these two items provides the competitiveness score.

Civil Liberties (or Government Coerciveness)

Because of the lack of reliable information on the extent to which governments recognize and respect civil liberties, this aspect of the system is measured

149,144

through the employment of an indirect method. The coerciveness of governments, which is treated as an opposite indicator of civil liberties, is estimated to this end.

All governments have coercive power, and they use it to maintain their systems. Because we have no explicit theoretical guidelines for the optimum or reasonable levels of coerciveness, a statistical estimation procedure is used. By regressing the number of sanctions employed on the social unrest indicators, for each year, we can estimate a line of optimum coerciveness for the real world. If a country employs more political sanctions than another given equal levels of unrest, we can describe it as a more coercive government, but if it employs fewer coercive actions, it can be ranked as less coercive. Then the difference between actual and predicted (estimated) values, the residuals, can provide a measure of coerciveness, or lack of liberties.[39]

After annual scores are assigned to the sample of countries for the years between 1948 and 1982, the annual score of participation is multiplied by 1 plus the score of inclusiveness. Then, the raw scores for each component are transformed into T-scores with mean values of 40 and standard deviation of 10. The final score of "democraticness" is calculated by subtracting the degree of coerciveness from the sum of the other components.[40] Thus, the equation for the democraticness score is:

Score of democraticness =
[(Participation x (1 + Inclusiveness)) + Competitiveness] – Coerciveness

The annual scores for the 35 years from 1948 through 1982 range from the minimum 29 to the maximum of 109 for the group of independent countries studied; the sample size varies between 65 and 150 for different years. (For the annual scores for each country, see Appendix B.) The mean score for the total of 3,873 cases is 73.

RELIABILITY AND VALIDITY OF
THE MEASURE OF "DEMOCRATICNESS"

Although estimated from a set of nominal indicators, the measure of political democracy takes on some properties of an interval scale. The reliability of this new scale was measured by using the appropriate tests developed for additive scales,[41] and the tests provide confirmatory results. The commonly used reliability measure, Cronbach's alpha, which is based on the interitem correlation, is .94 for our measure. A reliability measure over .80 is generally considered to be satisfactory.[42]

The measure is based on the structural-procedural definitions of "democracy," and the item indicators are chosen on the basis of their face validity. Although this measure is developed to overcome the weaknesses of previous measures, the only criterion for its construct validity seems to be these earlier measures despite their inadequacies. A summary of the previous measures and their correlations with the new measure is presented in Table 2.1, where letter *r* refers to the correlation coefficient, and *n* indicates the number of cases that are common to both the measures and included in the correlation analysis.

The validity of the new measure is tested against these indices for the overlapping countries and years. For the cumulative indices—i.e., the indices by Cutright, Cutright-Wiley, Adelman-Morris, Neubauer, Smith, and Coulter—for the comparable years the average values on the new measure are employed. For example, since Smith's score was cumulative for the years from 1946 to 1965, the average of the annual scores for those years on the new measure was calculated for each country.

As can be seen in Table 2.1, the correlations are generally high and positive, though the highest correlation appears to be with my earlier index (r = .95) and with Bollen's index (r = .90 for both time points), which are the most recent and sophisticated measures. The negative correlations are with those developed by Dahl, Adelman-Morris, and Fitzgibbon-Johnson; all are rank-order scales. The other measures, based on similar scales, yield high positive correlations, the lowest being with Neubauer's, which is limited to only advanced democratic countries.

LIMITATIONS OF THE NEW MEASURE OF DEMOCRATICNESS

Although it yields high reliability and validity scores, even this new measure of democracy should be interpreted carefully. Countries that rank high on this scale should not be considered as having reached the highest possible level. It is an interval level measure, not a closed-ended construct, without any minimum or maximum points defined. Even the country given the highest aggregate score may fall short of full popular control of its government. As phrased by MacIver, "Democracy is a form of government that is never completely achieved."[43] This new measure of democracy is developed with that observation in mind, leaving room for improvement in all countries.

Moreover, unavailability and incompatibility of data require the use of rather crude indicators. Information on judicial autonomy and effectiveness and on freedom of press are left out. Items used for government coerciveness are based on reported incidents, and some major indicators of coerciveness (such as arbitrary arrests and imprisonments, and disappearances) cannot be included because such information is seldom documented. Although reliable information on these items can be obtained for a few countries for a few recent years, it is not available for the large group studied here, and certainly not for 35 years for any country. Subtle coercive strategies frequently employed by governments to suppress freedoms cannot be captured. Strategies of suppression through intimidation, such as the blacklisting of the 1950s in the United States or the situations that lead the press to employ self-censorship, are not included.

A procedure that can restrict all freedoms and rights granted by constitu-

Table 2.1   Previous Measures of Democracy and Their Correlations with the New Measure

Creator of Index	Number of Countries	Type of Countries	Period Covered	Type of Index	Correlation with New Measure r	n
Coleman (1960)	75	developing	1958/1959[a]	3-level rank order	.69	42
Cutright (1963)	76	various	1940–1960	cumulative interval level	.73	57
Neubauer (1967)	23	highly democratic	1940–1960[a]	cumulative interval level	.26	17
Cutright-Wiley (1969)	40	various	1957–1966	cumulative interval level	.81	39
			1947–1956		.80	39
			1937–1946			
			1927–1936			
Smith (1969)	110	various	1946–1965	cumulative and temporal interval level	.76	62
Adelman-Morris (1971)	74	developing	1963–1968	categorical	−.61	69
	73		1957–1962	(adjusted for rank)	−.69	62
Dahl (1971)	114	various	circa 1969	cumulative rank order	−.82	112
Jackman (1973)	60	noncommunist	circa 1960	semicumulative interval level	.65	52
Coulter (1975)	85	various	1950–1970	cumulative interval level	.70	55
Fitzgibbon-Johnson (1977)	20	Latin American	1975	annual rank order	−.57	20
			1970		−.61	20
			1965		−.66	20
			1960		−.67	20
			1955		−.66	20
			1950		−.76	20
			1945			
Bollen (1980)	123	various	circa 1965	semicumulative interval level	.90	106
	113		circa 1960		.90	104
Arat (1984)	131	independent	1948–1977	annual interval level	.95	2985

Note: a. Time period uncertain

tions is the proclamation of martial law, which is frequently employed in developing countries. However, even when such information is available, it is difficult to determine the duration of the proclamation and specify the regions within the country where the law was effective and what percent of the population was affected. Thus, the influence of the restrictions introduced under martial law is reflected in the number of government sanctions used to acquire the coerciveness measure.

Furthermore, the suffrage measure is limited to constitutional provisions. But governments have access to different means either to mobilize or discourage the electorate. Setting simple registration and election procedures and providing easy access to the ballot boxes (e.g., reaching remote areas, scheduling elections on weekends) encourage participation, but some other policies (such as requiring citizens to vote at their places of birth instead of their residence) restrict it.

Finally, the extent of citizens' control of representatives and their participation in decisionmaking through several means other than voting, such as direct access to the leaders and lobbying, are factors usually not equally available to all citizens and could not be measured.

Thus, a completely accurate measure of democracy has yet to be developed and is not forseeable in the near future. The scores assigned by the present measure serve as a proxy and should be treated with caution. Like IQ scores, they do not apprehend the actual state of the individual case, but rank the cases according to their performance on some standardized tests.

NOTES

1. Burnham, p. 243.
2. McKeon, p. 522.
3. Henry B. Mayo, pp. 25–26.
4. Bryce, p. 4 (emphasis added).
5. Henry B. Mayo, p. 21.
6. On Athenian democracy, see Finely, 1963 and 1983. For a brief review, see Held, chap. 1.
7. Sartori, 1965, p. 60.
8. Ibid.
9. Ibid.
10. See also Dahl, 1956, chap. 1, for a discussion of the drawbacks of the maximum intensity of self-rule.
11. Dahl, 1989.
12. Pareto; Mosca; Michels; Mills; Bachrach, 1967; and Parenti. A collection of essays representing views of elite theorists and their critics can be found in Backrack, 1971.
13. Sartori, 1968, p. 115. Although political scientists tend to treat ancient Athens as the only society that has experienced direct rule, anthropologists have discovered that the political organization of many tribal societies in precolonial Africa and the Americas can be defined only as direct democracies.
14. Sartori, 1965, pp. 22–23. Sartori explains Rousseau's skepticism about representation as a fear of "irrevocable representation." Rousseau believed that as soon as the exercise of power is transferred to the representatives, the institution of representatives becomes sovereign and power slips out of the hands of people, its "nominal holder," and becomes "an abstract titular right." Rousseau, then, suggested election of leaders without considering them representative. Sartori, however, opposes this and argues that "if he who is elected is not regarded as the representative of those who elect him, the election simply creates, per se, an absolute ruler," and points to the head of the Catholic Church as an example of a person who is elected but does not represent his electors and is not responsible to them.
15. Sartori, 1965, pp. 23–24.
16. Ibid., p. 66.
17. MacIver, p. 198.

18. Schumpeter, pp. 284–285.

19. Ibid., p. 285.

20. Lipset, 1959, p. 71.

21. Lineberry, pp. 28–35.

22. Coulter, p. 1. The term "liberal" as used by Coulter tends to emphasize civil liberties as opposed to classical liberalism or the nineteenth century's "liberal democracy." He explains his approach with a statement from Sartori's *Democratic Theory:* "To isolate liberalism from democracy, we say that liberalism calls for liberty and democracy for equality. To unite them, we say that it is the task of liberal-democratic systems to combine liberty with equality in Democratic Theory," (Coulter, p. 386).

23. Henry B. Mayo, chap. 1.

24. Ibid., p. 70.

25. MacPhearson.

26. Ibid., pp. 20–21.

27. Note that Downs also perceives democracy as a nominal category of political systems and states all these conditions as necessary to such a system. Although our conceptualization is different, such definitions are still helpful to build a scale of "democraticness" of a system on the basis of the extent of these conditions available in it.

28. Downs, pp. 23–24.

29. Dahl, 1956, p. 84.

30. Lipset, 1959, p. 73.

31. Coleman, 1960; Coulter; Cutright; Cutright and Wiley; Arthur K. Smith, Jr.; Neubauer; Jackman, 1973; Adelman and Morris; Dahl, 1971; Banks, 1972; Fitzgibbon and Johnson Index as reported by Kenneth F. Johnson, "Research Perspectives on the Revised Fitzgibbon-Johnson Index of the Image of Political Democracy in Latin America, 1945–75," in Wilkie and Ruddle, chap. 5; Bollen, 1979 and 1980.

32. Arat, 1984.

33. See Campbell, et al., pp. 99–100; Schattschneider; and Olson for a discussion of these arguments.

34. Coulter, p. 3.

35. Bollen, 1979, p. 580.

36. Data referring to participation and competition components were obtained from Banks, 1979. The coding and definitions as developed by Banks and explained in the users' manual for the data archive (see pages 17–20) have been used except for some changes. First, the legislative effectiveness for Turkey for the years 1971 and 1972 is recoded by the author from "effective" to "partially effective." The former legislative body was kept after the military intervention in March 1971, but the military forced the former effective executive (premier) elected by the legislature to resign. The military enjoyed a considerable influence over the selection and practice of successor executives for approximately two years. Second, the party legitimacy score for Israel was changed from "no restriction" to "some restriction" because the government prevented establishment of any party that would focus on the needs of the Arab citizens in this country. Finally, some factual mistakes on dates or inconsistencies among some variables were corrected. Explanations for the coding procedure and definition of the terms are adapted from Banks, 1979.

37. No distinction has been made between direct and indirect elections because it could be misleading to state that direct election provides higher levels of popular control. I prefer to consider this difference as a diversity in constitutional arrangements.

38. The data for this component are gathered from several sources, including Gorvin; Heard; McDonald, 1971 and 1989; Mackie; Banks; *The Europa World Book; The Statesman's Year Book;* Blaustein; Peaslee. A country study series sponsored by the Federal Research Division of the Library of Congress (Washington, D.C.) was used for several countries in the study. For a few countries, I contacted embassies in Washington,

D.C., United Nations offices, or New York City consulates for verification and clarification of information from secondary sources.

39. The number of government sanctions—defined by Taylor and Hudson as the "actions taken by authorities to neutralize, suppress, or eliminate a preceived threat to the security of the government, the regime, or the state itself" (Tayor and Hudon, Table 3.5)—within a year (Y_i) is regressed on the number of social unrest events encountered that year, such as the number of antigovernment demonstrations, assassination, guerrilla warfare, riots, general strikes, and deaths from domestic violence $(X_1\text{-}X_6)$. (See Appendix A.) The regression equation is as follows:

$$Y_i = a + b_1 X_{1i} + b_2 X_{2i} + b_3 X_{3i} + b_4 X_{4i} + b_5 X_{5i} + b_6 X_{6i} + u_i$$

The residual values (u_i) from this regression analysis provide a measure of government coerciveness. On the logic of this estimation process, see Duvall and Shamirs.

Data for social unrest variables, except for deaths from domestic violence, were obtained from Banks, 1979. Banks defines "assassinations" as "politically motivated murder or attempted murder of a high governmental official or politician." "General strikes" is defined as "any strike of 1000 or more industrial and service workers that involves more than one employer and that is aimed at national government policies or authority." "Riots" refers to "any violent demonstration and clash of more than 100 citizens involving the use of physical force." "Antigovernment demonstrations" includes "any peaceful public gathering of at least 100 people for the primary purpose of displaying or voicing their opposition to government politicies or authority, excluding demonstrations of a distinctly anti-foreign nature." The numbers of "deaths from domestic violence" were derived from Taylor and Hudson, Table 3.4, which refers to the "numbers of persons reportedly killed in events of domestic political conflict" where the "data refer to the numbers of bodies, not events in which deaths occur."

40. The same strategy—subtracting the measure of lack of liberties or coerciveness from the additive score—was pursued also by Bollen in development of an index of political democracy (POLDEM). Bollen mentions that "there is a built-in bias against countries with high political liberties to being with; the greater the freedom, the more negative sanctions the government can impose." Bollen, 1980, n. 7, p. 376. Because of its large magnitude, the coerciveness component was divided by 6 before it was subtracted from the addition of other components of democracy.

41. McIver and Carmines.

42. Krippendorff, p. 147.

43. MacIver, p. 175.

3

The Social and Economic Origins of Democracy

Democracy seems to be suitable only to a very little country.—Voltaire

That [democracy] worked at all is a near-miracle, explainable only by the abundance of a nation [the United States] that could afford a cumbrous and wasteful government system.—Karl Loewenstein

ROLE OF THE BOURGEOISIE IN POLITICAL DEMOCRATIZATION

Interest in the relationships between social classes and the political system is as old as written history. Aristotle, the first empirical social scientist, developed his typology for the Greek polis according to the size of the politically participant groups and their class origin. Although the modern literature does not necessarily treat democracy as class rule, it does stress the parallel development of certain social classes and of democracy.

Historical studies indicate that modern democracies can occur only under certain conditions of capitalist industrialization. Karl Marx identified the bourgeoisie as the major force behind the emergence of democracy in Western Europe. He argued that the capitalist class used parliamentary systems and democratic mechanisms to capture control of the state from the traditional elite, the aristocracy. Similarly, Barrington Moore, in his study of major Western democracies, and Albert Soboul, in his analysis of the French Revolution, stressed the role of the middle class or the urban bourgeoisie in the transformation of political systems into democracies.[1] Although he marked the importance of Protestantism in the development of Western democracies, Max Weber, in his well-known work *The Protestant Ethic and the Spirit of Capitalism*, emphasized the individualism and the sense of individual responsibility inherent in the Protestant ethic as the major catalyst for the development of burgher classes and of a democratic political culture.

In the early 1940s, Joseph Schumpeter highlighted the historical correspondence between the development of capitalism and democracy. He established a creed for the liberal democratic theorists who would treat capitalism

33

and the presence of an autonomous bourgeois class as requisites of development and democracy. In Schumpeter's words:

> The ideology of democracy as reflected by the classical doctrine rests on a rational-
> ist scheme of human action and of the values of life. This fact would in itself suf-
> fice to suggest that it is of bourgeois origin. History clearly confirms this
> suggestion: historically, the modern democracy rose along with capitalism, and in
> causal connection with it. But the same holds true for democratic practice: democ-
> racy in the sense of our theory of competitive leadership presided over the process
> of political and institutional change by which the bourgeoisie reshaped, and from
> its own point of view rationalized, the social and political structure that preceded its
> ascendancy: the democratic method was the political tool of that reconstruction.
> We have seen that the democratic method works, particularly well, also in certain
> extra- and pre-capitalist societies. But modern democracy is a product of the capi-
> talist process.[2]

The classical middle class (bourgeoisie) in non-Western societies, however, tends to display political attitudes and features different from those of
Western counterparts. Regardless of the school of thought to which they
belong, students of Third World politics agree on the weakness of the bourgeoisie in promoting democracy in developing countries. Referring to the historical studies on Western democracies just mentioned, Samuel Huntington
writes:

> The most significant manifestation of the social structure argument . . . concerns
> . . . the existence of an autonomous bourgeoisie. The failure of democracy to
> develop in Third World countries despite their economic growth can, perhaps, be
> related to the nature of that growth. The leading roles have been played by the state
> and by multinational enterprises. As a result, economic development runs ahead of
> the development of a bourgeoisie. In those circumstances where a bourgeoisie has
> developed, however, the prospects for democracy have been greater. The move to
> democracy in Turkey in the 1940s coincided with the move away from the étatisme
> of Kemalism and the appearance of a group of independent businessmen. More sig-
> nificantly, the ability of a developing country to have an autonomous, indigenous
> bourgeoisie is likely to be related to its size. Countries with small internal markets
> are unlikely to be able to sustain such a class, but large ones can.[3]

Here, Huntington attributes the failure of the bourgeoisie in leading a political movement toward democratization in developing countries to the absence
or small size of this class. According to him, the growth of the bourgeoisie has
been (1) prevented by the state that played a dominant role in the economy, (2)
curtailed by the multinational corporations that penetrated into the economies
of developing countries, and (3) limited by the small size of the internal markets.

Huntington's interpretation of state intervention into the economy—the
development strategy called "statism"—as an obstacle to democratization has
been shared by others.[4] Still overwhelmed by the Western experience, these
authors believe that the bourgeoisie holds an inherently progressive and liberal
spirit. They see a strong link between an economic system of free enterprise

and political freedoms and liberties, believing that the bourgeoisie, if given the free hand in the economy, would be a liberating force not only in the economy but also in politics. Following de Tocqueville's analysis of the US democracy, they expect the competitive economic system to create its competitive counterpart in the political arena. Free business associations and organizations would not only establish a social basis of pluralism, but would also prevent the concentration of political power and stimulate political compromise and accountability. According to these authors, statism, with its restrictions and control over private enterprise, does not allow the bourgeoisie to fulfill its historical role of the liberator and thus makes conditions more suitable for authoritarianism.

Evidence from developing democracies, however, shows that the emergence of market economies does not necessarily yield a liberating bourgeoisie. On the contrary, democracy may advance in economies not totally "free." Although some degree of statism has been pursued in most developing countries, it did not prevent democratization in all cases. India may be the best example to support this point. In fact, the empirical research supports the claim that state ownership and control in some industries and intervention in favor of social reform and income distribution have strengthened democracy in India by increasing its social basis and political support.[5]

Moreover, as demonstrated by several cases, statism does not prevent the development of a private sector and bourgeoisie; on the contrary, it may serve as a strategy to create and promote private enterprise. Thus, many developing countries, despite state regulations and investments, have a viable private enterprise and influential bourgeoisie. This class, supported by different forms of authoritarian rule, however, has not demonstrated a keen interest in democratic political structures.[6] The lack of interest is explained by Agbese:

> Democracy entails, among other things, the accountability of the rulers to the ruled. However, accountability, within the context in which access to state power is the major mechanism for private capital accumulation, threatens the very accumulative base of the ruling class. To preserve the process of capital accumulation, non-accountability of the ruling class becomes a fundamental ethos of the political economy.[7]

The second argument by Huntington, who treats multinational corporations as an impediment for the development of a national bourgeoisie, has been emphasized most by the dependency theorists. According to them dependent development not only squeezes the number of native entrepreneurs but also distorts the nationalistic values of the native bourgeoisie. The "comprador elite" in developing countries align their interests with those of multinationals rather than with those of their native country.[8] This latter point about the impact of foreign investment and dependent development on democracy constitutes a major explanatory factor in our analysis of the decline of democracies in developing countries and is discussed in detail in subsequent chapters.

The third argument by Huntington—that size of the internal market is a determinant of democracy—does not hold in the light of empirical findings.

The small size of the internal market may be an indicator of a small and weak bourgeoisie, but it can hardly serve as a predictor of the stability of democratic systems. In addition to many examples from Europe, the developing countries that maintain stable democracies are (with the exception of India) mainly small by many criteria, including geographic size, population, production level, and consumption patterns (e.g., Costa Rica, Trinidad and Tobago, Papua New Guinea, and Mauritius). Countries with more developed markets, on the other hand, are characterized by instability if they have ever established a highly democratic regime (e.g., Brazil). Thus, we may conclude that if any aspect of the bourgeoisie is related to the nature of political systems, it must be its attitude and interests rather than its size. In addition to the dependency theory that focuses on this point, alternative explanations regarding the attitude of the bourgeoisie in developing countries have also been developed by the students of Latin American politics.

Lipset, who applied the Weberian modernization theory to Latin American countries, treats economic development as a prerequisite of democracy. Although he does not explicitly specify "capitalist development" as a necessary condition, Lipset shares Schumpeter's views regarding the role of the bourgeoisie. He attributes the slow economic growth in Latin American countries to the lack of "entrepreneurial values" among their entrepreneurs. He argues that Latin American countries reflect "ascriptive and particularistic" values as opposed to being oriented toward "achievement and universalism," which are defined as the pattern-variables most favorable to the emergence of an industrial society.[9] Preindustrial values, he states, still prevail in Latin America, and the "prestige attaching to land ownership still leads many businessmen to invest the monies they have made in industry, in farms."[10] Lipset also points out that Latin American businessmen fail to reflect the "key aspect of entrepreneurship," defined by Joseph Schumpeter as "the capacity for leadership in innovation, for breaking through the routine and the traditional."[11] He observes that they are reluctant to take risks, and they "frequently prefer to make a high profit quickly, often by charging a high price to a small market, rather than to maximize long-range profits by seeking to cut costs and prices, which would take more effort."[12]

Although values are significant in determining attitudes and behaviors, Lipset's analysis puts too much emphasis on values without any discussion of their material basis. He makes no reference to "profitability" of a business, which is supposed to be the key concept in business decisions. If Latin American entrepreneurs, the bourgeoisie, adopt aristocratic values and investment patterns (investing in land or ranches instead of industry), it is not necessarily because of their desire to obtain prestige in a hierarchical society, as put by Lipset. Traditional investments may still be more profitable than investments in industrial or commercial enterprises. In fact, they are likely to be more profitable for the native entrepreneur if the industrial sector and trade have already been penetrated or controlled by multinational enterprises or by family companies owned by foreign entrepreneurs. In England, for example, the aristocracy acquired so-called bourgeois (or entrepreneurial) values and attitudes when it realized that commercial enterprise was more profitable than the traditional system of land tenure, and it did not hesitate to undertake the infamous enclosure movement. Thus, even if agricultural arrangements in Latin America are inefficient by Western standards, they have prevailed and have been preferred by the entrepreneurs because they have been more profitable than the alternative modern enterprises. Moreover, if the Latin American entrepreneur avoids investing under risk, this can be attributed to a habit formed in a protected economy rather than to the strength of ascriptive-particularistic values (such as fear of disgracing the family), as argued by Lipset. There is no hard evidence to support the belief that entrepreneurs in Latin America (or elsewhere in the developing world) are not as rational as their Western counterparts, even though they may not be as progressive, are more dependent on government protection, and are less willing to take risks.

Adopting a neo-Marxist approach, Kenneth Roberts explains why democratic regimes tend to be stable in advanced capitalist societies but unstable in Latin America.[13] Using Gramsci's theory of "ideological hegemony" exercised by the "dominant coalition" over subordinate social classes, Roberts explains that although capital is concentrated in the hands of a few, advanced capitalist societies have a large middle segment whose interest is tied to the bourgeoisie. This segment serves "as a buffer between the dominant and subordinate sectors." In these societies,

> the industrial working class represents a minority of the population, and substantial sectors of the working class fall under the ideological hegemony of the bourgeoisie. Therefore, democratic procedures pose little threat of altering the social formation or the state's dominant coalition, and political order is relatively easy to maintain.
>
> However, conditions are much different within the social formation of dependent capitalism in Latin America. The dominant coalition tends to be a tiny internationalized elite, and national legitimacy may be undermined by external linkages or domination. The middle class is generally small in comparison to the working class, the peasantry, and rural and urban marginal sectors. The ideological hegemony of the dominant coalition is often tenuous; ideological currents hostile to the social formation of dependent capitalism are common among students, intellectuals, and sectors of organized labor, and even filter down on occasion to the peasantry . . . .
>
> Hence, the dominant coalitions in Latin America's dependent capitalist societies have been less successful than their counterparts in advanced capitalist societies at preventing threats to their hegemony from emerging within the democratic process. Frequently, the liberties associated with democratic procedures—the opportunities for the mobilization and articulation of lower class demands and channels for electoral influence—have come to be viewed as threatening by the dominant coalitions. Frequently, they have been able to find allies within the military establishments and the middle classes when popular mobilization and demands threaten social and political order.[14]

The last portion of this argument is based on Guillermo O'Donnell's theory of "bureaucratic authoritarianism."[15] O'Donnell argued that in an effort to suppress rising political and economic demands of lower classes, the industrial and managerial bourgeoisie in Latin America established a coalition with the top echelons of the civilian and military bureaucracy and technocracy. This coalition, by excluding the masses from the political process, managed to sustain an inegalitarian economic growth. According to this explanation, the capitalist industrialization in late developers would be possible only under authoritarian rule.

What is important for the development of democracy in new nation-states is not the size of the bourgeoisie but the way that class has evolved and the kind of relationship it has established with the state authority. Barrington Moore, who agreed that the bourgeoisie was a democratic force in many societies, also pointed to the significance of its relationship with other social classes. He observed that the presence of the bourgeoisie did not always result in democracies, and the political outcome was authoritarian where the bourgeoisie established alliances with the conservative ruling classes. According to his reading of historical data, democracy is expected where the bourgeoisie is allied with progressive groups seeking social and political change.[16] Moreover, contrary to the liberalist argument that treats a strong bourgeoisie as a necessary condition for democracy, the political weakness of this class and its failure to establish itself as the dominant class are asserted as the underlying cause of democratic success in some developing countries. India is used to exemplify this relationship because the capitalist industrial class in India "has not yet been strong enough to undermine the economic importance of the class of rich farmers or to absorb them into giant capitalist agro-business enterprises; neither has it succeeded in colonizing the bureaucracy and molding it to suit largely capitalist goals."[17]

Thus, in order to understand why the bourgeoisie in developing countries has displayed attitudes different from those of its Western counterparts in regard to political liberty and equality, we should study the social and political conditions under which it emerged.

The Western bourgeoisie was involved in a class struggle against privileged aristocracy and absolute monarchy to protect its economic power and promote its social and political status. Especially in an effort to guarantee the security of its private property, it defended the protection of individual rights as natural rights that even the state cannot confiscate. In the case of England, the Magna Carta shows that even the aristocracy was an effective class in limiting the power of the monarchy. The bourgeoisie, in its effort to curtail the economic domain of the state, inevitably extended restrictions on the state's power to other areas and became an advocate of civil and political rights. The 1688 English Revolution and the 1789 French Revolution are often called "bourgeois revolutions" because of the principles on which they were based and because of the foundation they built for the "bourgeois democracies" that became the political systems of these countries during the subsequent centuries.

By contrast, the bourgeoisie in most of the developing countries did not have to struggle against a privileged aristocracy that held the state authority. On the contrary, it was developed and supported by the state and was given a privileged position in the economy. Thus, cushioned by the state, the interests of the bourgeoisie were advanced by a *limiting* rather than a *limited* state.

The economies of developing countries have been basically agrarian. During the colonial period the industrial and commercial sectors were small and controlled by European nationals. In a few countries that escaped direct imperialism, such as China and Turkey, Europeans dominated manufacturing and commerce through the extraterritorial privileges they had acquired. Conscious of the political consequences of economic weakness and dependence, the nationalist leaders in many countries that achieved independence planned to create a national bourgeoisie, which was perceived as an effective means to the national goals of economic development, or Westernization.

In most of these countries, the essence of these goals was defined as industrialization. Thus, the capital accumulation necessary for industrialization was encouraged, and the industrial entrepreneurs were supported through several privileges, especially after the world economic crisis in the 1930s. Many governments turned to import-substituting industrialization and declared statism as a strategy of development. Although statism, accompanied by development plans in many countries, called for active government involvement in production, governments in reality played more of a subsidiary and regulatory role. Government investments appeared mostly in areas requiring large capital beyond the means of the private entrepreneurs and offering small profit margins.

Under statism the state provided the infrastructure (e.g., railways, shipbuilding and navigation, utilities) and produced inexpensive raw materials for private industry. This kind of engagement made the state a producer that created bureaucratic entrepreneurial agencies, even though the goal was stimulation of private enterprise. The State Economic Enterprises (Kamu İktisadi Teşekülleri, KITs) in Turkey and the Costa Rican Development Corporation (Corporación Costarricense de Desarrollo Sociedad Anonima, CODESA) are examples of agencies established for this purpose. İsmet İnönü, a former prime minister of Turkey who introduced statism there, explained statism as a development strategy that would create an economy in which "the activity of state would not replace individual enterprise, but it would eliminate the obstacles that stand in the way of individual enterprise."[18] In fact, even though CODESA was frequently attacked soon after its creation in 1972 and became the target of a takeover by the US Agency for International Development under Ronald Reagan's privatization plans in the 1980s, Costa Rican industrialists have acknowledged that CODESA "invested in areas that the private sector had been reluctant to enter, because of the size of investment and the degree of risk involved."[19]

In addition to statism, developments in the 1930s led the young states to pursue a new strategy of development that ultimately benefited their emerging bourgeoisie. The world economic crisis caused a decline in the foreign capital flow[20] and allowed the developing countries to lean toward a protective economy and import-substitution policies. The government measures taken during this time created an economic environment suitable for capital accumulation and high industrial profits. In Turkey, for example, industrialists' profit margins increased between 1932 and 1935 from 28.8 percent to 36.6 percent, while the share of wages in the national income declined from 11.2 percent to 9.7 percent.[21]

The growth of the private sector under state protectionism, however, is not unique to Turkey or Costa Rica. Cardoso observed that a similar process took place in Latin American countries:

> Not until somewhat later did the entrepreneur groups take over responsibility for industrial development. Even then, they did so under the protection of the state, and therefore, with the benefit of the expansion resulting from government investment (in energy, oil, iron and steel), which opened up new sources of profit for private investment as a substitute for imports. . . .The existence of markets did not involve such values as free competition, productivity, etc., because the market was "protected" by state measures which benefited the industrialists. Similarly, our reference to society does not imply, in the conditions prevailing in Latin America, that a deliberate scheme existed for controlling the politico-social situation; much less does it imply commitment to the construction of a democratic community for the masses, on the terms usually attributed to the industrial societies.[22]

Thus, unlike the bourgeoisie in the West, the bourgeoisie in developing countries did not emerge autonomously. The seeds of the native bourgeoisie were planted and nourished by authoritarian states. The bourgeoisie did not resist democracy as long as the electoral success of sympathetic right-wing parties was taken for granted and governments followed policies in line with bourgeois economic interest. But when the lower classes were mobilized and the regime became actually competitive, democracy was perceived as a luxury. Thus, when authoritarian regimes replaced democracy, through either military interventions or emergency measures taken by civilian governments, the new systems were well received by the bourgeoisie. The new authoritarian rulers were welcome because they usually promoted business interests further by suppressing demands by labor and other groups that opposed favoritism and economic policies facilitating the inegalitarian distribution of wealth. Thus, the bourgeoisie in developing countries has not been a social class that defended individual rights and civil liberties nor one that has been suspicious of absolute state power. On the contrary, it has preferred a conservative and authoritarian state that would maintain the economic system and the social status quo.

The class analysis of democracy in developing countries leads to the conclusion that these democracies usually lack the support of the bourgeoisie, the economically strong class. When democratic institutions have arisen in any such society, this has happened without support of an economic class and mostly as a result of pretense by a group of intellectuals. Hence, some argue, without the support of an economic class, the democracy in developing countries is stillborn. Thus, we should not have the illusion of expecting them to be viable or stable.

COMPARATIVE RESEARCH AND
MODERNIZATION THEORY IN THE CONTEXT OF DEVELOPMENT

Despite the absence of a bourgeoisie or lack of support from this class, a wave of democratization took place in developing countries during the 1950s. Inspired by this trend around the world, social research focused on identifying the conditions that lead to or stimulate the process of democratization. Some writers, following Weber's lead, have searched for cultural requisites and the elements of a "democratic personality." A "civic culture" (Almond and Verba) and a "modern" personality (Lerner) have been identified as essentials of a participant (democratic) society.[23] The emphasis on culture appeared also in older literature. De Tocqueville, in his study of US institutions, pointed out the virtue of voluntary associations as the basis of social pluralism, which in turn nurtures democracy.

Almond and Verba, in their analysis of survey data from five countries, considered education as the most important factor in creating the attitudes and values vital for a participant culture.[24] Deutsch and Pye stated the necessity of an integrative system of mass communications to build the social cohesion crucial for the reinforcement of democratic procedures.[25]

All of these factors—education, communication, urbanization—are defined by Lerner and Lipset as a set of complex social and economic conditions essential to the development of the modern, rational citizenry needed for the establishment of democratic political systems.[26] Using survey data from Middle Eastern countries, Lerner identified these three factors as prerequisites for the process of democratic development. He viewed urbanization as a factor stimulating education, which in turn accelerates media growth and, eventually, democratic development.

Lipset linked these structural factors to a broader process: socioeconomic development. His cross-national analysis of aggregate data, with an emphasis on socioeconomic characteristics of societies as causal factors of democratization, initiated a new trend in which the focus shifted from individual characteristics to system characteristics. Lipset's argument, through its expansion by subsequent scholars, started a discussion about the impact of socioeconomic development or modernization—these two concepts are used interchangeably—on political democracy.

Lipset compared mean values and ranges of socioeconomic development for four groups of countries: (1) European and English-speaking stable democracies; (2) European and English-speaking unstable democracies and dictatorships; (3) Latin American democracies and unstable dictatorships; and (4) Latin American stable dictatorships. Finding the socioeconomic development scores considerably higher for the first group, he concluded that "economic development involving industrialization, urbanization, high educational standards, and a steady increase in the overall wealth of the society, is a basic condition sustaining democracy, it is a mark of efficiency of the total system." Thus, his analysis implicitly suggests a positive linear relationship between levels of socioeconomic development and democratic development. He added, however, that "the stability of a given democratic system depends not only on the system's efficiency in modernization, but also upon *effectiveness* and *legitimacy* of the political systems."[27] A possible conclusion is that by considering effectiveness and the legitimacy of the system as well as socioeconomic development, Lipset was arguing for socioeconomic development as a *necessary* but *not as a sufficient* condition for the establishment or maintenance of a democratic political system.[28]

Similarly, Coleman classified 75 developing countries as competitive, semicompetitive, or authoritarian on the basis of their democratic political performance in the late 1950s.[29] Comparing the mean scores of each group on indicators of economic development, as well as the individual scores of countries in each category, Coleman reached two conclusions:

> (1) The major hypothesis that economic development and competitiveness are positively correlated is validated when countries are grouped into major differentiating categories of competitiveness and when mean scores of economic development are employed; but (2) the hypothesis is weakened by negative correlations found when the economic scores and relative competitiveness of individual countries are considered. To this should be added the caveat that economic modernization constitutes only one dimension of the ensemble of determinants shaping political institutions and behavior in the countries with which we are concerned [developing countries].[30]

More sophisticated measures and methods were used to test the hypothesis, derived from the works of Lipset and Coleman, that socioeconomic development and "democraticness" of the system are positively related. Authors developed scale measurements of democracy more refined than the common dichotomous perception of it. Using such measures, the correlation and regression analyses by Cutright, Cutright and Wiley, Smith, and Coulter provided empirical support for a positive linear relationship between levels of economic development and democracy in a system.[31] The linearity of the relationship has been questioned by the "threshold phenomenon" argument of Neubauer and Jackman.[32] These two authors found no significant relationship between the two properties for highly developed countries; their thesis states that the level of democraticness increases with increases in the levels of economic development up to a certain development level, but after that point no systematic relationship follows between the two variables. Despite the disagreement about the form of the relationship—whether it is linear or not—the authors in both camps have reached some consensus that development leads to more democratic systems, at least in the earlier stages of development. Implicit in their analyses and conclusions is support for modernization theory, which studies political systems from a developmental point of view and considers democracy as an ultimate system approached with modernization.

Evolutionary theses in all fields of study had been popular since the Age of Enlightenment, and their social theoretical versions found ideological support among the ranks of liberalists. Democracy as the form of government ultimately sought by the modern citizen, the person of reason, was proclaimed by prominent political scientists and statesmen such as Woodrow Wilson:

> If Aristocracy seems about to disappear, Democracy seems about universally to prevail. Ever since the rise of popular education in the last century and its vast development since have assured a thinking weight to the masses of the people everywhere, the advance of democratic opinion and the spread of democratic institutions have been most marked and most significant. They have destroyed almost all pure forms of Monarchy and Aristocracy by introducing into them imperative forces of popular thought and the concrete institutions of popular representation; and they promise to reduce politics to a single pure form by excluding all other governing forces and institutions but those of wide suffrage and a democratic representation—by reducing all forms of government to Democracy.[33]

This contention has not been effectively challenged, and the thesis dominated the discussions of political democracy throughout the last century. On the other hand, it seems fair to question whether such linearity is validly demonstrated even for the less-developed countries. The countries that may be classified in the middle range, in particular, display a conspicuous fluctuation in the level of democraticness they have experienced.[34] The authors who identified either a linear or curvilinear relationship between socioeconomic development and democratization have based their arguments on findings from cross-national regression analysis of several countries at single time points or, more commonly, separate periods. The high correlation between the two factors and the significant regression coefficients displayed by such data have seemed to support their evolutionary hypothesis.

A CRITIQUE OF MODERNIZATION
THEORY AND EVOLUTIONARY THESIS

The validity of modernization theory, with its evolutionary thesis about democracy, needs to be verified with improved data and measurement. For this purpose we will seek answers to two groups of questions:

A: 1. If we consider a large number of countries at different levels of economic development and democratic performance, can we find a systematic relationship between the levels of economic development and democracy?
2. If there is a systematic relationship between the two char-

acteristics, what is its form? Specifically, is it linear or
curvilinear?
3. Does this relationship hold for different time points?
B: 1. If we consider each country for a number of years, do we see a
systematic relationship between the characteristics?
2. If there is a systematic relationship, is it the same as the one
obtained from the study of a number of countries at one time
point?

The three questions grouped under A require cross-sectional analysis of
countries at one time point and the repetition of the same analysis at multiple
time points. The questions grouped under B refer to the analysis of each country over time (longitudinal analysis). Thus, if what has been suggested by the
modernization theorists holds, we should find a statistically significant positive
relationship—linear or curvilinear—between socioeconomic development and
democracy. The same relationship should be observed for different time points.
Moreover, the individual countries should display the same relationship (linear
or curvilinear pattern) over time. That is, if the linearity argument holds, most
of the countries should display increasing levels of democraticness with
increasing levels of socioeconomic development. However, if the curvilinearity
hypothesis holds, most of the developing countries should manifest a linear
relationship, but the developed countries should not display any relationship, or
at least not a strong one. (See Figure 3.1 for an illustration of these hypothetical
relationships.)

To test for these arguments, the index scores of democracy discussed in
Chapter 2 are regressed on energy consumption per capita, an indicator of
socioeconomic development.[35] Frequent criticisms have been directed toward
the use of a single indicator for complicated concepts like socioeconomic
development or modernization.[36] Furthermore, using a consumption-oriented
measure as the indicator of development in our age of environmental consciousness feels disturbing, if not irresponsible. Nevertheless, energy consumption per capita has been employed for several reasons: First, it is the measure
used by many authors, especially by the modernization theorists and by those
whose work is cited here. Second, the measure captures conceptually the definition of modernization by a well-known theorist, Marion Levy:

> My definition of modernization hinges on the uses of inanimate sources of power
> and the use of tools to multiply the effect of effort. I conceive each of these two ele-
> ments as the basis of continuum. A society will be considered more or less modern-
> ized to the extent that its members use inanimate sources of power and/or tools to
> multiply the effects of their efforts. Neither of these elements is either totally absent
> from or exclusively present in any society.[37]

Finally, energy consumption per capita is preferred because of its strong correlation with and relative superiority over the other possible indicators. Research
based on data from 74 countries and for five commonly used indicators of
modernization reaches the following conclusion:

Figure 3.1 Possible Relationships Between Levels of Democracy and Economic Development

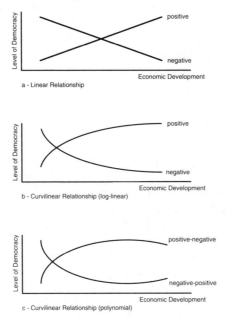

a - Linear Relationship

b - Curvilinear Relationship (log-linear)

c - Curvilinear Relationship (polynomial)

All five societal measures correlate quite highly with each other, and in an empirical sense, are not highly distinct from one another. The overall significance of the findings is that all of the societal measures, whether they are labeled modernization, societal differentiation, human resource development, or economic development, are apparently not measuring different aspects of societies, but rather some general underlying dimension. Considering data availability, coverage and accessibility, an argument is presented for use of "energy consumption" as the measure of societal modernity—development.[38]

First, to test for the linearity hypothesis, the democraticness scores of all countries are regressed on energy consumption per capita (ECO) for each year separately for the time period 1948–1982.

$$\text{Democraticness}_i = a + b\,(\text{ECO})_i + u_i \qquad (1)$$

For the curvilinearity hypothesis, two different models are employed for two possible curvilinear relationships: The first, a log-linear model, suggests that the level of democracy increases with economic development until a certain level of economic development is reached and then further economic development does not have a significant effect on democraticness. This is tested by regressing the scores of democracy on the logarithmic transformation of energy consumption per capita values.

$$\text{Democraticness}_i = a + b \, (\ln\text{ECO})_i + u_i \tag{2}$$

Next, a second-degree polynomial model suggests that the level of democracy increases with economic development until a certain level of economic development is reached, but it starts to decline with further economic development. This is tested by regressing the index scores of democracy on energy consumption per capita and the squared value of energy consumption per capita.

$$\text{Democraticness}_i = a + b_1 \, (\text{ECO})_i + b_2 \, (\text{ECO})_i^2 + u_i \tag{3}$$

A comparison of the results of these three regression models enables us to evaluate the strength of each hypothesis. If the linearity hypothesis of the early modernization theorists holds, the regression coefficient (slope = b) should be positive and significant and the coefficient of determination (R^2) should be high and significant. If the revised modernization theory holds, the log-linear model should yield a positive and significant regression coefficient (b) and a better fit to data than the linear model, with the better fit to data captured by a relatively higher and significant R^2. The third model, a slightly different curvilinear model, needs a positive regression coefficient for energy consumption per capita (b_1) and a negative significant regression coefficient (b_2) for its squared value, which refers to the decline after a certain level of economic development is reached. This last hypothesis is implicit in studies that emphasize the increasing state responsibilities and power and the rapidly expanding bureaucracies in modern industrial, or so-called postindustrial, societies.

The regression results of cross-national analysis for 35 different years confirm the findings of Jackman and Neubauer. The log-linear model (model 2) provides a better fit to the data for almost all years. The average R^2 for 35 years is .27 for this model as opposed to .25 for the polynomial model and .20 for the linear model (Appendix C). This finding indicates that at a given time point, relatively more developed countries tend to have more democratic systems, but the level of democracy does not increase with the level of economic development for countries located at the higher end of the economic development scale. Moreover, this relationship appears to be stable over time.

The same relationship is observed when the scores of democracy for all countries for all of the available years are regressed on socioeconomic development. It should be noted, however, that such an analysis of pooled data (longitudinal and cross-sectional data combined) treats each year for each country as a separate observation. It does not capture the pattern followed by an individual country over time. Thus, to check whether this curvilinear relationship holds over time when the relationship is studied for each country, scores of democracy from 6 to 33 years for each country are employed for the same three regression models.[39]

Contrary to the results from the cross-national analyses, the findings from the longitudinal application of data to the three models suggest more complex relationships. (See Appendix D for the regression analysis results for each country.) Although the short period of time with available data prevents us from deriving any comprehensive conclusions, the patterns manifested by each country can be sorted under seven major categories (Table 3.1) to display the variety of relationships illustrated by Figure 3.1.

The No Relationship category includes the countries that display no systematic relationship in terms of the three models tested, at .05 significance level. Countries are included in one of the Linear categories if there is a significant positive or negative linear relationship (Positive-Linear and Negative-Linear respectively) observed between economic development and democracy, and if neither of the curvilinear models provides a better fit to the data (i.e., a significant increase in the explained variance reflected by a significantly high R^2). While the Positive-Linear category includes the countries that become more democratic over time with increasing levels of socioeconomic development, the Negative-Linear category refers to change in the opposite direction (socioeconomic development appears with decline in democraticness).

Positive-Log-Linear and Negative-Log-Linear categories refer to the countries for which the log-linear model provides the best fit to the data. The Positive-Log-Linear category covers the countries that display an increase in democraticness with increasing levels of economic development until a certain level of economic development is reached, and no relationship appears after that level. Similarly, the Negative-Log-Linear category refers to continuous decline in the level of democracy with increasing economic development up to a certain level of economic development.

Countries are classified as Polynomial Positive-Negative or Polynomial Negative-Positive if the second-degree polynomial model provides a better fit in comparison with the other models. The Positive-Negative category covers the countries for which an increase in democraticness is observed with increasing levels of economic development until a certain level of economic development is reached, and then further increase in economic development appears with a decline in democraticness. The Negative-Positive category refers to the reverse of this relationship.

If the evolutionary thesis suggested by the modernization theorists is to hold, most of the "developing countries" should appear in the Positive-Linear category, and most of the "developed" countries should appear in the No-Relationship category. However, as seen in Table 3.1, only a few countries fit the models suggested by modernization theory. Out of 146 countries, only 21 experience increasing levels of democracy with increasing levels of economic development. Moreover, the category is not limited to developing countries. Even though most of them can be considered as developing countries, several economically advanced countries demonstrate a linear pattern. Other developed countries, along with the rest of the developing countries, are spread into the other categories, each of which refers to a different pattern of relationship.

Table 3.1 Countries Classified According to the Relationship Between Their Levels of Democracy and Economic Development

Linear		Log-Linear		Polynomial		No Relationship	
Positive	Negative	Positive	Negative	Positive	Negative	Negative	Positive
Australia	Comoros	Algeria	Bahrain	Afghanistan	Brazil	Angola	Qatar
Bahamas	Gambia	Austria	Barbados	Albania	Burma	Argentina	Sao Tome and Principe
Belgium	Guyana	Canada	Cameroon	Bulgaria	Cape Verde	Bangladesh	Seychelles
Colombia	Kenya	Costa Rica	Chad	Burundi	Central African R	Benin	Sierra Leone
Czechoslovakia	Madagascar	Denmark	Fiji	Congo	Chile	Bolivia	Singapore
Equitorial Guinea	Mozambique	Dominican R	Haiti	Jordan	China	Cyprus	Sudan
Ethiopia	Niger	Egypt	Iraq	Mauritania	Cuba	Gabon	Suriname
Finland	Panama	El Salvador	Malawi	Mexico	Ecuador	Ghana	Syria
Iceland	Philippines	Germany, DR	Rwanda	Mongolia	France	Grenada	Thailand
India		Germany, FR	Somalia	Nepal	Greece	Guatemala	Trinidad
Ireland		Indonesia		Paraguay	Hungary	Guinea	Turkey
Kampuchea		Iran		Peru	Laos	Guinea-Bissau	Uganda
Korea		Italy		Tunisia	Lebanon	Honduras	United Kingdom
Libya		Ivory Coast		Uruguay	Nigeria	Israel	United States
Morocco		Japan		Yemen, AR	Poland	Jamaica	Upper Volta
Netherlands		Korea, DPR		Yugoslavia	South Africa	Liberia	Vietnam, PR
Portugal		Kuwait			Switzerland	Malaysia	Vietnam, S
Romania		Luxembourg			Togo	Malta	Vietnam
Spain		Mali			USSR	Mauritius	Yemen, PDR
Sweden		New Zealand				Nicaragua	Zaire
Western Samoa		Norway				Oman	Zambia
		Saudi Arabia				Pakistan	Zimbabwe
		Senegal				Papua New Guinea	
		Sri Lanka					
		Tanzania					
		Venezuela					

On the basis of these findings, it can be concluded that increasing levels of economic development do not necessarily lead to higher levels of democracy, even for the less-developed countries. When such a relationship has been observed through the study of cross-national data, it suggests only this: At a given time point, the countries with more democratic political systems happen to be the ones that are economically more developed. As Rustow emphasized in his critique of the "Lipset-Cutright genre," "correlation is not the same as causation."[40]

Developing countries, on the other hand, do not display a linear relationship but instead more complex patterns or no systematic relationship at all. In fact, most of these countries, especially the ones located in the middle of the development axis, experience higher levels of instability—a continuous back-and-forth shift—on the scale of democracy. Huntington classifies these unstable political systems in his "cyclical model" of democratization and divides them into two groups on the basis of their regularity in oscillation between two forms of systems. In countries such as Peru, Ecuador, Bolivia, Argentina, Ghana, and Nigeria, where the oscillation is quite regular, "the alternation of democracy and despotism is the political system"; in others, "the shift from a stable despotism to a stable democracy is a change in political systems."[41]

DEMOCRATIC INSTABILITY AND ECONOMIC DEVELOPMENT

A method to measure instability of a democracy, based on the scale discussed here, was developed to identify patterns of oscillation. For each country, the sum of the absolute values of the annual change in democracy scores was divided by the number of years in the time period covered (which varies for each country according to the date of independence and data availability) to obtain an average score of "change in the level of democracy." This calculation follows the logic that the more frequent or larger the shifts a country displays on the scale of democracy, the higher it will score on democratic instability. Out of 152 countries included in Table 3.2, Suriname (11.2), Bolivia (10.6), Bangladesh (9.8), Guatemala (9.7), Argentina (9.5), and Peru (9.3) compose the most unstable group with instability scores higher than 9. Bahamas, Bhutan, Tunisia, Qatar, Malta, Austria, Papua New Guinea, United Arab Emirates, and Mauritius constitute the most stable group with instability scores less than .7, with the mean value being 3.33. It should be noted, however, that the instability score is not a general measure of political instability but rather a specific measure of the instability in regard to the level of democraticness. That is, countries ranking high on this scale experience more frequent and larger shifts between relatively more authoritarian and democratic systems.

To test for the hypothesis that the middle-range developed countries (MDCs) experience higher levels of democratic instability than do the least developed and advanced developed countries (LDCs and ADCs), a regression model that captures the curvilinearity of the relationship between economic

Table 3.2   Democratic Instability Scores of Countries

Country	Score	Country	Score
Bahamas	.40	Germany, FR	1.86
Bhutan	.50	Italy	1.86
Tunisia	.54	Germany, DR	1.87
Qatar	.61	Costa Rica	1.95
Malta	.62	Ivory Coast	1.97
Austria	.65	Finland	2.01
Papua New Guinea	.65	Algeria	2.11
United Arab Emirates	.66	Israel	2.17
Mauritius	.69	Poland	2.20
Ireland	.75	Libya	2.23
Sao Tome and Principe	.79	Afghanistan	2.24
Malawi	.83	Burundi	2.26
Sweden	.84	Central African R	2.30
Iceland	.85	Haiti	2.37
Korea, DPR	.88	Australia	2.38
Bulgaria	.89	Malaysia	2.40
New Zealand	.91	Chad	2.44
Maldive Islands	.92	Czechoslovakia	2.46
Tanzania	.95	Paraguay	2.47
Romania	.96	Canada	2.49
Gambia	1.01	Cyprus	2.51
Jamaica	1.04	Iraq	2.55
Belgium	1.12	South Africa	2.61
Oman	1.12	Mali	2.66
Guyana	1.14	Cameroon	2.67
Barbados	1.14	Rwanda	2.70
Switzerland	1.22	United Kingdom	2.71
Mongolia	1.22	India	2.79
Albania	1.24	Equatorial Guinea	2.84
Zambia	1.24	Yemen, PDR	2.90
Vietnam, PR	1.25	Mauritania	2.92
Botswana	1.29	Lebanon	3.00
Kenya	1.29	Togo	3.04
Singapore	1.30	Nepal	3.17
Yugoslavia	1.33	Venezuela	3.17
Ethiopia	1.38	Gabon	3.27
Fiji	1.38	Hungary	3.29
Liberia	1.41	Portugal	3.34
Sri Lanka	1.45	United States	3.35
Japan	1.46	Trinidad and Tobago	3.39
Luxembourg	1.52	Colombia	3.44
Denmark	1.57	China	3.45
Guinea	1.58	Guinea-Bissau	3.47
Kuwait	1.61	Philippines	3.49
Norway	1.61	Yemen	3.50
Bahrain	1.62	Dominican Republic	3.55
USSR	1.63	Jordan	3.56
Saudi Arabia	1.65	Nicaragua	3.61
Senegal	1.65	Somalia	3.67
Netherlands	1.66	Spain	3.72
Mexico	1.68	Madagascar	3.85
France	1.80	Lesotho	3.85
Niger	1.81	Indonesia	3.98
Western Samoa	1.86	Uruguay	4.06

(continues)

Table 3.2. *(continued)*

Country	Score	Country	Score
Panama	4.07	Turkey	6.71
Zaire	4.08	Zimbabwe	6.85
Egypt	4.23	Comoros	6.91
Chile	4.26	Nigeria	6.94
Iran	4.34	Upper Volta	7.02
Benin	4.38	El Salvador	7.07
Cape Verde Islands	4.40	Greece	7.11
Swaziland	4.60	Korea	7.12
Congo Republic	4.68	Vietnam	7.23
Angola	4.70	Sierra Leone	7.35
Laos	4.74	Honduras	7.36
Burma	4.89	Pakistan	7.89
Vietnam	4.93	Grenada	8.00
Uganda	4.97	Thailand	8.24
Syria	5.27	Ghana	8.32
Ecuador	5.45	Seychelles	8.36
Brazil	5.71	Peru	9.33
Morocco	5.76	Argentina	9.50
Cuba	5.76	Guatemala	9.69
Kampuchea	5.90	Bangladesh	9.75
Mozambique	5.97	Bolivia	10.62
Sudan	6.69	Suriname	11.21

development and instability is employed. The instability scores for the countries listed in Table 3.2 (except Bhutan, Botswana, Lesotho, the Maldives, and Swaziland, which are excluded for lack of data on energy consumption) are regressed on the logarithmic values of their average energy consumption per capita (AVECO) and the squared value of this indicator of economic development. Logarithmic transformation of average energy consumption values is employed to smooth the highly (positively) skewed data.

$$\text{Instability}_i = a + b_1 (\ln AVECO)_i + b_2 (\ln AVECO)_i^2 + u_i$$

In this second-degree polynomial model, if the regression coefficient b_1 is positive but b_2 is negative and they are both significant, we can say that there is a curvilinear relationship between the instability of the political system and the development level of the country, meaning that the MDCs tend to display higher levels of instability.

The analysis supports the hypothesis with a considerably strong and significant correlation ($R = .36$) and with a confirming regression equation:

$$\text{Instability} = .823 + 1.41 (\ln AVECO) - .15 (\ln AVECO)^2$$

The findings display that an evolutionary thesis based on the analysis of cross-national data for a fixed time point is misleading. Our findings support the hypothesis that MDCs experience more frequent or larger shifts between

Figure 3.2 Plot of Democratic Instability and Economic Development

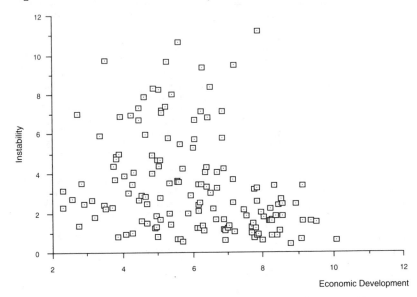

more and less democratic systems as opposed to LDCs and ADCs. A scatter-gram of the instability and economic development scores illustrates the curvi-linear relationship (Figure 3.2).

If we ignore the positive change in the score of democraticness and examine the average decline in the annual scores, again MDCs appear as the group that experiences highest levels of decline.[42]

CONCLUSION

The two major findings from the analyses presented here provide sufficient evidence to question modernization theory, which considers democratic development as an evolutionary phenomenon. First, a longitudinal analysis yields widely varied relationships between levels of socioeconomic development and democracy. It is clear that democracy is not a one-way ladder that countries climb as their economy and social structures develop. If there has been any linearity in the democratization process, it was on one of its components: inclusiveness of the electoral process. All countries that hold elections, regardless of the strength of their democratic institutions, have extended their electoral basis. Today, only a handful of countries exclude women or racial and ethnic groups or require literacy. Suffrage tends to be universal, and the minimum voting age is being reduced. The other components of democracy, however, do not manifest any particular pattern of progress through time.

Second, shifts on the scale of democracy are observed in a considerable number of countries. They tend to be highest in countries located near the middle of the development scale. These countries have experienced high rates of democratic instability within the 1948–1982 period. Therefore, the positive correlation between economic development and democracy displayed by the cross-sectional data but not confirmed by the longitudinal data supports the early arguments of Lipset and Coleman. These authors identified economic development as a necessary but not a sufficient condition of democratic development. However, those who attempted to test their hypothesis neglected this major assertion, treated economic development as almost the single determinant, and limited their study and discussions to a linear/curvilinear argument. Thus, forty years later, they left the same question unaddressed or largely unanswered: What might be the other conditions of democracy? Or, as this study poses it: Which conditions of middle-range development and what other factors might be related to the decline of democracy?

NOTES

1. Moore, 1967; Soboul.
2. Schumpeter, pp. 296–297.
3. Huntington, 1984, p. 204.
4. See Diamond, Linz, and Lipset, especially the introductions; Weiner, "Empirical Democratic Theory," in Weiner and Özbudum; Baker.
5. Solid analysis and strong evidence for this argument are provided by Atul Kohli in his comparative analysis of Indian states. See Kohli, 1987.
6. Richard Robinson; Swaison; Nafziger; Lubeck; Fatton, 1988 and 1990; Therborn.
7. Agbese, p. 41.
8. Baran; Frank; Amin, 1974 and 1976; Wallerstein, 1974; Delacroix and Ragin; Evans and Timberlake.
9. Lipset, 1967.
10. Ibid., p. 9.
11. Ibid., p. 23.
12. Ibid., p. 15.
13. Roberts.
14. Ibid., pp. 15–16.
15. O'Donnell.
16. Moore, 1967.
17. Bardhan, p. 215.
18. Boratav, p. 84.
19. Vega, p. 143.
20. Tekeli and Ilkin, p. 46.
21. Ibid., p. 24.
22. Cardoso, 1967, p. 102.
23. Almond and Verba, 1963; Lerner.
24. Almond and Verba, 1963.
25. Deutsch, 1966; and Pye.
26. Lerner; Lipset, 1959 and 1960.

27. Lipset, 1959, p. 86. Lipset's later work on the subject (Lipset, 1981) reflects the same premises and conclusions.

28. Although Lipset's argument is the most interesting of its kind and more comprehensive than his successors', his analysis suffers from certain methodological inadequacies. First, he categorizes the countries on the basis of a rather ad hoc criterion. Second, such nominal categorization masks considerable variation within the groups of countries. Third, the cumulative character of his measure prevents him from identifying the conditions that lead to instability. And more important, he does not make a distinction between conditions needed to establish a democracy and those required to maintain such a system. He uses these two terms casually by neglecting the signficant conceptual differences between them. Finally, although he emphasizes the importance of effectiveness and legitimacy of the system, he leaves them as abstract concepts without concrete linkage to their social and economic origins.

29. Coleman, 1960.

30. Ibid., p. 544.

31. Coulter; Cutright; Cutright and Wiley; Arthur K. Smith, Jr.

32. Neubauer; Jackman, 1973.

33. Quoted in Almond and Verba, 1980, p. 7.

34. Lijphart, p. 38; and Huntington, 1984.

35. The energy consumption data used in this study were obtained from Banks, 1979.

36. The pitfalls of using a single indicator of a complex concept like socioeconomic development or modernization and the changes in the implications of such indicators over time have been discussed and displayed by Banks, 1981.

37. As quoted in Safranko, Nolan, and Bealer, p. 302.

38. Ibid., p. 301.

39. The number of years included is determined by the independence date of the country and the availability of data.

40. Rustow, 1970.

41. Huntington, 1984 p. 210.

42. The explained variance for the decline model increases by 2 percent compared with the instability model.

4

Democracy in Developing Countries: Its Correlates

[The citizens of the United States] will avoid the necessity of those overgrown military establishments which, under any form of government, are inauspicious to liberty, and which are to be regarded as particularly hostile to republican liberty.—George Washington

DEMOCRACY DOES EXIST IN DEVELOPING COUNTRIES

Both the class analysis of democracy and the empirical tests of modernization theory defined the prevailing conditions as unsuitable for the advancement of democracy in developing countries and predicted an unpromising future. Nevertheless, some developing countries have established democratic political institutions, and a few of them have managed to maintain fairly stable democracies.

Among 128 developing countries[1] for which we have data, at least 51 made serious attempts to establish democratic systems. But less than half of these maintained stable democracies; others experienced vacillations between highly democratic and authoritarian systems. Including some relatively young states whose political capabilities have not been fully tested, we can identify 20 developing countries as stable democracies. Although their annual scores of democracy vary—some score over 100, some in the high 80s or 90s, and some fluctuate between these levels—once they obtained an annual·democracy score higher than 82, their scores remained above that level for subsequent years. The Bahamas, Barbados, Botswana, Colombia, Costa Rica, Cyprus, the Dominican Republic, Fiji, Gambia, Guyana, India, Jamaica, Malta, Mauritius, Papua New Guinea, Venezuela, and Western Samoa have maintained highly democratic systems. The same appears true of Sri Lanka, Trinidad and Tobago and of Zimbabwe, but the political turmoil observed in the first two during the late 1980s and in 1990 and the move toward a one-party system initiated in the latter in 1987 may qualify them for a category other than that of "stable democracies." Brazil, Burma, Chile, El Salvador, Greece, Grenada, Guatemala, Honduras, Lebanon, Madagascar, Malaysia, Nigeria, Panama, Peru, the Philippines, Somalia, Suriname, Turkey, and Uruguay, established highly democratic structures, but experienced either major declines from which they could not recover or cycles of democratic and authoritarian rule. A third group of countries evidenced brief episodes of democratic rule within a mainly authoritarian setting. Although their experiences with different forms of rule have not been equal, and some leaned toward democracy more than did others, Argentina, Bolivia, Cameroon, Congo, Cuba, Ecuador, Indonesia, the Korean Republic, Lesotho, Laos, Pakistan, and Sierra Leone can be counted in this group.

What differences among these groups of countries account for their success or failure in maintaining democratic structures? Major differences are apparent in socioeconomic matters: The stable democracies tend to reflect higher levels of socioeconomic equality. The neglect of social and economic rights puts pressure on the system and eventually leads the civil and political rights that are ingredients of a viable democracy to draw a declining curve. A review of the destabilizing factors that have been presented by others and of their relevance to this argument is useful before further elaborations of our human rights model of declining democracies.

PARTY SYSTEM AND ELECTORAL LAWS

Ever since the failure of the Weimar Republic in Germany and the Fourth Republic in France in maintaining their competitive electoral systems and democratic stability, students of democracy have identified the multiparty system and proportional representation as destabilizing political factors. Two party systems and electoral rules that reduce the power of small parties through some mechanism of thresholds or through single-member constituencies are considered to yield more suitable conditions for government and regime stability.[2] Having a large number of parties, it is argued, frustrates the consensus-building process and prevents the establishment of strong governments. When the seats in the parliament are parceled among several small parties, with no one party able to maintain the majority, governments would be either minority or coalition governments. Minority governments, lacking parliamentary support, would be unable to take decisive measures and would be weak. The coalition governments, composed of two or more parties—especially if the parties are ideologically diverse—not only would be weak, but would also tend to act irresponsibly due to the diffusion of responsibility among the member parties. Each partner in the government would try to avoid responsibility on difficult issues and blame the other partner(s) for unpopular decisions. Moreover, when composed of several parties, coalition governments would rarely reach consensus on major issues. Fewer parties—ideally, two-party systems—on the other hand, would establish majority governments that would rule according to their party programs and function as "responsible governments."[3]

Some scholars who believe that democracy survives in consensus societies

also argue that political cultures and electoral systems that yield only a few ideologically close parties are more auspicious for the stability of democracy.
Extremist parties on either side, but especially those on the left, would exacerbate conflicts and accelerate polarization. Thus such parties should be restricted
or eliminated either by setting high thresholds in the electoral system or by ban-
ning them.[4] In fact, the Federal Republic of Germany has followed this strategy
to avoid a recurrence of the problems of the Weimar Republic that would lead
to another era of instability.

Preventing party proliferation and polarization, however, is not easy.
Manipulation of the party system through restrictive party laws or electoral systems seems to be the most common strategy. But imposing the procedural
restrictions that would produce a few large and ideologically close parties can
be counterproductive for democracy. Juan Linz argues that regime stability
largely depends on the number of the regime's supporters, and it can be
increased through co-option of larger groups into the mechanisms of political
participation and decisionmaking.[5] Restricting the political arena, then, would
only weaken the democracy by pushing the adherents of small or ideologically
extreme parties outside of the system, to challenge its legitimacy. In contrast,
allowing extremist parties and especially those on the left may challenge the
centrist or social democratic governments to undertake some reforms and
improve those social and economic rights that would increase the system's
legitimacy and reinforce stability.

Evidence, both from the old democracies of Europe and the younger ones
in developing countries, shows that neither multiple parties nor their ideological
diversity necessarily results in political breakdown. Arend Lijphart's analysis of
21 European democracies concludes that the "responsible-party model" based
on majoritarianism tends to be the exception rather than the rule.[6] In addition to
coalition governments, minority cabinets are quite common in Europe and in
many countries have appeared at least once in every twenty years. In
Scandinavian and lowland countries, governments based on parliamentary
minorities composed half of the cabinets established since 1945.[7] Moreover,
these systems in fact are open to political diversity. So-called extremist parties
have been allowed to share the political platform to discuss issues, to propose
alternative policies, and to run in elections. Such parties rarely garner more than
1 to 2 percent of the votes; exceptions are the Flemish separatists in Belgium
and so-called "extreme" left-wing and right-wing parties in Italy and
Luxembourg.[8] Nevertheless, they present choices, and by challenging the larger
mainstream parties, they force governments to be more responsive to popular
demands. This is best displayed in Italy, which is described by LaPalombara as
a stable democracy despite its high governmental turnovers and "extremist"
political parties.[9] Although the Italian Communist Party (recently renamed the
Democratic Party of the Left) has been kept out of political office through political maneuvering, the approximately one-third of the votes it receives makes it
visible and keeps pressure on other parties.[10]

CONSTITUTIONAL STRUCTURE:
PRESIDENTIAL VERSUS PARLIAMENTARY SYSTEMS

As occurred on the issue of party structures and electoral systems, discussions on the relative merits of parliamentary and presidential systems in regard to their support for stability accelerated after the failure of the German and French democracies. When parliamentary systems failed to provide strong executives, especially in the case of multiparty systems, both students of politics and lawmakers began to treat presidential systems as a viable alternative. An executive elected directly by and responsible to the people, rather than to its representatives in the legislature, would be a cure to the problems of proliferation and polarization. Thus, the French Fifth Republic designed a presidential-parliamentary system by investing the president with considerable executive power.

After decolonization, most developing countries instituted parliamentary democracies modeled after the British Westminster style, though the Latin American countries adopted the presidential system of their neighbor, the United States. Some countries later expanded the power of originally symbolic heads of state by endowing them with the right to veto parliamentary decisions or to dissolve the parliament if it reaches a stalemate, but they maintained the essence of the parliamentary system by keeping the cabinet and its head, the major executive (premier), responsible to the parliament.

The merit of the presidential system for maintaining stability becomes a debatable issue in the light of evidence from the Latin American countries. Presidential democratic systems in these countries have mostly failed to open the decisionmaking process to the whole citizen body and have been subject to frequent military takeovers. These factors forced political scientists to introduce some further qualifications. They argued that in a political environment where political institutions are weak and political leaders are strong (as it is in many Latin American countries where the *caudillo* tradition prevailed), presidential systems with strong executives may lead to dictatorships. Moreover, it was held that executive power centralized and concentrated in the hands of one person, and not controlled or balanced with a strong legislature, would reinforce the corporatist system[11] and respond to the interests of the elite rather than to those of the public.[12] In Latin America, where such problems have been acute, there has been some effort to curtail the power of individual leaders. In Uruguay, for example, José Batlle y Ordóñez, a two-term president who believed that presidents in Latin America were too strong and easily became dictators, initiated a collegial executive rule that was used from 1917 to 1933. In 1951 the *colegiado* system was reestablished by popular vote but failed to solve the problems of the country. The executive council functioned more like a problematic coalition government and led the system to stalemate and paralysis.[13]

Thus, we may conclude that the presidential or parliamentary composition of the executive office does not by itself determine the stability of the system. Political tradition, the level of institutionalization, and other prevailing cultural factors in a society may establish a milieu more suitable for one type of constitutional arrangement than the other. In fact, in addition to several failures, we see examples of success from both types of system: Costa Rica, Colombia, and Venezuela have maintained relatively successful presidential democracies, whereas India, Sri Lanka, Jamaica, Papua New Guinea, Barbados, and Guyana have demonstrated that a parliamentary system does not necessarily yield instability.

ETHNIC, LINGUISTIC, AND RELIGIOUS DIVERSITY

The social and political impact of ethnic, linguistic, and religious diversities has been a puzzle for social scientists for a long time. These factors, confirmed as causes of past wars, are considered as challenges for national unity and democracy in contemporary societies. Theories of modernization treat people's emphasis on their ethnic or religious identity, as opposed to national identity, as a trait of traditionalism and view communal consciousness as a dysfunctional factor that should be suppressed or eliminated in the process of nation-state building.[14] Modern societies are expected to reflect social pluralism based on cooperation around the national interest, which transcends ethnic or religious differences. But because development of a national identity in the new "nation-states" is not completed—or may not even be possible due to their borders being arbitrarily drawn by the colonial powers—the ethnic, religious, and tribal differences are held responsible for their political instability.

Ethnic, religious, or linguistic conflicts continue even in some Western countries that are "modern" and economically advanced, such as Canada and Belgium—which illustrates that modernity does not necessarily warm the melting pot. There are two explanations for this. First, civil and political rights were included in constitutions as "constitutional rights" around the time when societies were reorganizing and establishing nation-states. In an effort to create a national identity, ethnic and linguistic differences were overlooked and cultural hegemonies were established. Thus, the wave of social unrest observable in contemporary societies today represents struggles for "cultural rights" that are yet to be included in modern constitutions. Second, political demands and social unrest associated with cultural groups are usually class-related and entail struggles for social and economic equality. Today we know that economic and political factors were more important for undertaking the Christian Crusades, although religion served as a persuasive tool for mobilizing masses. Similarly, in contemporary societies, ethnic, religious, and linguistic rivalries are more likely to be facades for struggles for economic and political justice. The denial to certain groups of the benefits of economic development and national wealth creates resentment and frustration and turns the disadvantaged groups against the system. While such demands are more likely to be suppressed in authoritarian systems, democracies, which allow demands to be vocalized and encourage groups to organize around issues, are more susceptible to secessionist movements and social unrest. Even in the Soviet Union, a country not defined as highly democratic by any scale, it is no accident that ethnic conflicts and demands became more frequent and visible under glasnost.

Ethnic, religious, and linguistic differences transform into a major political problem if they correspond to significant social and economic inequalities. They provide a source of identity and a common bond for the socially and economically deprived groups. In other words, communal conflicts and secessionist movements are more likely to arise when ethnic, religious, and linguistic combinations transform into class configurations.

Das Gupta, who defines ethnic action "as a form of collective action conveniently using emotional affinity to make claims on the powers that decide who should be the beneficiaries of the development process," explains the ethnic conflicts in India as reactions to the interregional and intraregional economic discrepancies.[15] Similarly, Shah argues that the "grass-roots mobilization in politics [in India] has resulted from ethnic as well as economic issues."[16] Das Gupta adds that because the initiative for development and investments in India has originated mostly from the central government, "if the government has chosen a design of development that selectively dispenses benefits to certain ethnic groups, then excluded groups will naturally feel that ethnic mobilization may yield access to central power and therefore to the desired opportunities."[17] This observation can be extended to many countries that reflect communal diversity and unrest. In fact, a similar argument is presented by a student of African politics, Dov Ronen, who finds the solution to ethnic hostilities in political decentralization:

> No clear-cut evidence has been found to support the view that ethnic diversity is in itself the cause of instability. . . . The utilization and manipulation of ethnic identities appears to be the single most important factor in political instability. This occurs when ethnic groups are mobilized by political leaders stuggling to gain the *centralized* political power. If power were to be decentralized, the struggle for power would be bound to decline, and, with it, the intensity of political instability.[18]

FORMER COLONIAL EXPERIENCE

Although all colonial rules were based on extreme inequalities between the rulers and the ruled and were authoritarian in essence, they varied in style and in the extent to which they co-opted the natives into the decisionmaking process at the national or local levels. Because most of the former colonies that experimented with democratic systems or even established stable democracies are former British colonies, many scholars reached the conclusion that British colonialism was more co-optive and better prepared the natives for self-rule through democratic institutions.[19] The British created a national elite who were educated in the British liberal tradition and whose members were later recruited into the civil service system. The national elite were allowed to participate in the decisionmaking process at least at the local level, and although it was limited, when the electoral system was introduced it allowed the natives to gain experience. In contrast, it was claimed that French rule lacked many of these properties, and Spanish colonial rule was characterized by a hierarchical authoritarian structure.

The empirical evidence, however, suggests that the British colonialists were given too much credit. The raw number of former colonies that established stable democracies is a misleading measure. If we consider the fact that the British Empire ruled more territories than the other colonial powers and eventually gave way to more independent countries (Table 4.1), we would conclude that the overall influence of the British is not significantly more democratic than that of the others. (It should be noted that the style of British rule varied from one colony to another. The prototype rule described here is not valid for Britain's later colonies, especially for those areas designated as British mandates or protectorates after World War I.)

Typically, the formation of democracy in India and its persistence despite its socioeconomic disadvantages are explained by the protodemocratic political traditions inherited from its colonial past.[20] One cannot help questioning the validity of this view given the political experiences of Pakistan and Bangladesh, two countries that came out of the same colonial rule, the British Raj. Moreover, by the end of 1951, British-type political institutions and universal suffrage were introduced by the British in virtually in all of their remaining colonies. The impact of such exposure during colonial rule on the type of political systems established after independence has not been always democratic. Even the British were not confident about the final outcome. The British government's decision to implant British parliamentarism in the colonies was found fruitless even by its own officals, who compared the effort to the translation of belles lettres and asserted that "even in the best translations the essential meaning is apt to be lost."[21]

Among the 128 developing countries for which we have data, 42 experienced British rule, but the record of democracy among these countries has been one of extreme contrasts. Although 15 of them established highly democratic and stable systems and 6 tried it unsuccessfully, half of these countries appear at the other end of the spectrum without any major experience in democracy. In comparison, although only four of them have been stable democracies, virtually all Spanish colonies experimented with democracy. In fact, the average score of democraticness for the countries that experienced British rule is 73.8, approximating the overall average of 73 for the study. This is only slightly higher than the 73.3 average for the former Spanish colonies. Similarly, the average regime instability score for these countries (3.1) is not significantly lower than the overall average (3.1). Although the political changes in some of these countries have been in the direction of democratization, the relatively low average on the score of decline in the level of democraticness in the former British colonies is

Table 4.1 Developing Countries and Their Foreign Rulers

Britain	Spain	France	Other Western	Non-Western	No Direct Foreign Rule
Bahrain	Argentina	Algeria	Libya	Albania	Afghanistan
Bahamas	Bolivia	Benin	Somalia	Bulgaria	Hungary
Bangladesh	Chile	Central African R	Burundi	Czechoslovakia	Bhutan
Barbados	Colombia	Chad	Zaire	Greece	China
Botswana	Costa Rica	Comoros	Indonesia	Korea, PR	Ethiopia
Burma	Cuba	Congo	South Africa	Korea, R	Iran
Cyprus	Dominican R	Gabon	Suriname	Mongolia	Israel
Egypt	Ecuador	Guinea	Cameroon	Romania	Liberia
Fiji	El Salvador	Haiti	Togo	Saudi Arabia	Nepal
Gambia	Equatorial	Ivory Coast	Western Samoa	Sudan	Poland
Ghana	Guinea	Kampuchea	Angola	Yemen, R	Thailand
Grenada	Guatemala	Laos	Brazil	Yugoslavia	Turkey
Guyana	Honduras	Lebanon	Cape Verde		
India	Mexico	Madagascar	Guinea-Bissau		
Iraq	Nicaragua	Mali	Mozambique		
Jamaica	Panama	Mauritania	Sao Tome and Principe		
Jordan	Paraguay	Morocco	Papua New Guinea		
Kenya	Peru	Niger			
Kuwait	Philippines	Senegal			
Lesotho	Uruguay	Syria			
Malawi	Venezuela	Tunisia			
Malaysia		Upper Volta			
Maldives		Vietnam			
Malta		Vietnam, PR			
Mauritius		Vietnam, S			
Nigeria					
Oman					
Pakistan					
Qatar					
Rwanda					
Seychelles					
Sierra Leone					
Singapore					
Sri Lanka					
Swaziland					
Tanzania					
Trinidad					
Uganda					
UA Emirates					
Yemen, PDR					
Zambia					
Zimbabwe					

not statistically significant when compared to the other developing countries.[22] If we include the countries not ruled solely or directly by the British—that is, where Britain was only one of the colonial powers (e.g., Suriname, Togo, Somalia) or where British political culture was introduced by another Western power such as the United States (e.g. Philippines, Cuba)—the number of countries exposed to Anglo-Saxon traditions increases to 52. But that does not improve the British record of democratic influence.

One may argue that the length of the British presence varied from ten years to over two centuries, with the colonial rulers more likely to make a stronger cultural impact the longer they stayed. The correlation analysis, conducted to test the hypothesis that "the longer the British rule in a country, the lower its democratic instability score" yielded no significant correlations between the two ($r = .11$ and F-value is $.46$). However, I would not totally reject the reasoning that political traditions, colonial or native, that prevailed before independence would be influential in determining the fate of the democratic system. Thus, some experience in electoral systems and in open political discussions would serve as reinforcing factors. However, it should be noted that if these practices were directly introduced by the colonial powers, they may be rejected as a part of the foreign, imperial heritage, as has been the case in many countries following their independence movements.

The way the colonies mounted their independence movements, I believe, is a more significant factor in determining the success of the postcolonial democratic systems than is identifying the colonial power involved. Many colonies gained their independence through armed struggle. The higher the extent to which the independence movement was led or controlled by military leaders or relatively organized military groups, the less favorable the outcome was for the development of democracy. This matter leads us to analysis of the political role of the military and its impact on the stability of democracy.

POLITICAL ROLE OF THE MILITARY

Elected democratic governments in developing countries are often overthrown by military coups d'état. Thus, the nature of the military becomes a central point in discussions regarding democratic stability. The military elements in developing countries establish themselves as rival but strong political entities for several reasons. First, in societies where institutionalization is weak, the military appears to be the most professional and best-organized group. Second, as the armed forces of the nation, the military is the best equipped in coercive power. Third, with its rigid rank-and-file structure and strong emphasis on discipline, the military represents order and authority, the qualities that become virtues in situations of political chaos and power vacuum. Moreover, if the political movement during the period of transition—from colonialism to independence or from monarchy to republic—is led by the military, the military may also claim a traditional political role.

Only in a very few young democracies have the democratic leaders managed to curb the political ambitions of their military rivals. Costa Rica took a radical step and abolished its traditional military organization. Some countries avoided a military takeover because international developments forced them to keep a weak military (e.g., Japan). Some others, despite maintaining a strong military, managed to keep it out of politics (e.g., India). However, any such steps would be difficult to take in countries where the military had played an important role in the independence movement (many African and South American countries) or in the establishment of a republic after the decline of monarchies (e.g., Turkey). Democratic rulers in these countries have to take their military counterparts into account.

Some military forces expand their role from maintaining law and order into the economic domain. According to a declaration of the National Conference of Bishops of Brazil, "National security doctrines originating in Latin American military schools after World War II stressed the firm link between national security and economic growth, indicated that threats to security existed both inside and outside the country, and assigned to the military the role of maintaining the security vital to economic growth."[23] National security at the War College in Brazil "was seen to a great extent as a function of rationally maximizing the output of the economy and minimizing all sources of cleavage and disunity within the country."[24] Some observers, such as former US ambassador to Brazil Ben Stephansky, even argue that "Brazil considers the violation of human rights a necessary condition for economic development."[25]

Similar views on national security were common among some Chilean officers in the 1970s. In July 1970, the official publication of the Army General Staff included an article by Major Claudio Lópes, who identified underdevelopment as a threat to national security and argued that the function of the armed forces should not be limited to maintaining order and repressing subversion, but should also include avoiding the outbreak of violence even if it requires repression.[26] Many students of Latin America agree that this national security doctrine has been "adopted by many of Latin America's armed forces with encouragement of the United States military," and as "an integral part of the military's function to insure national defense" it was expected to "take control of the national government in order to reform national society, implement an economic development program, and remove other obstacles to modernization."[27]

Maintaining high levels of economic growth at all costs is likely to be a goal for the military where it holds corporate shares and, as a result, is not impartial to economic interests and conflicts. In Turkey, where the military has interrupted the democratic process approximately every ten years, the military controls a huge investment fund called Army Mutual Aid Cooperative (Ordu Yardimlaşma Kooperatifi, OYAK) accumulated through obligatory and voluntary contributions of military personnel and through investment profits. Established in 1960 after the first coup, OYAK has made sizable investments in various industries, such as auto, truck, tractor, tire, cement, petrochemical, food processing, retail, and service. It owns profitable manufacturing plants, such as those of International Harvester agricultural machinery, Renault cars, and Goodyear tires. As partners of foreign and domestic firms, the military shares the economic concerns of the civilian entrepreneurs. OYAK, as a holding company, provides "management positions virtually assured to top office-holding generals as they retired"[28] and, through its investments, makes the economic security of both active and retired military personnel dependent upon the profitability of large capitalist enterprises. With a "military capitalist sector" created,[29] the corporate interests of the military "expanded into the areas of labor law, trade unionism, monetary policy, corporate taxation, tariffs, investment banking, and related matters."[30] The close link between military and corporate interests has been evident in the policy choices of the military governments. The martial law period of 1971–1973, which followed the 1971 military intervention, for example, was characterized by the imposition of severe and frequent bans on union activity that resulted in a decline of the income shares of labor.[31] During the same period, the number of lockouts showed a significant increase.[32]

Similar investment opportunities accrued to the Philippine military through presidential initiatives provided by Ferdinand Marcos. The martial law years during the Marcos regime also correspond to the "aggrandizement of the military" in both political and business spheres.[33] As noted by an observer:

> Through presidential directives, military-run business establishments were established, such as the PEFTOK Investment and Development Corporation, which provide investment opportunities to Korean War veterans and their dependents. Later, a similar corporation, the Philippine Veterans Development Corporation (PHIVIDEC), was also created in July 1973 to "provide investment opportunities" for retired military personnel. It was provided an initial capital outlay of U.S. $500,000 (Government provided 20% of this) with tax benefits which increased in 1974 to P10 Million. It was opened to active-duty military personnel during the same year.
>
> In sum, for the Marcos regime, the military was not only to contain political threats but to also principally assist in national development goals by either actively participating in it or providing the necessary conducive atmosphere to allow unhindered national growth.[34]

Because most military officers are recruited from the lower classes, it is often assumed that military governments would be more likely to pursue egalitarian policies and that the military, as the most modern and professional institution in the country, would lead the society toward modernization. Although such tendencies are likely to be observed among lower-rank officers, and leftist-oriented military interventions are not completely absent, military takeovers are more likely to result in repression of the lower classes and their economic interests. In addition to the reasons already presented, the right-wing tendency of the military is explained by the higher-ranking officers' upper-class origin or access and assimilation to the upper-class life.[35] Even if they come from modest families, as military officers advance they may invest in business activities or acquire rural property and start to identify with the upper-middle class, to which they aspire. Their "access to the social milieu" of the upper classes makes them "subject to pressures to intervene in politics to prevent the coming to power, or to remove from power, leftist or populist movements which threaten the existing distribution of property."[36] In other words, as stated by Huntington, they "become the guardians of the existing middle-class order" because "their historical role is to open the door to the middle class and close it on the lower class."[37] This has been evident in Latin America, where modernizing, industrializing coups of the 1960s gave way to "labor-repressive institutional coups" in the 1970s.[38]

In sum, the military in developing countries does not manifest professional, rational, and apolitical features of the "military mind" as identified by Huntington, for whom the military ethic "holds that war is the instrument of politics, that the military are the servants of the statesman, and that civilian control is essential to military professionalism."[39]

POLITICAL CONSENSUS VS. POLARIZATION

While some observers define politics as the art of compromising, some regard compromising and consensus building as essential for the stability of political systems, at least for the democratic ones. Polarization, however, is perceived as a destabilizing factor.

A minimum level of consensus—agreement about the rules of the game—would be necessary for the continuity of a democratic system. Seeking further consensus, however, would mean the denial of an essence of the representative democratic system: choice. Although this is a quality not adequately measured by any quantitative scale of democracy, including mine, competitiveness required for democracy would demand some differences between the competing groups. If all the competing parties (or the major ones) reach a consensus on everything, then the system is not competitive. Although their view did not shift until later in their careers, even those writers who originally emphasized the significance of consensus building in democracies (e.g., Robert Dahl and Charles Lindblom) began to see divergence rather than consensus as an essential component of meaningful democracies.[40]

But how much divergence can a democracy tolerate? Political polarization was observed before the breakdown of many democratic regimes.[41] Ideological differences both at the mass and elite levels and the elites' unwillingness to compromise are often identified as invitations to military takeovers. Many authors agree on polarization as a cause of the breakdown of democracies, but they seldom discuss the causes of polarization. Why would people take extremely diverse paths? What is at stake that precludes them from attempting to compromise? The answer must be "a lot" in a highly inegalitarian society. Those in a disadvantaged position would demand more from the system; the privileged would struggle to maintain the status quo. As we will see in later chapters, extreme polarization, evident in social unrest, is observed in societies where economic inequalities are higher.

POLITICAL LEADERSHIP

According to Schumpeter, the first condition for the success of democracy is that "the human material of politics—the people who man the party machines, are elected to serve in parliament, rise to cabinet office—should be of sufficiently high quality."[42] Although this sounds reasonable and convincing, the analytical value of his statement can be questioned from a number of points of views. First, "high quality" is a subjective term and may apply to a number of qualifications varying from technical expertise to professional competence to manipulative strength or to holding certain moral standards (each of which may have multiple definitions depending on the views of the reviewer). Second, even if we agree on its definition, can we say "high quality" leadership is a requirement for stability only in democratic political systems? And most important, is the "high quality" requirement for leadership compatible with the democratic principle of equality—rule by the people—that should allow common citizens to exercise some control over their lives?

Nevertheless, leaders, whether they were democratically elected or came to power through other means, perform important functions in developing countries. Max Weber, in his threefold classification of political organization, points to the significance of leaders in societies at the transitional stage between patrimonial and bureaucratic rule. Even if they do not follow an exactly Weberian path, there is no doubt that developing countries today can be classified as transitional on a number of dimensions. They experience various kinds of change at a rapid pace. They are in transition from foreign hegemony to independence, from agrarian economy to industrialization, from a mainly rural society to urbanization, from using the plow to generating computer technology, and from subsistence production to conspicuous consumption. The rapid change taking place in all aspects of life does not miss social institutions. By weakening some and making others obsolete, change leaves these societies without stable institutions. Thus, leaders become important not only in shaping the society but also in legitimizing the transformation and the newly established structures.

The absence of strong institutions, however, allows the leaders in developing countries to escape the control mechanisms that would hold them accountable to the public. The heavy reliance on leaders and their unaccountability create a situation in which leaders can easily became corrupt or dictatorial, traits that of course weaken the legitimacy of the democratic system. Moreover, the leaders have a more crucial role in younger democracies because of their decisive position. Their capacity to solve the multiple and complex problems of the society determines the legitimacy of their systems. In this sense, developing democracies have greater need for visionary, strong, and effective leaders than do the older, stable states.

In addition to the individual characteristics of leaders, the relationship between the leaders of opposing groups in a democracy is also crucial for the stability of the system. Peeler, in his analysis of Latin American political systems, argues that the three relatively stable democracies of Latin America (Costa Rica, Colombia, and Venezuela) maintained stability because the key members of the elite groups self-consciously accommodated each other and established policy consensus on a mixed economy and "ameliorative rather than structurally radical social reforms."[43] Similarly in India, none of the "proprietary classes" was able to dominate the political scene, rather, they established a coalition among themselves and co-opted lower classes and castes as they gained organizational strength.[44]

POLITICAL CULTURE

Tolerance, accommodation, and consensus building are considered to be critical characteristics of the democratic elite by Schumpeter also:

> It must be possible for every would-be leader who is not lawfully excluded to present his case without producing disorder. This may imply that people stand by patiently while somebody is attacking their most vital interests or offending their most cherished ideals—or as an alternative, that the would-be leader who holds such views restrains himself correspondingly. Neither is possible without genuine respect for the opinions of one's fellow citizens amounting to a willingness to subordinate one's own opinions.[45]

Some writers further argue that these and other characteristics not only should prevail among the political elite but should manifest themselves as dominant cultural traits of the nation for the democracy to succeed.[46] The most well-known work on this line of argument is by Almond and Verba, who aggregated and combined some individual political attitudes under an umbrella term: *civic culture*. In Almond's words, the civic culture is largely based on "the 'rationality-activist model' of democratic citizenship, the model of a successful democracy that required that all citizens be involved and active in politics, and their participation be informed, analytical, and rational." This model, however, is considered to be only "*one* component of the civic culture, but not the sole one." Almond writes: "Indeed, by itself this participant-rationalist model of citizenship could not logically sustain a *stable* democratic government. Only when combined in some sense with its opposites of passivity, trust, and deference to authority and competence was a viable, stable democracy possible."[47] But, if civic culture is, at least partially, based on "passivity, trust and deference," which are correlated to "apathy," one can only question its compatibility with democracy, which demands participation. Eckstein, who also emphasizes the role of culture, seeks an overall participant culture that transcends politics as necessary for the stability of democracy. He explains the political stability in

Britain by the congruence of authority patterns in the family, school, and voluntary associations; he associates the political system and the instability of the Weimar Republic with the incongruence of the authoritarian structure of the German family with the participant nature of the polity.[48]

Another cultural theory of democracy is presented by the students of Latin America. If civic culture is an outcome of Western liberalism, the absence of it, argue Howard Wiarda and Claudio Veliz, is the reason for the failure of democracy in Iberia and Latin America. According to these authors, the Iberian culture is inconsistent with if not resistant to the liberal values of the West. The Iberian political tradition— called "centralist" by Veliz and defined as "authoritarian and corporatist" by Wiarda—would not accommodate a structure involving the dispersion of authority or the mobilization of the masses for political participation.[49]

Although certain cultural traits may be more suitable for the development of democracy, it is risky to regard culture as the major factor that explains the variation in political structures. The relationship between political culture and structure must be treated as a two-way street, where structural elements are often used consciously to create or reinforce specific values and norms.[50] As Almond and Verba admit, political socialization is a lifelong process, and, especially immediately after a regime change, political institutions are mobilized for this end.[51] Moreover, values change through time, and it would be misleading to treat culture (or dominant culture) as a static element.

Needler presents a critique of the "Hispanic cultural tradition" as an explanation of the failure of democracy in Latin America. He argues that "norms of hierarchy, inequality, and authoritarianism were no more prevalent in Hispanic culture of the colonial period than they were in contemporary Anglo-Saxon or other cultures; and . . . as survey results suggest, present-day attitudes in the Latin American countries are just as conducive to democratic systems as are attitudes in countries elsewhere in which such systems exist."[52] Needler treats the social and economic structures as more influential in determining the political structure of a country, a conclusion he reaches by examining historical evidence and comparing the demographics and economics of North and South America:

> Inequality, hierarchy, and authoritarianism did not particularly characterize purely Hispanic societies more than societies of other cultural identities of the same period of time, but emerged only where there were substantial concentrations of Indian population, or where African slavery was introduced. Inequality of social condition . . . resulted where circumstances favored the establishment of various forms of unfree labor; put in other way, it grew from the existence of concentration of wealth. *Inequality and authoritarianism grew out of social and economic conditions and not culture.* Costa Rica [the most democratic country in that hemisphere], for example, is no less Hispanic than anywhere else in the hemisphere; in fact it is more Hispanic . . . 97.38 percent of the population spoke Spanish.[53]

EXTENT OF GOVERNMENT INVOLVEMENT IN ECONOMY

The discussion in Chapter 3 about the role of the bourgeoisie made clear that those who see the capitalist entrepreneur as a liberating force also see the free enterprise economy as a necessary condition of democracy. For them, state intervention into the economy is the major impediment to the development of democracy. A competitive economic system constitutes a necessary condition for competitive political systems. Given the fact that the older and stable democracies are also the ones that were the first market economies, the defendants of this argument believe it is empirically justified.

Moreover, since Alexis de Tocqueville explained the success of US democracy largely by the prevalence of the voluntary associations in that society, the liberal democratic theorists identify state intervention into the economy as an obstacle for the development of such voluntary associations, especially for the formation of business associations. Most of all, the pluralists, who view the free competition of interest groups as the essence of democracy, regard state activity in the economy as a restraint for the evolution of the competitive process. Some further argue that tolerance and compromise, the essential cultural traits of democracy, are characteristics of the free entrepreneurs, the bourgeoisie:

> The bourgeoisie who is primarily absorbed in his private concerns is in general—as long as these concerns are not seriously threatened—much more likely to display tolerance of political differences and respect for opinions he does not share than any other type of human being. Moreover so long as bourgeois standards are dominant in a society this attitude will tend to spread to other classes as well.[54]

The experience of developing countries presents contradictory evidence. In the absence of private capital accumulation, virtually all developing countries had the state as the major economic entrepreneur. However, even though all developing countries have experienced some level of statism, their expectations from state intervention into the economy have differed. Whereas some countries tried to use state power to establish an infrastructure and to subsidize the initially weak private enterprise, others mobilized state authority toward redistributive ends. Contrary to the liberalist arguments, the democracies that followed the second course have been more successful in maintaining stability. Furthermore, although state strength is generally linked to the strength of the civil society, and associational organizations are found to be more numerous and influential in capitalist societies, empirical studies documenting their democratization impact in developing countries is yet to be provided.[55]

FOREIGN INFLUENCE

Those who believed in the ultimate victory of democracy over any other form of government also believed that those countries that first went through the process of democratization would lead the others on this route. William B. Munro was confident when he wrote in the 1920s: "It is hardly an exaggeration to say . . . that the democratization of the entire civilized world, largely through the influence of Anglo-Norman leadership, is the most conspicuous fact in the whole realm of political science."[56]

Human beings, however, turned out to be politically more innovative than they were given credit for at the turn of the century. They not only created diverse political systems, but also started a competition for dominance among them. After the polarization of the world political system during the cold war years and the division of the Northern Hemisphere into Eastern and Western blocs that were organized in the form of political and military alliances, some Western scholars started to interpret the affiliation with either of the two alliances as a determinant of the political system of developing countries.[57] Because the Eastern Bloc was composed of Marxist-oriented one-party governments and the Western Bloc included multiparty electoral systems, countries that established closer ties with the Western Bloc nations have been expected to be more democratic. Moreover, due to the role the Allies played in "liberating" Europe and Asia from German and Japanese expansion and authoritarianism and then installing democratic political structures in these countries, Western democracies developed an image as "liberators." This image has been challenged, however, by those who argue that "the struggle against Nazism and fascism during World War II was mainly geopolitical in character, and only incidentally did the Allied victory result in ending patterns of severe violations of human rights on the part of the defeated countries" and establishment of democratic regimes.[58]

A closer examination of the relationship between Western democracies and developing countries would not yield an image of a "liberating West." First, democracy at home did not necessarily lead these countries to seek democratization abroad. Their foreign policies were based on their national economic or political interests rather than on some globally applied principles of humanism or democratic ideology. Colonial rule, which can be best characterized as authoritarian, in some instances replaced functional democracies. In sub-Saharan Africa, for example, many precolonial African governments reflected the characteristics of institutional pluralism and mass political participation. Functionally differentiated institutions checked each other's power. The gerontocratic leadership—based on respect for age, but with respect not automatically granted unless the leader continued to earn it—was balanced by mass participation.[59] But colonial rule undermined these structures and even sought their annihilation.

After decolonization, despite the change in the rhetoric, national economic interests of the Western powers continued to define their foreign policies. For example, even after respect for human rights was designated as a criterion for determining the foreign aid policy of the United States, its foreign policy record shows that this criterion was usually overruled by other nationalist concerns, even during the Carter administration that introduced the qualification.[60] Foreign policy analysts mention democratic values at the end of the list of reasons for US involvement in Latin America: "The rationale for continuing America's military and political involvement in the region centers around permanent national interests: defending the homeland; maintaining access to strategic raw materials, markets for U.S. exports, and investment opportunities; strengthening the international order; and fortifying democratic values."[61]

In the 1970s and 1980s, even as several military or martial law regimes increased their coercive measures, US aid continued to flow in at the same rate or was accompanied by generous increases. During Marcos's martial law regime, US aid to the Philippines continued to increase. Secretary Cyrus Vance's official explanation stated that "whatever the human rights violations, assistance could not be reduced because of 'overriding security considerations.'" In 1969, 60 percent of US investments in South Asia were in the Philippines; immediately after the declaration of martial law, and an accompanying set of "economic reforms" to liberalize the economy, US investments in the Philippines jumped from US $19.99 million in 1972 to US $103.96 million in 1973.[62]

Despite the lip service paid to promoting democracy and human rights in other countries by various administrations, the United States often took steps in the opposite direction by supporting authoritarian coups to oust elected democratic governments (e.g., Guatemala and Iran in 1953, Chile in 1973) or by assisting rulers who demonstrated no respect for human rights and were concerned only with staying in power (e.g., Zaire, the Shah's Iran, the Philippines in the 1970s). Moreover, it is well documented that US specialists trained military and police officers in many oppressive countries, especially in Latin America, in techniques of counterinsurgency and civic action. These include guidance of intelligence, use and maintenance of arms and machinery, and methods of guerrilla warfare.[63] Chilcote classifies US involvement in the region's affairs under three categories: (1) overt, "including hundreds of incidents of direct attack by military force"; (2) covert, including organization by the Central Intelligence Agency (CIA) of coups and other destabilization activities; and (3) corporate, including destabilization activities and blockades by multinational corporations.[64]

Although the decline in their power limited the influence of European democracies in shaping world affairs as individual governments after World War II, as a group they composed a significant power base. European countries played a significant role for the democratization of some countries in their region. Most of these countries have subscribed to the European Convention on Human Rights, which emphasizes civil and political rights, is monitored by the investigatory European Human Rights Commission, and is enforced by the European Human Rights Court. When the European Economic Community became a vital economic force and its political component, the European Parliament, started to reinforce democratic procedures in member countries, democratization, as a condition sought for full membership, was encouraged at least for those countries whose developing economies needed opportunities provided by the European Common Market. Thus, foreign influence, indirectly and in the form of economic incentives, contributed to the democratization processes that took place in Greece, Portugal, and Spain in the 1970s and in Turkey in the 1980s. Similarly, the economic advantages of the Marshall Plan stimulated the transition to multiparty politics in Greece and Turkey after World War II. It would be difficult to argue, however, that the Western democracies made any conscious and direct effort or took decisive steps toward promoting democracy in developing countries outside of their region.

Western countries have frequently used economic sanctions to protest coercive measures and human rights violations in countries with centrally planned economies. The response to such violations in free market economies, however, has been weak and characterized by tolerance.[65]

In sum, European or American, the Western foreign influence generally, has been unfavorable to the advancement of democracy in developing countries. The economic and military power of the industrialized countries is used to create capitalist markets and protect the economic interests of the donor.

Likewise, unilateral aid from the United States and other Western countries, as well as aid and loans from international organizations such as the International Monetary Fund (IMF) or the World Bank have been more generous when governments agreed to liberalize the economy and took coercive measures to maintain stability. Although the World Bank and the IMF were hesitant to support elected governments that pursued the policy of import-substitution industrialization or semisocialist development strategies, they supported liberal economies of authoritarian or martial law regimes.[66] The diversions from the originally socialist development path in Yugoslavia and India are seen as compromises of governments to obtain IMF loans.[67] In 1976, when martial law had been in effect in the Philippines for three years, the generosity of the World Bank, the IMF, and the US Agency for International Development (USAID) made the Philippines the top aid recipient among Third World countries.[68]

The United States, as a major financial power with a vote on the board of directors of several international financial agencies (e.g., the World Bank, the IMF, and the Inter-American Development Bank), plays a major role in determining the lending policies of these agencies. It should be noted, however, that other nationalities on the board (mostly Western capitalist countries) and the permanent staff of these institutions tend to hold views not very different from those of US officials.

As a reaction to Salvador Allende's nationalization plan, the multinationals in Chile not only cooperated to influence US foreign policy toward the new Chilean government but also those of the international lending agencies. The memoirs and research of an Allende official provide some insight:

A few weeks after Allende's inauguration, a number of them—ITT, Anaconda,

Kennecott, Bethlehem Steel, Dow Chemical, Firestone Tire and Rubber, W. R. Grace, Charles Pfizer, Ralston Purina, and the Bank of America—formed a "Chile Ad Hoc Committee." According to a memorandum on the committee's first meeting, prepared by a Bank of America official who attended, "the thrust . . . was toward the application of pressure on the [US] government wherever possible to make it clear that a Chilean takeover would not be tolerated without serious repercussions following. ITT believes that the place to apply pressure is through the office of Henry Kissinger. They feel that this office and the CIA are handling the Chile problem." Both ITT and Anaconda representatives told of meetings with Arnold Nachmanoff of Kissinger's staff. The Anaconda representative reported that Nachmanoff had "indicated that the U.S. will apply quiet pressure [on Chile] along economic lines. . . ." The meeting also discussed the need to bring pressure "upon the international lending agencies to cease activity in countries that threaten or actually expropriate private investments." The minutes of the meeting give further information about the discussion of lending agencies. "Ralph Mecham of Anaconda said that the World Bank people had been in Santiago this past week talking to officials of the Chilean government telling them that no more loans would be made."[69]

When the US Export-Import Bank rejected the Chilean request for credit in summer 1971, the press interpreted this as the first application of White House policy, developed under the pressure of US companies, to refuse credit to foreign countries that nationalize private property owned by US interests.[70] Soon after this, the World Bank and the Inter-American Development Bank stopped giving loans to Chile, and by spring 1972, short-term credits from North American banks to Chile declined to $20 million from $220 million, the amount approximately a month before Allende's election.[71]

The liberal economic bias of the International Monetary Fund has been frequently addressed by its critics. Some even argue that "the Fund is bound by its articles of Agreement to promote the smooth running of the capitalist international system, and to oppose restraints on international payments and trade."[72] In fact, the typical economic stabilization program of the IMF would entail reduction in government spending, reversal of nationalization, encouragement of privatization, a freeze on wages regardless of the prevailing rate of inflation, removal of subsidies on basic consumer items such as public utilities and transportation, and discontinuance of food rationing. All of these measures of *economic stabilization,* however, demand more sacrifice from the wage earners and other lower-income groups and establish causes of social unrest and *political destabilization.*

Moreover, the policy advice provided by the IMF does not entail recommendations that would guide these countries on strengthening their economy toward self-sufficiency. The IMF provides tips on how to qualify for more credit, which would, of course, reinforce the cycle of dependency. Dependency, in turn, weakens the roots of democracy in developing countries by distorting the views of the national bourgeoisie, by restricting the autonomy of the national government, by skewing the income distribution, by setting priorities on economic stability as opposed to equality, and by equipping the authoritarian institutions with coercive tools of the most advanced technology.

CONCLUSION

Evidence from developing countries indicates that most of the conditions usually pointed out as determinants of the democratic success are either ineffective or inconclusive. The only two factors clearly linked to the decline of democracy are the influence of Western nations and the politicized military of the country. The other factors—the type of colonial experience, having either presidential or parliamentary constitutional arrangements, the number of political parties and their diversity, the cultural heritage and ethnic diversity of the society, and the extent of government intervention into the economy—do not present a clear picture of how they affect the success of democracy. The direction of their impacts is linked to their relation to the socioeconomic conditions in the society: If these factors stimulate socioeconomic equality in the society, they have a reinforcing impact on democracy. But if they incite inequality or help to uncover social injustice, their impacts on democracy are negative. Thus, we turn next to the relationship between socioeconomic rights and political rights and how the balance between them can influence the stability or instability of democracy.

NOTES

1. Developing countries are defined here to include all non-Western countries except Japan, including the East European countries except West Germany and the USSR.
2. See Duverger. Also for a critique of this position and an empirical analysis of the impact of electoral laws, see Rae.
3. Ranney.
4. Weiner, *PS*, Fall 1987.
5. Linz, in Linz and Stepan.
6. Lijphart.
7. Strom.
8. Kavanagh, at p. 25.
9. LaPalombara.
10. See Apter.
11. A working definition of "corporatist system" is provided by Schmitter, pp. 93–94. It is

> a system of interest representation in which the constituent units are organized into a limited number of single, compulsory, non–competitive, hierarchically ordered and functionally differentiated categories, recognized or licensed (if not created) by the state and granted a deliberate representational monopoly within their respective categories in exchange for observing certain controls on their selection.

12. Ebel.
13. Needler, 1987, pp. 131–132.
14. For a review of these theories, see Huntington and Dominguez, especially pp.

66–96.
15. Das Gupta, 1988, pp. 145–146.
16. Shah, p. 299.
17. Das Gupta, 1988, p. 146.
18. Ronen, p. 201.
19. Weiner, *PS*, Fall 1987.
20. Kohli, 1988, p. 9.
21. From the Simon Commission writings in 1930, as quoted in Peter Lyon's "Transfer and Transformation: An Introduction," in Lyon and Manor, p. 3.
22. Eta^2 is .12, and the F value is 1.62 and significant at .5 level.
23. Wood, at p. 166.
24. Stepan.
25. Wood, p. 166.
26. Boorstein, p. 77.
27. Needler, 1987, pp. 7–8.
28. Keyder, "The Political Economy of Turkish Democracy," p. 51.
29. Ahmad, pp. 280–281.
30. Magnarella, p. 52.
31. Özbudun and Ulusan.
32. Bianchi, p. 266.
33. Abinales.
34. Ibid., p. 136.
35. Needler, 1987, pp. 53–68.
36. Ibid., p. 59. Needler further argues that the military officers in Latin America "are also subject to pressures from the United States embassy, generally, though not always, in the same political direction" (p. 59).
37. Huntington, 1968, p. 222.
38. Varas, in Varas, ed.
39. Huntington, 1985, p. 79.
40. Shapiro and Reeher.
41. Linz and Stepan; Hale; Dodd.
42. Schumpeter, p. 290.
43. Peeler. A similar argument is presented by Karl.
44. Bardhan; Frankel; Shah.
45. Schumpeter, p. 295.
46. Schumpeter, pp. 294–296; Dahl, 1971; Linz, in Linz and Stepan; Almond and Verba, 1963 and 1980.
47. Almond and Verba, 1980, p. 16.
48. Eckstein.
49. Wiarda, 1980; Wiarda and Kline; Veliz.
50. For philosophical and methodological critiques of the "civic culture" study, see Almond and Verba, 1980, especially the essays by Arend Lijphart, "The Structure of Inference"; Carole Pateman, "The Civic Culture: A Philosophical Critique"; and Jerzy J. Wiatr, "The Civic Culture from a Marxist Sociological Perspective."
51. Almond and Verba, 1980, p. 29.
52. Needler, 1987, pp. xi, 11–28.
53. Ibid., p. 13.
54. Schumpeter, p. 298.
55. Bratton.
56. Munro, p. 1.
57. Weiner, *PS*, Fall 1987.
58. Falk, p. 233.
59. Ayoade, p. 30.

60. For a collection of papers that provides an assessment of Carter's human rights policies, see Farer. Carter's human rights policies were also criticized for being proleftist and responsible for weakening pro-U.S. governments such as Somoza's rule in Nicaragua and the Shah's rule in Iran. For such critiques, see Wiarda, 1982; and Baumann. Jeane J. Kirkpatrick's articles in the last two volumes not only criticize Carter's administration but also present a justification for the policies of its successor, the Reagan administration.

61. Martin E. Anderson, p. 95.

62. Abinales, pp. 156–157.

63. Wood; Barber and Ronning. For a review of the US foreign policy and CIA activities in Latin America, see Omang; Boorstein; Black; Immerman; and Needler, 1987, pp. 43–54. For the US policy of intervention in other regions, see Chomsky and Herman; Garwood; Eveland; and Powers.

64. Chilcote, p. 15.

65. See Dominguez et al.; pp. 14–15; and Ullman.

66. For the Philippines, see Abinales. For a detailed discussion of IMF policies and their impacts on the economies of various countries, see Payer. Payer hypothesizes that "where the most powerful opposition to the government in power is rightist and friendly to the US (as in Brazil, Argentina, and Indonesia before their respective military coups [in the 1960s]), the government is likely to receive more severe treatment from the IMF" (p. 43).

67. Payer, pp. 117–142 and 166–183.

68. Abinales, p. 160.

69. Boorstein, p. 84.

70. Payer, p. 191.

71. Ibid., p. 192.

72. Ibid., p. 220.

5

Structural Determinants and Policy Causes of Decline

Equality breeds no revolution.—Solon

Democracy and violence can ill go together. The States that are today nominally democratic have either to become frankly totalitarian or if they are to become truly democratic, they must become courageously non-violent. It is a blasphemy to say that nonviolence can be practiced by individuals and never by nations which are composed of individuals.—Mahatma Gandhi

THE LEGITIMACY CRISIS IN DEVELOPING COUNTRIES

As discussed in Chapter 1, the criteria for government legitimacy have changed over time. The new criteria of social and political equality that require governments to play a positive role in meeting basic human needs and establishing justice, and the capacity of governments to fulfill them, pose major dilemmas for governments in the modern world—and even more so for the governments of developing countries, because the sequence of the changes is as important as the changes themselves.[1] Early developers in the West experienced social and political problems sequentially and enjoyed the opportunity of resolving them gradually as highly autonomous political entities. In contrast, developing countries today confront more complex and intricate problems that occur not sequentially but simultaneously.[2] In the wake of emerging as new nation-states and facing worldwide pressure to adopt democratic political institutions, the late developers lack the resources or willingness to provide material security or a more egalitarian distribution of wealth. By setting a strategy that aims at fast and immediate economic growth and that usually lacks the egalitarian distribution of benefits, leaders in developing countries expose themselves to a chain of problems, and these eventually result in democratic governments evolving into or being replaced by more authoritarian ones. An illustration of this transformation of regime in developing countries is provided by the conceptual model in Figure 5.1.

The two-stage policy construct suggests that certain socioeconomic conditions (system demand and input) lead to certain policies being formulated and implemented. The impact of these policies results in another set of social con-

Figure 5.1 Conceptual Model for Declining Democracies

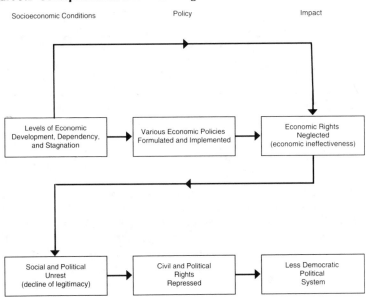

ditions (social unrest) that demands response from the government. The government's response—coercive policies—leads to the decline of democracy. Given low levels of economic development and high levels of dependency, a rapid economic growth rate appears to be the major concern of governments in developing countries, as opposed to an egalitarian distribution of the benefits of growth. Governments pursue policies that increase social and economic inequalities.

Simon Kuznets's study of income distribution in European countries found a curvilinear relationship between the levels of economic development and inequality.[3] The countries in his study demonstrated an increase in income inequality as they economically advanced, but then, at higher stages of development, they started to reduce the gap between different income groups. Kuznets's findings and the work of others who identified a similar pattern of inequality began to be used to popularize neoclassical economics and justify inegalitarian economic growth strategies. Economic inequality is treated as a cost necessary to pay for economic growth at the earlier stages of economic development. Because high-income groups have a larger propensity to save, it is argued, they should continue to receive a larger share so they can continue to accumulate capital for further investments and economic growth. Moreover, uneven and rapid economic growth is expected to have a "trickle-down effect" resulting in all segments of the population being better off in the long run.

Thus, politicians have argued that first they had to enlarge the pie, then they could slice it equally. They have not, however, taken the social and political cost of inequalities into consideration. Inegalitarian development policies, either initiated by domestic leadership or imposed by foreign institutions through high levels of economic dependency and indebtedness, cause the system to be perceived as unresponsive or ineffective by the lower-income groups. The result is a decline of legitimacy. Contrary to the famous J-curve theory of revolution—which predicts revolutions will occur in a period of economic stagnation following a period of rapid economic growth—the revolutions in Mexico, Cuba, and Nicaragua took place following a period of economic growth, not stagnation. The growth in each of these three cases, however, was uneven.

Confuting neoclassical economic theory, some studies on developing countries find that distributive efforts do not necessarily impede economic growth. In fact, investments in basic needs, looked upon as investments in national human resources, can yield returns in the form of higher rates of economic growth.[4] Such evidence, however, is usually overlooked by policymakers overwhelmed by the success of the Western economic development model, which was also inegalitarian. The model, however, is not replicable because policymakers in the twentieth century are dealing with a much more politicized public connected to the rest of the world through the means of mass communication.

Lucian Pye observes that in England, considered to be "the model of modern democracies," the crises arose sequentially and were resolved gradually: "The English developed a sense of national identity early, the issue of the legitimacy of the monarchy and government was well established before the problem of expanding participation appeared and, finally, serious issues of distribution did not arise until after the political system was relatively well integrated."[5] Huntington points out the differences in the historical experience of the late and early developers:

> In the modernization of the non-Western parts of the world, however, the problems of the centralization of authority, national integration, social mobilization, economic development, political participation, and social welfare have arisen not sequentially but simultaneously. The "demonstration effect" which the early modernizers have on the later modernizers first intensifies aspirations and then exacerbates frustration.[6]

The historical interaction between the early and late developers also set certain terms that have been favorable for the development of democracy in the first group of countries but detrimental for the second group. First, colonialism and indirect imperialism equipped the early developers with a sense of power and strength, but for the colonies they meant imposition of foreign rule characterized by authoritarianism and suppression of genuine opposition. Thus, no matter which country was colonial ruler, the cultural legacy of colonialism has been one based on domination and coerciveness. Second, under imperial policies, the first developers not only exploited the resources of their colonies, penetrated their markets, and curtailed the development of their native industries and "nationalistic" bourgeoisie, but also used these opportunities to increase the imperialist country's national wealth to a level at which the standard of living for lower classes could be increased without a radical redistributive effort. Thus, the loyalty of lower classes could be bought without alienating the upper classes. Finally, colonization helped the old developers to reduce the population pressure that inevitably results from industrialization and economic growth. Emigration to the new and underpopulated land eased tension in the "old country." Late developers, however, lack such an outlet. Those who seek opportunities in industrialized countries, sometimes disguising themselves as refugees, are shipped back home, only to continue living in poverty. As Olson also pointed out: "The underdeveloped countries cannot afford modern welfare measures as well as the advanced nations can. But it is perhaps also true that they need these modern welfare institutions more than the advanced countries do."[7]

Unjust social conditions prevailing under several elected administrations are likely to weaken citizens' confidence in the electoral system. The stagnation of electoral representative systems, which are supposed to provide an avenue of influence and change under normal circumstances, leads those struggling with unemployment and declining real wages to take actions threatening the foundations of the political system. Violence becomes a political resource when the traditional "bargaining process provides no other alternatives."[8] Confronted with high levels of social unrest, governments without resources to meet economic needs immediately respond with coercive measures to suppress unrest. This means a less democratic government. Students of Indian politics agree that the political crisis in the country corresponds to the era of "awakening" of India's voters, who became increasingly aware of the logic of the electoral process, representation, and political responsiveness.[9] As described by Manor:

> Voters became more assertive and competitive, and their appetites for resources from politicians grew. Interest groups crystallized and came increasingly into conflict, so that it became harder to operate a political machine that could cater to every organized interest, as Congress [Party] had very nearly done in the Nehru years. India became increasingly democratic and difficult to govern.[10]

Similarly, in Latin America, the transition to "bureaucratic-authoritarianism" from democracy is argued to be a deliberate effort by the propertied and professional classes to suppress the demands of lower classes and maintain a capitalist development strategy with unequal distribution.[11]

WHY INEQUALITY?

Kuznets's finding of the curvilinear relationship between economic development and inequality was further tested and confirmed by using cross-national data.[12] Although their explanations are different, both developmentalists and dependency theorists agree that the middle-range developed countries experience higher levels of economic inequality. The first approach emphasizes internal factors and argues that the economic development level and some other intermediary factors (themselves determined by levels of economic development) establish the roots of social and economic inequality. The second approach directs attention to external factors and points to dependency as the major determinant of inequality as well as some other problems facing developing countries. The internal factors are treated as secondary or intermediary.[13]

By again using the European experience, developmentalists perceive social and economic inequality as inevitable in the middle stages of the modernization process. Economic development, modernization, and industrialization lead to a breakdown of the traditional social structure and its replacement with new class relationships and patterns of social stratification.[14] Although some developmentalists recognize the process of modernization as a destabilizing one, members of this school generally hold an optimistic view for the future. Once the economy is advanced and the society is reorganized in modern terms, they believe, the new society will be more egalitarian socially, economically, and politically.

Dependency theorists associate penetration by foreign capital and increasing levels of dependence on the international capitalist market with inegalitarian development models.[15] According to this school, the domination of the world economy by the core countries (industrial capitalist countries) results in economic inequalities in the peripheries (dependent developing countries) through several processes. First, dependency prevents any egalitarian redistribution by retarding economic growth and development in the periphery. Profits on foreign investment and interest on foreign credit transfer value from the periphery to the core country, hampering the development of the periphery.[16] Second, dependency stimulates inequality by distorting the social and economic structure of developing countries. Foreign capital supports the "semi-feudal" or "comprador" elites in developing countries,[17] and the external interests align themselves with local dominant groups, with the effect that the local dominated class suffers the equivalent of double exploitation.[18] Moreover, the world division of labor pushes peripheral economies to externally oriented production and specialization in primary commodities. These factors may not retard development per se, but they increase inequalities within these countries as a result of "national elite control of the export economy."[19] It is also argued that concentration both in product and market results in sectoral income inequality in peripheries.[20] The composition of trade in peripheries is characterized by the reliance on export of a few primary products and on trade with a single buyer.

Foreign investments also cause high levels of inequality by distorting the evolution of the labor-force structure. Evans and Timberlake argue that "foreign capital may draw a poor country's population into the market economy and into the non-agricultural labor force, but it does not appear to play a significant role in the expansion of employment opportunities in the secondary sector."[21] On the contrary, the capital-intensive technology imported by foreign capital fails to absorb the labor surpluses, resulting in a rapidly growing proportion of the labor force being employed in the tertiary sector.[22] The work of Evans and Timberlake provides empirical support for this argument and displays the inegalitarian impact of the rapid growth of the tertiary sector. Portes adds that "while the working sector associated with the multinationals may evolve into a veritable labor aristocracy, the masses remain in a subsistence situation where unemployment, scarcity of bare essentials, and lack of access to expanding social and economic benefits are the norm."[23] Economic development and industrialization under the dominance of foreign capital promote an inegalitarian social structure. Those employed in the "modern" sector, who are able to purchase its products, compose a self-contained minority, effectively divorced from the majority.[24]

Finally, economic dependency stimulates inequality by working through political means. The strong links between elites on the periphery and in the core create a "bridgehead" of interests and connections that lead these "liaison elites" to suppress policies and leaders seeking to mobilize balanced autonomous development.[25] The liberal economic bias of international lending agencies like IMF is frequently observed. Foreign loans and assistance from industrial capitalist societies are usually obtained by developing countries under the condition that they suspend government subsidies, privatize and deregulate industries, and reduce government spending on welfare. Dependency theorists further argue that dependency promotes right-wing authoritarianism because international and transnational institutions that lend to peripheries stand behind the operations of transnational companies in maintaining "a good climate for foreign investment."[26] Richard Falk discusses the negative impact of the international elite collaboration on human rights:

> The basic mixture of statism and imperial geopolitics that dominates international politics is not conducive to the promotion of minimum human rights, especially given patterns of gross inequality, ethnic animosities, high population growth, and mass poverty that are characteristic for such a large part of the planet. In effect, state power is typically exercised on behalf of a privileged minority of the total society, while the majority population of most national societies endures misery of various types and is repressed to the extent that its representatives challenge as unacceptable the patterns of benefits and burdens prevailing in a particular polity. This primary hierarchy is reinforced by imperial geopolitics, creating and shaping relationships of mutual benefit between the hegemonial elites of dominant governments and their counterparts in dependent, weaker states.[27]

Regardless of the differences in their explanations of inequality and in their prescriptions for the problems of developing countries, the empirical research from both schools finds that dependency is positively related to income inequality,[28] and that peripheral countries are less democratic than core nations, even when controlling for the effect of economic development levels.[29]

IMPACT OF INEQUALITY AND
SOCIAL MOBILIZATION: SOCIAL UNREST

As previously mentioned, equality, political or economic, has become a condition sought in the contemporary world by the masses and has been included among the responsibilities of governments. Recent empirical studies provide further support. A cross-national analysis by Muller and Seligson of the determinants of political violence identifies inequality, especially income inequality, as a major causal factor.[30]

Social mobilization—defined by Karl Deutsch as the process by which "major clusters of old social, economic and psychological commitments are eroded or broken and people become available for new patterns of socialization and behavior"[31]—is often identified as a source of instability.[32] Similarly, because that definition of social mobilization is closely linked to modernization and economic development, development too is characterized by such destabilizing factors:

> Since economic growth is associated not only with capital accumulation, but with the advance of education, skill, and technology, it will be connected in underdeveloped countries with an increasing knowledge of the possibilities of a better life, of new ideologies, and of new systems of government. It will be associated with a "revolution of rising expectations" that is apt to involve, above all, rising expectations about what governments should do.[33]

Such arguments are supported by empirical research. The analysis of coups d'état in "Black Africa" yielded a strong positive relationship between the level of social mobilization and the number of attempted and actual military takeovers.[34] The effort to explain why social mobilization would lead to instability, however, requires including other factors in the analysis. Social mobilization may be a necessary condition for social and political instability, but it is not a sufficient condition. Its interaction with the economic welfare of citizens needs to be taken into consideration. Mobilization brings pressure for the expansion of governmental services and the improvement of social welfare. Only if expectations in this area exceed the responsiveness of government does the dissatisfaction of a large portion of the population lead to social unrest.[35] Thus, social mobilization would have destabilizing impacts in the absence of social welfare, but is not a sufficient condition for social unrest. Even in the absence of social justice or welfare, as long as those discontented with the system have low intensities of preferences, the system does not face strong demands originating at the mass level. "Preference intensities" increase as the problems grow in magnitude amid high levels of social mobilization.[36] Compared with village life, for example, urban living makes socioeconomic inequalities more visible and the development of a sense of "relative deprivation" more likely.

Through widespread media and communication networks, citizens of developing countries today can compare their standard of living with that of the upper segments of their own societies or of more developed countries, become aware of inequalities, and consequently levy more pressure on their political system for higher standards of living.

> The communications process also performs an amplifying function by magnifying some of the actions of individuals to the point that they can be felt throughout the society, in a sense transforming mere "man-sized" acts into "society-sized" acts. To an important degree the communications process informs the members of a community about the extent to which they can and should legitimately question the motives and intentions of those initiating political actions. In short, with an effective communications process people can more readily gain a realistic sense of the domain of the relevant in comprehending political motives.[37]

Although the development of communications, urbanization, and education may also have a consolidating impact, it is unrealistic to expect this to occur among the disadvantaged segments of the society. Communications would cause problems to gain in momentum and to grow both in dimension and scope. As Cnudde and Neubauer state: "When leaders do not or cannot produce outcomes which are valued by citizens, problems develop for which no solutions are being offered. As the problems grow in magnitude, citizens' awareness and, eventually, preference intensity increase. With increasing intensities will come greater probabilities for demands from the citizenry for solution."[38]

Impotence of governments in providing solutions to problems instigates manifest social unrest, but as Gurr says: "People are less likely to attack their political leaders, or to engage in violence against others, if they have a high positive regard for their political system."[39] Thus, "before violence can become a factor, there must be a governmental failure to maintain or support legitimacy; otherwise there would be no basis for a serious threat to it."[40] Crane Brinton identifies three preconditions for revolutions, the extreme case of social unrest and declining system legitimacy: (1) the fruits of progress are not distributed evenly; (2) government is ineffective; and (3) the intellectuals are developing a social consciousness.[41]

As observed by Moore: "The breakdown of routines of daily life that tie people to the prevailing order, such as getting food and going to work, leads the people to rebel against the rules and authorities associated with their everyday activities."[42] Jackson and others further argue that the development of social distortions and inequality in the economic sphere, stemming from the failures of domestic leaders or high levels of dependency, leads to "the rise of grievances of class against class and group against group within society."[43] In fact, social unrest is often observed soon after the implementation of austerity measures required by the IMF. The correlation between several indicators of IMF conditions and the presence of protest activities is consistently positive and significant.[44] Similarly, the analysis by Boswell and Dixon concludes that both economic dependence and military dependence promote violent social unrest through their facilitating impacts on income inequality and regime repressiveness.[45]

Of course, social unrest may appear in different forms. For example, workers can protest by striking, but the unemployed cannot strike and thus riot in the streets.[46]

RESPONSES BY GOVERNMENTS
AND POLITICAL ELITES: COERCIVE POLICIES

When such institutional disruptions by the disadvantaged segments occur, governments unable to offer an immediate positive response must choose between two alternatives: to ignore or to repress.[47] Cnudde and Neubauer agree that "political leaders in the face of citizen demands that are difficult to satisfy" have few alternatives:

> They may attempt to minimize these demands by changing the rules of the game, thus creating limitations on citizen influence on policy making. On the other hand, political leaders may become or even actively attempt to maintain the status quo. As a result of this, unsatisfied demands lead large numbers of the population to become politically frustrated or alienated. If such a situation continues, new demands to change the rules of the game will find support among these citizens."[48]

Unrest is more likely to be ignored when disruption is not central to the system; repression appears to be more likely when central institutions are affected.

Given that one of the major obligations of government is to maintain peace and order, continuous and widespread social unrest causes the middle class to perceive the government as unresponsive and ineffective because it is unable to provide security, and their status is threatened by such violent actions. "If the status of major conservative groups is threatened," Lipset says, "the legitimacy of the system will remain in question."[49] Indeed, the last century witnessed a vast number of cases of authoritarian takeover under such a threat to the middle class.[50]

It is also argued that high levels of social unrest generally result in more coercive measures in dependent countries because the regime is engaged in "keeping conditions stable for foreign investors."[51] An additional point made is that "the principal means of attaining [a] high level of coercion which are available to a relatively *poor* state must be through some form of *dependence.*"[52] Although the ultimate decision regarding the use of coercion resides with the national political elite, it has been made possible and encouraged through the technology transfer, technical assistance, military aid, and other financial and advisory means provided by the industrial world.[53]

Repression may occur as an incremental policy that gradually curtails civil and political rights at different junctures or as an absolute transformation of the regime either by the incumbent or the opposition (counterelite). It is common to witness a democratic political elite taking authoritarian measures with a

Machiavellian pragmatism while still regarding democracy as the best form of government. Moreover, as stated by Huntington, democratic "institutions come into existence through negotiations and compromises among political elites calculating their own interests and desires," and political leaders promote democracy either "because they are convinced of the ethical and political superiority of democracy and, hence, view democracy as a desirable goal in itself," or because they "view democracy as a means to other goals, such as prolonging their own rule, achieving international legitimacy, minimizing domestic opposition, and reducing the likelihood of civil violence."[54] By the same token, political leaders may curtail democracy if the system becomes a counterproductive means of achieving these other goals. Dictatorship, revolution, and democracy are equally rational choices for political leaders. These choices present alternative strategies of political competition, and political leaders select the most effective strategy of competition regardless of their ideal or desirable political systems.[55]

Incrementalist policies of repression are likely to be followed by the incumbent elite and may appear in the form of constitutional amendments, changes in legal codes, proclamation of martial law, and increasing governmental sanctions; an absolute transformation of the regime may occur in the form of social revolution or coup d'état. In each case, the democratic nature of the system declines. A less democratic government may be unable to meet the demand for an increase in social and economic rights, but it will almost certainly be more successful in suppressing such demands. Coercive policies, however, serve only as temporary solutions. As "cyclical policies," they alternate between one option and another to cope with the problem, rather than eliminating its causes.[56] Thus, the coercive policies that lead to decline of democracy are not expected to eliminate the socioeconomic causes of social unrest, but rather to control it.

MEASUREMENT AND DATA ANALYSIS

The conceptual model illustrated by Figure 5.1 and discussed here treats the decline of democracy as a function of multiple and interacting factors following a causal order. It suggests that although all of the factors included in the model influence the level of decline, their influence is not necessarily direct. Most of the factors lead to decline of democracy through their impact on other intervening variables. From right to left, the model indicates that decline is most immediately an outcome of suppressive political and civil rights policies pursued by government, the incumbent or its replacement. Governments that are unstable due to major social and economic problems employ coercive policies to cope with the increasing levels of social unrest, which is the masses' reaction to inegalitarian economic conditions. The economic conditions, in turn, are, at least in part, consequences of unresponsive or ineffective policies implemented by governments that may have little choice given the structural constraints. The

Table 5.1   Correlations with the Decline in Democracy

Indicators	All Countries	Developing Countries
Purges	.21[a]	.21[a]
Political sanctions	.19[a]	.19[a]
Political executions	.06[a]	.06[a]
Constitutional changes	.54[a]	.54[a]
Coups d'état	.58	.57[a]
Cabinet changes	.29[a]	.31[a]
Government crises	.16[a]	.18[a]
Deaths from domestic violence	.13[a]	.11[a]
Assassinations	.09[a]	.09[a]
General strikes	.06[a]	.07[a]
Guerrilla warfare	.03[c]	.03
Riots	.09[a]	.14[a]
Antigovernment demonstrations	.06[a]	.13[a]
Armed attacks	.04[c]	.07[a]
Unemployment rate	−.01	−.10
Inflation rate	.16[a]	.15[a]
Income inequality—Gini	.08	.04[c]
Social mobilization	−.15[a]	.04
Economic development	−.13[a]	−.09[a]
Economic growth rate	−.11[a]	−.12[a]

Notes: a. Significant at .01 level.
b. Significant at .05 level.
c. Significant at .10 level.

structural or relatively more stable factors, such as levels of economic development and economically and politically dependent status in the world system, affect the change in the level of democracy indirectly.

Based on the availability of data, several variables were selected as the indicators of the factors outlined in the model and the hypothesis suggested by it, and these were tested using correlation analyses.[57] Table 5.1 provides a list of these variables and their correlation with the magnitude of annual decline in the index score of democracy for our sample of countries.[58]

Frequently, in preceding pages, I have referred to the causes of *decline* in democracy. The thrust of most of the earlier studies was to explain the causes of the development or *rise* of democracy. One could readily assume that the causes of decline are simply reverse values of the determinants of the rise of democracy. A bit of reflection, however, raises the possibility of a "ratchet effect," that is, the factors causing authoritarian change may not be at all the inverse of those that encourage democracy. As argued by Ake, "What destabilizes one political system may stabilize another one and may be quite irrelevant to the stability of yet another political system."[59] Or as more explicitly stated by

O'Donnell and Schmitter: "Political and social processes are neither symmetric nor reversible. What brings down a democracy is not the inverse of those factors that brings down an authoritarian regime."[60] Economic advancement, social mobilization, or other factors associated with the rise of democratic practices may well be unidirectional in their change, at least over the long run. Yet the empirical fact is that reversals seem to occur rather quickly. Common-sense observation, therefore, suggests (without adopting the full thrust of an evolutionary explanation) that relatively long-term historical forces may be operative in encouraging democratic development, but rather different factors precipitate reversals.

In brief, the causes of positive and negative changes in democraticness seem to be much different. As stated earlier, coercive civil and political rights policies, hypothesized to result in a decline in democracy, are cyclical policies employed to cope with social unrest rather than to eliminate its socioeconomic roots. Thus, a democratic improvement can take place when such coercive policies loosen or are reversed, but the underlying socioeconomic factors that led to their employment do not have to be improved from the time when those coercive policies were implemented.

The factors that might lead toward democratization seem to be more effective in the long term. The worldwide popularity and diffusion of democratic ideology and its capacity to function as a source of legitimacy—a political system based on people's power and will—are the first such factors that can be noted. Evidence shows that even when a less democratic government takes over, a more democratic one in the near future is promised (e.g., military governments of Zia-ul Hak in Pakistan and of Pinochet in Chile). The formation and the background of political elites, the relative power and attitude of organized groups, and the alliances of these organizations and ruling groups with other prodemocratic institutions in the world are some other factors to be considered. Our insight suggests that democratic groups that are relatively strong enable the system to return to the former level of democracy, even though they were not strong enough originally to prevent it from a decline.

Because the measure of democracy employed in this study treats the concept of democracy as a continuum, along which theoretically all countries can experience change, even if it is marginal, the study is concerned with the explanation of the *magnitude of decline* in the score of democracy rather than the presence or absence of a qualitative characteristic of the political system. Thus, the focus is on cases for which the annual change in democracy score was *negative*.

The indicators of the explanatory factors listed in Table 5.1 are grouped according to the way they are organized in the conceptual model, with each group corresponding to a box on Figure 5.1. The measures of coercive political and civil rights policies refer to government actions that result in violation or limitation of the civil and political rights of citizens. Political executions, political sanctions, purges, and major constitutional changes are the four categories defined. Government sanctions cover "actions taken by authorities to neutralize, suppress, or eliminate a perceived threat to the security of the government, the regime, or the state itself."[61] Similarly, purges include "any systematic elimination by jailing or execution of political opposition within the ranks of the regime or the opposition."[62] Major constitutional changes are "the number of basic alterations in a state's constitutional structure, the extreme case being the adoption of a new constitution that significantly alters the prerogatives of the various branches of government," but the "constitutional amendments which do not have significant impact on the political system are not counted."[63] Although normally some constitutional changes may be in the direction of introducing or restoring civil and political rights and democratic institutions, they are likely to be in the reverse direction when the focus is on the decline in democracy. As the correlation coefficients in Table 5.1 indicate, these repressive policies all have negative impacts on democracy. The magnitude of decline increases as more incidents of repression occur. The most dramatic impact on decline appears to be through constitutional changes ($r = .54$). These are followed by purges and political sanctions, which are close in the extent of their impacts, and by political executions. Moreover, the strength of the relationship between coercive measures and the magnitude of decline is congruous regardless of countries' development levels.

The second group of indicators refers to instability or unrest at the elite level, the extent of the circulation of the executive group. Because the type of executive renewal is as important as its extent, two indicators of government turnover, either through conventional or unconventional means, are used. The number of major cabinet changes within a calendar year and the number of coups d'état are employed as the measures of conventional and unconventional government turnover, respectively. The number of coups d'état, as stated by Arthur Banks, who compiled the data, refers to the number of "extraconstitutional or forced changes in the top government elite and/or its executive control of the nation's power structure in a given year. The term 'coup' includes, but is not exhausted by, the term 'successful revolution.' Unsuccessful coups are not counted."[64] The major cabinet changes are measured by "the number of times in a year that a new premier is named and/or 50% of the cabinet posts are occupied by new ministers."[65] In addition to these two indicators, the number of government crises, defined as "any rapidly developing situation that threatens to bring the downfall of the present regime—excluding situations of revolt aimed at such overthrow," is used to capture the weakening of the legitimacy of the system as felt at the executive level.

Coups d'état explain a major portion of the decline in the level of democracy. Their strong impact is understandable: They represent a change in regime and are acts of coercion because they violate the political rights of citizens, especially if the coups are against an elected government. Moreover, governments installed by coups d'état tend to employ more sanctions. The correlations between coups d'état and coercive policies are all positive and significant.

Coups are usually undertaken by military groups, and although the military sometimes steps in with the claim of protecting the regime and promising to restore the democracy that was deteriorating in the hands of incompetent civilians, findings reported here tell a different story: Democracy does not follow coups. Though the correlations are not as strong as for coups d'état, the other two indicators of executive instability, the numbers of government crises and cabinet changes, are also positively related to the magnitude of decline.

The numbers of guerrilla wars, deaths from domestic violence, assassinations, general strikes, antigovernment demonstrations, riots, and armed attacks are used as seven different indicators of social unrest.[66] As hypothesized, all seven are positively related to the decline of democracy: the higher the level of social unrest, the higher the level of decline. It should be noted, however, that the impact of each indicator on the magnitude of decline varies among different types of countries. Riots, antigovernment demonstrations, and armed attacks have more devastating impacts on democracy in developing countries.

When we examine the relationship between social unrest indicators and the other factors used to explain the decline in democracy (Table 5.2), we find them to be positively related to the indicators of executive instability as well as those of coercive measures. The data indicate that social unrest stimulates executive instability and leads governments to employ repressive policies.

Although the available data are limited, three particular economic problems that involve ineffectiveness in fulfilling social and economic rights are included: economic inequality, measured by the Gini coefficient for income distribution; economic instability, measured as the annual percentage change in consumer prices (inflation rate); and the unemployment rate. The first two indicators are viewed as influenced by redistributive policies, with the Gini coefficient capturing the long-term distribution of income, and the annual increase in consumer prices reflecting the short-term distribution. Unemployment refers to the violation of a major socioeconomic right, the right to work.

These indicators are not, of course, adequate in measuring the overall economic effectiveness of a government in reinforcing social and economic rights. Because the economic conditions that reflect these rights can be influenced directly or indirectly by macroeconomic policies and social programs, policymakers can deal with economic problems in various ways. Indicators of welfare policies and social services (e.g., the extent and distribution of health services, nutrition, literacy, and education) are important in measuring economic inequality and governmental respect for social and economic rights. These indicators need to be included in a comprehensive measure of economic ineffectiveness. Data on these variables, however, are limited mostly to developed countries and for a small number of years (largely starting in the late 1960s). Including them in the analysis would limit us to a small and unrepresentative group of countries.

Another problem in comparing economic effectiveness is the difficulty in identifying the individual policy instruments so that they can be incorporated in

Table 5.2 Correlations Between Social Unrest Indicators and Other Determinants of the Decline in Democracy

	Deaths from Domestic Violence	Assassinations	General Strikes	Guerrilla Warfare	Riots	Antigovernment Demonstrations	Armed Attacks
Purges	.20[a]	.08[a]	.14[a]	.17[a]	.18[a]	.12[a]	.08[a]
Political sanctions	.18[a]	.08[a]	.17[a]	.14[a]	.28[a]	.25[a]	.20[a]
Political executions	.37[a]	.05[a]	.05[a]	.13[a]	.03	.02	.07[a]
Constitutional changes	.10[a]	.05[b]	.03	.09[a]	.03	.02	.01
Coups d'état	.14[a]	.08[a]	.09[a]	.11[a]	.08[a]	.04[b]	.02
Cabinet changes	.13[a]	.08[a]	.13[a]	.12[a]	.10[a]	.04[b]	.03
Government crises	.17[a]	.24[a]	.29[a]	.31[a]	.23[a]	.12[a]	.06[a]
Unemployment	.09[b]	.08[c]	-.004	-.03	-.01	-.005	.08[c]
Inflation	.17[a]	.25[a]	.16[a]	-.002	.01	.03	.04[c]
Income inequality—Gini	.06[b]	.005	.02	.08[b]	.008	-.08[b]	.02
Social mobilization	-.19[a]	.03	.06[b]	-.05[c]	.15[a]	.21[a]	.03
Economic development	-.11[a]	-.03	-.01	-.07[a]	.07[a]	.15[a]	.03
Economic growth rate	-.14[a]	-.01	-.02	-.07[a]	-.05[b]	-.02	-.04[c]

Notes: a. Significant at .01 level.
b. Significant at .05 level.
c. Significant at .10 level.

a wide cross-national analysis. Although it is often argued that policy outcomes provide a more valid comparison base than policy outputs,[67] less egalitarian income distribution and high inflation rates may also be unintended impacts of some policies. In such cases governments might have even considered as defined policy goals lowering inequality levels and inflation rates, but the outcome may still be the same if policies formulated and implemented to accomplish those goals turn out to be ineffective. In fact, administrative ineffectiveness is often stated as a common problem in developing countries.[68] The structural elements play a considerable role in determining the outcomes by limiting the integrity of implementation as well as the policy options.[69] Thus, individual policies that may result in or are ineffective in curing inegalitarian income distribution and high inflation are not represented in our model. This component of the system is treated as a "black box."

The extent of income inequality is measured by the Gini coefficient. The Gini coefficient is a frequently used measure of inequality. Based on income distribution, it can take a value between 0 and 1 (or 0 and 100 in percentage values), representing perfect equality and inequality in a society (See Appendix E). Gini coefficient values employed in this analysis were obtained from Paukert[70] and, by using the same formula employed by Paukert, were calculated for some years and countries on the basis of income distribution data reported by Ahluwalia[71] and by the World Bank in the *World Development Report* (see Appendix D for the formula). Inflation rates were calculated from the consumer price indices reported in *Statistical Yearbook* of the United Nations and *Statistical Abstract of Latin America*.[72] These two sources were used also for the unemployment data.

Table 5.1 shows that both inflation rates and income inequality are positively related to the magnitude of decline, the inflation rate having a stronger impact. Unemployment rates are found to be insignificant, though this may be attributed to the nature of data. Because information on unemployment is available mostly for Western industrial countries, the overrepresentation of this group might have skewed the direction of the relationship. When we examine the relationship between economic indicators and social unrest variables, we observe the impact of inflation on social unrest as the most potent (Table 5.2). Inflation rate is positively correlated with deaths from domestic violence ($r = .17$), assassinations ($r = .21$), and general strikes ($r = .16$). Noteworthy is the variation in the relationship between the measures of economic ineffectiveness with those of social unrest. Different economic problems seem to invoke different kinds of public response. Income inequality, for example, is positively correlated with deaths from domestic violence and with guerrilla warfare, and negatively correlated with antigovernment demonstrations. But the latter two display no significant relationship with the other two economic problems. Again, the number of armed attacks is moderately related to both unemployment and inflation but not to income inequality. Also, unemployment, which appears to have no direct impact on the decline of democracy, seems to be working indirectly by stimulating social unrest such as evidenced by deaths from domestic violence, assassinations, and armed attacks. These already have been pointed out for their cataclysmic impacts on democracy. Economic problems, especially inflation and inequality, are positively correlated to executive unrest. The correlations between inflation and coups d'état, cabinet changes, and government crises are all .08; their respective correlations with income inequality are .10, .16 and .10.

The structural factors included in the correlation analysis—economic development level, economic growth rate, and social mobilization—yield either negative or insignificant correlations with the magnitude of decline in democracy. (Another structural factor that we emphasized, dependency, is discussed separately in the next section because of the categorical nature of its measurement.) Economic development level, measured by energy consumption in kilograms of coal-equivalent per capita,[73] reflects a strong but negative relationship with the level of decline in democracy (Table 5.1), although the relationship becomes slightly weaker when analysis is focused on developing countries ($r = -.09$ for developing countries, but $r = r -.13$ when other countries are included).

Similarly, economic growth rate, measured by the annual percentage changes in the gross national product per capita (GNP/capita), yields a negative correlation with the magnitude of decline in democracy. As reported in Table 5.2, it is negatively correlated also with social unrest indicators. These findings contradict the argument that rapid economic growth is a destabilizing factor and support the thesis that democratic instability is instead a function of inegalitarian growth. The significant negative relationships may also provide some support for the argument that social unrest and political instability are a function of economic stagnation.

Finally, the analysis of the impact of social mobilization reflects its dual role, consolidation and destabilization. To capture the complex nature of this concept, an index was constructed by factor analysis of several measures of physical mobility and communication levels: railroad passengers per mile; (per capita) automobiles, telegrams, telephones, all mail, radios, newspaper circulation, primary school enrollment, secondary school enrollment, university enrollment, percent of literacy, and population of cities of 100,000, of 50,000, of 25,000, and of 20,000. The factor analysis uncovers that there is more than one common factor for these 15 variables, but the first factor obtained from the analysis captures more than 50 percent of the common variance for these variables and provides consistent results over time. Thus, this first dimension is used as an indicator of social mobilization.

The correlation of social mobilization index scores with the level of decline in democracy is -.15 when all countries with data are included in the analysis (Table 5.1), suggesting that social mobilization promotes democratization. However, when the analysis is limited to developing countries, a positive but insignificant correlation coefficient is obtained. The difference between these two correlations reinforces the argument about the interactive role of social mobilization. Social mobilization fortifies democracy in economically sound and balanced settings, but serves as a destabilizing factor in the presence of problems and injustice. Again, analysis of the relationship between this indicator and social unrest variables produces either negative or insignificant correlations with social unrest indicators that imply more violence (e.g., deaths from domestic violence) and positive correlations with less violent forms (e.g., antigovernment demonstrations) that are positively correlated with economic development level.

Finally, a regression analysis of the decline of democracy with all of the variables included in the model yields a Multiple-R value of .94. This means that these variables explain 88 percent of the variance in the magnitude of decline in democracy.

We have established that most of the variation in the magnitude of the decline is explained by the events that occur on the verge of decline (e.g., coups d'état and coercive measures by governments). Although they have high explanatory powers, closeness of these events to the event of decline itself does not allow these indicators to be useful predictors as warning signals to policymakers. Thus, in an effort to identify a parsimonious model with predictive value, a stepwise regression analysis of decline was conducted by excluding the numbers of coups d'état, purges, government sanctions, and constitutional changes. The outcome was a simple model with only three indicators: inflation, cabinet changes, and deaths from domestic violence.

> Decline in democracy =
> $-.28 + .02$ Inflation $+ 2.9$ Cabinet changes $+ .03$ Deaths

This model—which yields a Multiple-R value of .58 and explains 33 percent of the variance in the magnitude of decline suggests that we should expect a major decline in the democraticness of the regime if prevailing conditions are high inflation rates, frequent cabinet changes, and large numbers of deaths from domestic violence.

DEPENDENCY

Dependency has been identified as an important structural factor that prevents both development and democracy. Considering interactions between nations and the levels of influence they exercise over each other, the world system is divided into three components by some dependency theorists: the core (or center) societies, peripheral societies, and semiperipheral societies. Chiro states the characteristics of each as follows:

- Core societies: economically diversified . . . rich, powerful societies that are *relatively* independent of outside controls.
- Peripheral societies: economically overspecialized, relatively poor and weak societies that are subject to manipulation or direct control by the

core powers.
- Semi-peripheral societies: societies mid-way between the core and periphery that are trying to industrialize and diversify their economies."[74]

Galtung highlights the intermediary position of a semiperipheral society and points to its role in the world system as a "go-between":

> Concretely, it would exchange semi-processed goods with highly processed goods upwards and semi-processed goods with raw materials downwards. It would simply be located in between Center and Periphery where the degree of processing of its export products is concerned.
> In another version of the same conception the go-between nation would be one cycle behind the Center as to technology but one cycle ahead of the Periphery; in line with its position as to the degree of processing. This would also apply to the means of destruction and the means of communication.[75]

For the analysis of the relationship of dependency with the decline of democracy and its other determinants, Snyder and Kick's categorical measure of dependency is adapted with some modifications. These authors measure the dependency level of countries by their world system status, which is operationally defined "according to four types of international networks: trade flows, military interventions, diplomatic exchanges and conjoint treaty memberships."[76] Using block-model analysis, they obtain ten blocks that classify countries accordingly. Then they aggregate the blocks into three groups of countries—core, periphery, and semiperiphery. For the present research the classification by Snyder and Kick is revised for statistical and theoretical concerns by using a reasoning similar to that pursued by some other researchers.[77] Two blocks located between the periphery and semiperiphery blocks fall closer to the latter in most dimensions, and thus for this study are included in the semiperiphery group, although they are considered as peripheries by the original authors. Moreover, countries with centrally planned economies, most of which appear in a single block in Snyder and Kick's analysis, are grouped in a new category different from the three common ones. These countries were classified originally as semiperipheral because despite the differences in their domestic system, they operate in a capitalist world market dominated by the core countries. Although this explanation is valid, it overlooks the difference between these countries and the other semiperipheral ones. State intervention and control of the economy are much higher in these countries, and the integration between native capitalist classes and the international capitalist elite does not apply to these cases.[78] Thus, the measure of dependency, or world system status, of countries is built as a variable with four categories: core countries, semiperipheries, peripheries, and centrally planned economies (Table 5.3).

Because dependency is defined as world system status and measured as a categorical variable, mean differences instead of correlation analysis is used to assess the impact of dependency. Table 5.4 presents the average values of all

Table 5.3   World System Status of Countries

Core	Centrally Planned	Semiperiphery	
Australia	Albania	Argentina	Kenya
Belgium	Bulgaria	Bolivia	Korea, R
Canada	China	Brazil	Lebanon
Denmark	Cuba	Burma	Malaysia
France	Czechoslovakia	Chile	Mexico
Germany, FR	Germany, DR	Colombia	Nicaragua
Iceland	Hungary	Costa Rica	Pakistan
Italy	Korea, PR	Cyprus	Panama
Japan	Mongolia	Dominican R	Paraguay
Luxembourg	Poland	Ecuador	Peru
Netherlands	Romania	El Salvador	Philippines
New Zealand	USSR	Finland	Portugal
Norway		Greece	Saudi Arabia
Sweden		Guatemala	South Africa
Switzerland		Haiti	Spain
United Kingdom		Honduras	Sri Lanka
United States		India	Taiwan
		Iran	Turkey
		Iraq	Uruguay
		Ireland	Venezuela
		Israel	Vietnam, PR
		Jordan	Yugoslavia

Note: Countries not listed are classified as peripheries.

Table 5.4   Average Values of Indicators by World System Status

Indicator	Core	Centrally Planned	Semiperiphery	Periphery
Democracy score	98.28	60.02	73.94	66.02
Change in democracy	.47	−.01	.12	−.37
Coups d'état	.00	.01	.05	.06
Cabinet changes	.41	.25	.53	.46
Government crises	.33	.10	.35	.14
Armed attacks	30.65	10.68	14.38	14.86
Political sanctions	9.52	18.45	10.28	3.90
Political executions	.01	16.68	2.96	3.96
Constitutional changes	.02	.05	.09	.18
Deaths from violence	4.21	22.99	42.42	36.46
Assassinations	.14	.04	.32	.09
General strikes	.20	.03	.17	.03
Guerrilla warfare	.18	.16	.43	.21
Purges	.06	.63	.43	.14
Riots	.97	.37	.94	.18
Antigovernment demonstrations	.96	.33	.59	.16
Unemployment rate	3.64	2.87	6.10	7.30
Inflation rate	6.4	1.66	14.30	11.75
Income inequality—Gini	3.6	.22	.46	.44
Energy consumption (per capita)	4679.78	2635.79	694.18	885.30
Economic growth	8.65	8.15	8.03	8.32
Social mobilization	1.24	.27	−.26	−.87

variables that were used in this research in explaining the decline of democracy by the world system status of countries.

Economic ineffectiveness of governments has already been identified as a destabilizing factor by the correlation analysis. Table 5.4 illustrates that economic performance in semiperipheries and peripheries has been poorer compared with core countries and centrally planned economies. Unemployment rates in semiperipheries and peripheries have been higher, 6.1 percent and 7.3 percent on the average, while core countries and centrally planned economies have had much lower rates, 3.6 percent and 2.9 percent, respectively. Similarly, inflation rates have been less than 2 percent for the centrally planned economies and around 6.5 percent in core countries, but jumped to 11.8 percent for peripheries and 14.3 percent for semiperipheries. Thus, the economic milieu in dependent countries is more pertinent to social unrest.

Although core countries are not free from social unrest, it tends to appear in these countries in less violent forms, such as antigovernment demonstrations or strikes. In countries with dependent status, however, social unrest takes more violent forms, producing high death tolls. Dependent countries rank high also on executive unrest indicators. Although core countries are likely to experience frequent government crises and cabinet changes, these events are more common to semiperipheries and peripheries. Finally, coups d'état have been completely unknown to the core nations and have seldom occurred in centrally planned economies, but dependent countries have encountered them frequently. Consequently, changes in regime in these countries appear to be in the direction of decline in the level of democracy. While the average change in the score of democraticness for core nations has been a positive one, .47, semiperipheries experienced moderate increases, and peripheries with an average score of -.37 suffered from major declines.

Thus, we can conclude that dependent status does not establish a favorable environment for the development or stability of democracy in developing countries. Either as a result of the policy preferences of their elite, or due to foreign control and impositions, or as a consequence of both, developing countries lack the relatively egalitarian economic ground that would stabilize their democratic structures.

NOTES

1. Binder et al.; Nordlinger, 1971.
2. Huntington, 1968, p. 46; Olson, p. 551; Pye, p. 66; Das Gupta, 1989.
3. Kuznets.
4. See the study by Hicks. His research, based on a regression analysis of data from developing countries reaches three important conclusions: (1) "It would appear that countries making substantial progress in meeting basic needs do *not* have substantially lower GNP growth rates"; (2) "the attainment of a higher level of basic needs satisfaction appears to lead a higher growth rates in the future"; (3) "measures of health improvement (life expectancy) are as strongly related to growth and productivity as

measures of education attainment" (p. 992).

5. Pye, p. 66.
6. Huntington, 1968, p. 46.
7. Olson, p. 551.
8. Thomas Rose, in Thomas Rose, ed., p. 30.
9. Field; Manor.
10. Manor, p. 72.
11. O'Donnell; Collier.
12. Kravis; Paukert; Ahluwalia; Weede, 1980; Weede and Tiefenback, 1981.
13. For dependency theorists who criticize the modernization approach for its emphasis on internal development factors, see Zolberg; Cardoso, 1977; Portes.
14. Olson; Lenski.
15. Baran; Frank; Galtung; Wallerstein, 1974; Amin, 1974 and 1976; Cardoso, 1977.
16. Frank; Chase-Dunn; Portes.
17. Baran.
18. Cardoso, 1977, p. 13.
19. Furtado.
20. Galtung.
21. Evans and Timberlake, p. 540.
22. Portes; Evans and Timberlake.
23. Portes, p. 76.
24. Furtado.
25. Galtung; Sunkel.
26. Hyter. See also the discussions and references under "Foreign Influence" in the previous chapter.
27. Falk.
28. Kaufman, Chernotsky, and Geller; Evans and Timberlake; Bollen, 1983.
29. Bollen, 1983, p. 477.
30. Muller and Seligson.
31. Deutsch, 1961, p. 494.
32. Deutsch, 1961; Cornelius; Olson; Hoselitz; Huntington, 1968.
33. Olson, p. 541.
34. Jackman, 1978; Johnson, Slater, and McGowan.
35. Deutsch, 1961; Feierabend, Feierabend, and Nesvold; Gurr; Hibbs.
36. Cnudde and Neubauer, p. 530.
37. Pye, pp. 154–155.
38. Cnudde and Neubauer, p. 530.
39. Gurr, p. 605.
40. Gude, p. 739.
41. Brinton.
42. Moore, 1969.
43. Jackson et al., p. 631.
44. Walton and Ragin.
45. Boswell and Dixon.
46. Piven and Cloward.
47. Ibid.
48. Cnudde and Neubauer, p. 520.
49. Lipset, 1959, p. 89.
50. Linz and Stepan; O'Donnell, Schmitter, and Whitehead; Collier, 1979; Roberts, p. 21.
51. Roberts; Jackson et al., p. 634; Hyter.
52. Jackson et al., p. 652.

53. Several case studies document the coercive impact of dependency. In addition to the literature discussed under "Foreign Influence" in Chapter 4, see Lopez and Stohl.

54. Huntington, 1984, p. 212.

55. Chaffee.

56. On cyclical policies, see Richard Rose, "Models of Change," in Richard Rose, ed.

57. Information for most of the variables was obtained from Banks, 1979. Data for domestic violence and the number of government sanctions were acquired from the "Events Data" collected by Charles Taylor and his associates and provided by the Interuniversity Consortium for Political and Social Research (ICPSR) Data Archive.

58. The sample includes all countries for which we have assigned a democracy score. The number of years that a country is included in the analysis depends on the availability of data on its other indicators. Thus, the sample is a sample of convenience. Because it is not a random sample, statistical significance tests are not meaningful, but they are reported here as some implicit measures of the strength of the relationship between the respective variables.

59. Ake, p. 215.

60. O'Donnell, Schmitter, and Whitehead, p. 18.

61. Taylor and Hudson.

62. Banks, 1979, p. 14.

63. Ibid., p. 18.

64. Ibid., p. 17.

65. Ibid., p. 19.

66. See Chapter 1 for information regarding the sources and definitions of these indicators.

67. Leichter.

68. Pye.

69. Hofferbert and Ergrüder.

70. Paukert.

71. Ahluwalia.

72. United Nations, *Statistical Yearbook; Statistical Abstract of Latin America* (Los Angeles: University of California, Latin American Center).

73. See Chapter 2 for justification of selecting this indicator over another. The data on this indicator as well as on economic growth rate and social mobilization are obtained from Banks, *Cross-National Time-Series Data Archive*, provided by the Center for Economic and Social Research at the State University of New York at Binghamton.

74. Chiro, p. 13.

75. Galtung, p. 104.

76. Snyder and Kick, p. 1105.

77. Bollen, 1983.

78. Wallerstein, 1976.

6

Policy Implications for Democratic Rulers: Lessons from Costa Rica, India, and Turkey

Parliament and democracy are only considered desirable by the possessing class so long as they maintain existing conditions. That is, of course, not real democracy; it is the exploitation of the democratic idea for undemocratic purposes. Real democracy has had no chance to exist so far, for there is an essential contradiction between the capitalist system and democracy. Democracy, if it means anything, means equality; not merely the equality of possessing a vote, but economic and social equality.—Jawaharlal Nehru

COUPS AS CYCLICAL POLICIES

The empirical findings presented in the previous chapter provide support for the thesis that a democratic system can be attained through the adoption of a set of democratic rules, but it cannot be maintained without an infrastructure based on *balanced* economic development. In other words, civil and political rights, essentials of democracy, cannot be sustained absent a minimum level of socioeconomic rights. In fact, structural changes toward eliminating economic discrepancies are treated as a prerequisite for genuine and effective political democracy by many Latin American specialists. Coercive civil and political rights policies, implemented one after the other, result in important qualitative changes in political systems, transforming more democratic systems into less democratic ones. These policies do not eliminate socioeconomic problems, however, and they leave a nation with a high probability of experiencing similar qualitative transformations in the future.

Among those analyzed, coups d'état appear to be among the most important events leading to high rates of decline in democracies. If we examine individually some cases with high levels of decline and coups d'état and follow the changes in other factors for three or four years prior to and after the coups, the cyclical character of coercive policies can be seen clearly. These cases show that although economic and structural factors are relatively constant, generally the social unrest that was high before a coup is reduced or completely eliminated soon afterward.

The Afghan coup of 1973, four coups in Argentina (1955, 1962, 1966, and 1976), the 1960 Bolivian coup, the 1964 military takeover in Brazil, the 1972 coups in Chile and Ghana, the 1963 coup in Honduras, the 1966 coups in Indonesia and Nigeria, the 1962 and 1968 coups in Peru, and the 1960, 1971 and 1980 military takeovers in Turkey are some of the cases that display the cyclical character of coercive policies. Military rules successfully suppress unrest, but because they do not treat the socioeconomic causes of it, once the coercive measures are removed, the cycle of social unrest and suppression starts again.

However, it would be misleading to see the military as the only coercive group. The responsibility of civilian governments in bringing about decline should not be overlooked. Elected governments do not hesitate to employ government sanctions in the face of persistent social unrest, and such actions not only reduce the level of democraticness in the country but also pave the way for further coercion and military intervention. In fact, such sanctions can justify and legitimize subsequent military takeovers. For example, in many countries that experience high levels of social unrest, we see martial law put into effect by civilian governments. This justifies military intervention (1) by admitting the incompetence of the civilian law enforcement institutions in handling social unrest, (2) by consolidating the image of the military as an effective force in maintaining social order, and (3) by politicizing the military.

SOCIAL MOBILIZATION AND SOCIOECONOMIC INEQUALITY

The findings reported in the previous chapter suggest that attention should be directed to the causes of social unrest if an effective and stable solution to democratic decline is to be found. They show clearly that social unrest indicators are largely explained by economic inequality and instability rather than by the extent of social mobilization. This observation has a couple of important implications.

First, it confirms that social mobilization, per se, is not a destabilizing phenomenon, though it has been treated as such because of the social change component inherent in its definition (including increasing levels of education, urbanization, and communication). Identifying these factors with instability has even led decisionmakers to consider policies that would slow the expansion of literacy, education, means of communication, and urbanization. Our analysis, however, suggests that reassessments of developmental policies aimed at slowing these aspects of social mobilization are unnecessary and counterproductive.

Second, the positive relationships between income inequality, social unrest, and the decline of democracy challenge arguments such as those of Robert Moss, who is afraid that egalitarian policies and the welfare state will be the end of democracy in Britain. Classical liberal theory presented in the writings of J. S. Mill and de Tocqueville also treated individual liberties as incompatible with equality. They believed that "freedom and liberty were the most valuable accomplishments of societal development which deserved to be protected, under all circumstances, from the egalitarian threats of mass society."[1]

Their critics, however, stress the positive interaction between democratic politics and welfare economics. Claus Offe, for example, argues against the presence of a trade-off between the two, emphasizing the fact that they reinforce each other. He concludes that the welfare state makes things safer for a democracy.[2] Our findings also support the argument that democratic institutions have survived in countries like Britain largely because of the welfare policies and the relatively more egalitarian nature of the system.

It is no wonder that Harold Laski emphasized economic equality in addition to political equality in his definition of "democracy" published half a century ago. First, Laski stressed that "the basis of democratic development is the demand for equality, the demand that the system of power to be erected upon the similarities and not the differences between men." Then, he emphasized the inadequacy of political equality without the supplement of economic equality:

> It is because political equality, however profound, does not permit the full affirmation of the common man's essence that the idea of democracy has spread to other spheres. . . . In the absence of economic equality no political mechanisms will of themselves enable the common man to realize his wills and interests. Economic power is regarded as the parent of political power. To make the definition of the latter effective, the former also must be widely diffused. To divide a people into rich and poor is to make impossible the attainment of a common interest by state action. Economic equality is then urged as the clue upon which the reality of democracy depends.[3]

Referring to historical development in the perception of the interaction between economic equality and the fundamentals of democracy, Laski concluded that "for new democratic theory liberty is necessarily a function of equality."[4] Finally, Laski pointed to the role of the state in establishing a more egalitarian society and maintaining it. He referred to the accomplishments by the movements for social and economic equality and argued that "there is a kind of eminent domain which entitles the state deliberately to intervene to mitigate the consequences of social inequality."[5] Laski's call for state intervention, contradicting modernization theorists and liberal economists, is also advocated by some economists for both its social and economic value:

> Free markets are powerful systems for producing the goods and services for which there is an effective demand, but the demand generated in such a system may not always be the most desirable from a social point of view. One problem is that such a system may not lead to the fastest growth of which the economy is capable. Therefore, there is room for government policies for promoting the rapid accumulation and full use of productive sources and the advancement of technology. There is also need for policies to influence the allocation of resources to different sectors of the economy, such as agriculture and industry, which also influence the rate of growth. . . .

> One of the most serious problems of a liberal economic system is that, under
> certain conditions, the resulting distribution of income may be very unequal, and
> the inequality may increase over time in a cumulative way. Therefore it is desirable
> for the government to follow policies to improve the distribution of income.[6]

The impact of laissez-faire economy is argued to be more devastating in
least developed countries because it results in food shortages that would subject a large portion of the population to severe malnutrition and fuel popular
resistance to increasing food prices.[7] However, it is well known that states or,
more precisely, governments do not have unlimited power under conditions of
an increasingly dependent world system that limits policy choices and capacities.

AVOIDING DEPENDENCY

The present study also found that world system status is a significant factor in
determining economic equality and instability. These economic conditions in
turn have a significant effect on decline of democracy, and from this one can
conclude that development in the contemporary world, both economic and
democratic, cannot be achieved by mere repetition of earlier development models. Early developers did not face the complex world structure that has evolved
in the course of the present century—the increasing power of multinational corporations, strong international trading alliances, a large gap between technologically powerful rich nations and technologically weak poor ones, and increasing
levels of indebtedness of the latter to the former.

Although the detrimental impact of dependency is clear, we cannot easily
conclude that policies overemphasizing self-reliance result in better conditions
for democracy or equality. Earlier studies show that "autarky combined with
political modernization for development has been successful only in large states
which control big internal markets, such as China and the Soviet Union. Small
nations that cut themselves off from the world risk isolation and stagnation,
e.g., Burma," and peripheral countries that attempt to bring an ultimate solution
to "their dependency on the core risk subversion or invasion, e.g., Chile."[8]

One reasonable strategy to eliminate the problems of dependency would be
controlling inputs from the core and assuring their compatibility with balanced
development. State intervention, in this respect, has been recommended by several authors who stress the significant economic role played by states, even
those Western countries that went through their major economic transformation
at a time when the world structure was less complex and more egalitarian.[9]
Effective state control, however, is difficult in a quite competitive world in
which multinationals are largely uncontrolled but consequential actors.
Nevertheless, through the close regulation of foreign investments, some countries—Japan, India, and Yugoslavia—have managed to benefit from foreign
capital inflow without paying high costs. Empirical findings indicate that states

that are both "viable" and "active" are the most successful in "overcoming the dependency-induced obstacles to underdevelopment."[10] Several students of democracy argue against state intervention into the economy, believing that statism will prevent the growth of economic associational groups and that these retard democratic development.[11] But reformist state intervention is more likely to have a positive effect on democratization because of its redistributive impact. Kohli presents a strong argument in favor of state intervention in his study of Indian states. He finds the states run by left-of-center and interventionist parties are more successful in undertaking economic reform and in reducing poverty.[12] Here, it may be necessary to restate that the process of gradual democratization within a laissez-faire economy as experienced by the West does not establish a viable model for the developing countries of the twentieth century. In fact, even Western democracies felt the need for state intervention and transformed their liberal states to welfare states in the face of economic crisis.

THREE CASE STUDIES

The indicators of economic effectiveness used in the data analysis presented in the previous chapter are rather crude measures. Several other measures of inequality and instability are required for a more realistic picture of the economic performance of governments. Moreover, the cross-national nature of the analysis and the reliance on correlations conceal the causal order of the events. Furthermore, because of scope, time, and data limitations, the individual policies that might result in effective performance (or reversal), are not included in the analysis. Macroeconomic policies, welfare policies, social services, development projects, and the like all have direct or indirect effects on economic effectiveness. These policy variables, interactions among them, and their impacts on the system need to be studied to provide more specific policy guidance. The lack of data and the problems of compatibility with the available data do not allow us to undertake such a comprehensive study, global in scope. However, these questions can be addressed and some generalizations drawn through case study research if comparable and illustrative cases are selected for analysis.

Costa Rica, India, and Turkey are chosen as cases for comparative analysis because these countries established their prevailing political systems about the same time, soon after World War II. Turkey moved from one-party absolutism to multiparty politics in 1946. India gained its independence from Britain in 1947 and subsequently established a parliamentary democracy. Costa Rica had experience with elected governments before, but its democratic process was interrupted by a civil war, and it entered an era of stable democratic rule in 1948.

The levels of success with democracy, however, have been different in these three countries. Turkey experienced three military interruptions, in 1960, 1971, and 1980. Between periods of military rule, democratically elected governments often sacrificed some principles of democracy by putting martial law into effect to cope with social unrest. India has been praised for the continuity of its democracy until 1975, when Prime Minister Indira Gandhi declared a state of emergency that lasted two years. Costa Rica, more successful than the other two, has managed to maintain a stable democratic system.

Factors commonly identified as the determinants of the success of democracy are mostly inconclusive, except for the role of the military, when we compare these three countries:

1. The *size* of the country seems to be irrelevant. Costa Rica, a tiny country with a small population and often referred to as a city-state, and India, a subcontinent, have been more successful in maintaining stable democracies than Turkey, a middle-size country.

2. The *homogeneity of the population* in these countries also varies considerably. Turkey and India could be ranked at the extremes on a scale of homogeneity. Turkey is highly homogeneous in its racial, religious, linguistic, and ethnic composition, with only one significant ethnic minority, the Kurds. India is the opposite; it is composed of hundreds of groups divided by various combinations of linguistic, religious, and ethnic differences. Costa Rica lies in between.

3. *Statism* is often identified as an obstacle for democratization because government intervention into the economy is believed to prevent the development of an autonomous bourgeoisie that played a liberating role in Europe. All three countries have mixed economies in which the state has been an active participant in the economy not only to regulate it but also to produce both goods and services. Moreover, especially in Turkey and India, statism and import-substituting industrialization have been used to support the development of a national bourgeoisie. However, the political power held by the bourgeoisie in these two countries varies considerably. India's bourgeoisie has not yet established itself as the dominant class,[13] but its Turkish counterpart has been referred to as a major player in the decisionmaking process even during times of authoritarian military rule. A study conducted by Euromoney after the 1980 coup ranked the business sector as "the most influential civilian source of power" in Turkey and only slightly below the military junta.[14] Moreover, the members of this class as well as its various associations allied themselves with conservative groups and right-wing parties to welcome any government changes that suppressed labor activities and demands for social justice.[15]

4. The diversity in the *constitutional arrangements* of these countries does not allow us to conclude that either presidential or parliamentary systems are more preferable for the stability of democracy. India and Costa Rica can be classified as typical examples of parliamentary and presidential systems, respectively. Turkey began as a parliamentary system, and although it went through several revisions that extended the power of the presidential

office, especially after the 1980 coup, it kept trust in parliamentary responsibility.

5. The political role of the *military* has been crucial for the fate of democracies, with elected governments often ousted by military juntas. Consequently, the strength of the military is treated as a significant factor in determining the stability of democracy. The three countries analyzed here reflect two extremes in terms of their military strength. Costa Rica does not have a military force in the traditional sense; Turkey maintains a huge army, its major contribution to the NATO forces; and India is a continental superpower equipped with atomic weapons.

Although the size of the military may not be an important factor in explaining the variation in the democratic experiences of these countries, the historical role of the military was consequential for the differences between India and Turkey. As already mentioned, where the military plays a major role in the establishment of the modern state, it is more likely to acquire a political role and see itself as a political alternative. Thus, despite the relative similarity in their size and strength, the military forces of Turkey and India have different political roles. India, as a country that resisted colonial rule without a full-fledged armed struggle, has a strong but apolitical military. The Indian officers serving in the British army at the verge of independence were all very young and low in rank, so could not establish a political threat to the experienced and charismatic civilian leaders of independence.[16] Thus, the military was easily transformed into a bureaucratic instrument of the state. But, even then, there was a conscious effort on the part of the civilian leadership to confine the power domain of the military. It is claimed that the first prime minister, Nehru, "was wary of the military and tried to keep it as small as possible as long as possible."[17] Moreover, he pursued a "divide and rule" strategy against the armed forces, and successors Shastri and Indira Gandhi adhered to the same strategy.[18] Turkey, on the other hand, owes its emancipation from Western occupation after World War I and the establishment in 1923 of the republic to the progressive military cadres of the Ottoman Empire. This group and their successors continued to hold important political offices; all but one of the elected presidents were recruited from the military. Even if they did not assume political titles, the officers were indoctrinated to serve as guards of the republic, a task assigned to them by its founder, Atatürk. This was used as the rationale for frequent interventions into politics. Efforts of the civilian leaders focused on having the military on their side rather than depoliticizing the military or bringing it under objective state control. Moreover, as discussed in Chapter 4, by assuming entrepreneurial roles and becoming shareholders in major corporations, the Turkish military, like many of its Latin American counterparts, started to see any threat to the socioeconomic status quo as a threat to national security.

However, even the military is not immune to some political accountability, and it cannot justify an intervention if the current government appears legitimate and there is no major evidence of social unrest. Thus, I focus on the main thrust of the theoretical model previously discussed to examine the economic policies and distributive efforts of the governments to explain the stability or instability of democracy in these three countries. After all, as stated by a student of Latin American politics, "Democracy rests on equality, and equality in political rights on equality in the distribution of property."[19]

LEADERS' ATTITUDE AND IDEOLOGY

The transitions to democracy in India and Costa Rica were led by socialist or social democratic leaders. Even though they failed to apply it fully, the victors of the civil war in Costa Rica, organized as the Partido Liberacion Nacional (PLN), had a social democratic program that stated as a goal the transformation of the country into a welfare state.

In the case of India, its first prime minister, Jawaharlal Nehru, a Fabian socialist, was not secretive about his ideology and was able to influence the Congress Party program and the government structure to undertake social reforms. These included the programs of affirmative action and positive discrimination of the "scheduled castes" and "scheduled tribes" to overcome the age-old discrimination imposed by the caste system of Hinduism. Although the reformist spirit of the Congress Party faded by the 1960s, either as a result of intraelite co-option or as a consequence of compromises with international lending agencies,[20] agrarian discontent and unrest forced the party to reinstate it in the 1970s. *Garibi hatao* (remove poverty) became the slogan for the 1971 election and continued to be the main topic of political debates throughout the decade. A study of value commitments of local leaders in four countries (India, Poland, United States, and Yugoslavia) in the 1960s found Indian leaders emphasizing economic equality more than anything else (second only to economic development)—and more so than the leaders in the three other countries.[21]

In Turkey, however, the Democrat Party (which composed the first elected government to replace the authoritarian rule of the Republican People's Party) had no socialist or social democratic pretense, and it even attempted to reverse the limited populist reforms of the former authoritarian government. It was not until 1961 that the concepts of social reform and the welfare state were included among the responsibilities of the state, and even then, they were initiated by the military, not by a political party. Major political parties were slow in responding to public demands, and they acted more like followers than leaders in including social reform and equality in the public agenda. Only in the early 1970s did one of the major parties, the Republican People's Party, declare itself as a party of the "democratic left."

In Costa Rica, steps toward adoption of welfare policies were taken after the world depression by the Calderanista conservatives before the PLN institutionalized such measures. Although their motive is open to dispute, there is little disagreement about the commitment of the Costa Rican governments to

their welfare state. Some attribute this orientation to the ideological commitment of the populist or social democratic leaders.[22] Others treat it as a strategy
of social control and argue that social reform has been used by an essentially
inegalitarian elite as a co-optive tool, an "escape valve" to maintain their hegemony over the masses.[23] Regardless of the original motive, welfare programs in
Costa Rica continued to grow, with both conservative and social democratic
parties contributing to their expansion.

ECONOMIC GROWTH AND INFLATION

India pursued a slow but steady growth by allowing price vacillations, but
avoided a continuously climbing inflation rate (Table 6.1). Costa Rica maintained lower inflation rates until the 1970s, but failed to control price increases
during the oil crisis in the 1970s and the world depression in the 1980s. Turkey
pursued a rapid and inflationary economic growth strategy. As illustrated by
Figure 6.1, India and Costa Rica managed to keep their inflation rates below 10
percent for most of the years during the last four decades (especially before the
1970s), but the inflation rate in Turkey has been mostly above that level, sky-
rocketing in the years preceding the military interventions. Between 1948 and
1987, the average annual increase in consumer prices in Turkey has been 19
percent, while it has been 9 and 7 percent in Costa Rica and India, respectively.
For the same period, the correlation between GNP per capita and the inflation
rate is .79 for Turkey, .60 for Costa Rica, and only .21 for India. The rates of
inflation in India and Costa Rica reached their highest levels in the periods
1973–1975 and 1979–1981 following the oil shocks and world recession. But

Table 6.1　Average Annual Growth Rates and Changes in Consumer Prices

Country	1950–1960	1960–1970	1970–1980
India			
GNP	3.9	3.6	3.7
Inflation	2.0	7.2	8.5
Turkey			
GNP	6.3	6.2	5.0
Inflation	9.5	6.1	32.9
Costa Rica			
GNP	4.5	6.3	4.8
Inflation	1.8	2.0	12.2

Source: World Tables, 3d ed., vol. 1, Economic Data (Washington, D.C.: World Bank, 1983).

Figure 6.1 Inflation Rates for Three Countries

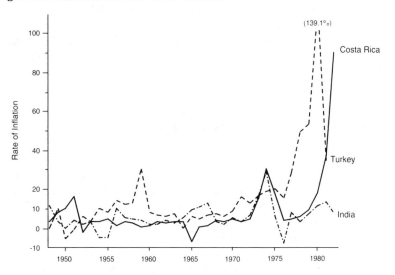

even during the 1970s, the rate of inflation in India was lower than in the majority of the OECD countries.[24]

It should be noted, however, that a high annual growth rate does not necessarily correspond to high inflation for a given year. The correlations between annual growth rate in GNP per capita and annual change in consumer prices are low and statistically insignificant for all three countries.

INCOME INEQUALITY

Table 6.2 provides information on the distribution of disposable household income in the three countries; included also are the Gini coefficients.

India, despite its large population living in absolute poverty, has maintained a relatively egalitarian distribution of income in which the Gini coefficient, calculated by using the data on the distribution of disposable income into quintiles, is 36.[25] Costa Rica lies in the middle with a Gini coefficient of 46.0, which is slightly lower than the 47.2 coefficient for Turkey but 10 points higher than that of India.[26]

A detailed study of income distribution in India implies that the government in this country has reinforced the redistribution of income through its tax policy. Compared with pretaxed income, concentration of disposable income is found to be less in India.[27] Because applicable data are not available for Costa Rica and Turkey, it is not possible to compare the effect of taxation on income

Table 6.2   Income Distribution and Gini Coefficients

Country	Lowest 20 percent	Second Quintile	Third Quintile	Fourth Quintile	Highest 20 percent	Highest 10 percent	Gini	Gini2
India								
1975–1976	7.0	9.2	13.9	20.5	49.4	33.6	36.0	40.2
Turkey								
1973	3.5	8.0	12.5	19.5	56.5	40.7	47.2	49.6
Costa Rica								
1971	3.3	8.7	13.3	19.8	54.8	39.5	46.0	48.6

Source: World Development Report, 1988 (Washington, D.C.: World Bank, 1988).

distribution in these countries. However, there are reasons to suspect that their tax policies have egalitarian impacts. Turkish tax laws have not been particularly progressive, and the tax burden has been mostly on fixed-income groups, such as government employees and wage labor. In Costa Rica, the contribution of income tax to the total tax revenues has composed too small a percentage to have a major redistributive impact.

A comparison of the change in the shares of the lowest and highest income groups shows that the trends in income distribution in India have been more egalitarian than in the other two countries (Table 6.3). The share of the lowest 20th percentile in India increased from 4.1 percent in 1960 to 7.0 per cent in 1975, while during the same period the share of the highest 5th percentile was reduced from 26.7 percent to 22.2 percent. Turkey and Costa Rica, in contrast, show a pattern of decline in the share of the lowest income groups. The change in the distribution of income in these two countries appears to favor the middle sectors. However, whereas in Costa Rica the share of the middle income groups seems to increase as a result of a reduction in the share of the highest income group, the transfer of income in Turkey seems to be from the lower income groups because the wealthy continue to maintain their share.

Despite the fact that a large portion of its population live in poverty, India's relatively egalitarian distribution of income contributed to the legitimacy of its young democracy. As noted by Charles Anderson in his analysis of Honduran politics in the 1960s, "Poverty itself, when national in scope and unmixed by grotesque contrasts between rich and poor, may in some measure have the effect of softening the political conflicts that are endemic to much of present-day Latin America."[28] It also should be noted that since independence India has managed to reduce poverty or keep it from increasing most of the time. The tendency of poverty to decline, however, has been modest, not sufficient to offset the growth of population. Both rural and urban poverty in India manifested patterns of fluctuation instead of continuous decline (Table 6.4).

SECTORAL INEQUALITIES

Table 6.5 reports the Gini coefficients for income inequalities between the

Table 6.3   Percentage of Income Received by the Lowest and Highest Income Groups for Selected Years

Country	Lowest 20 Percent	Highest 5 Percent
India		
1960	4.1	26.7
1964–1965	6.7	26.3
1975	7.0	22.2
Turkey		
1960	4.0	33.0
1963	4.2	33.0
1968	2.9	32.8
1970	3.0	32.0
1973	3.5	——
Costa Rica		
1960–1961	5.7	33.0
1970	5.4	23.0
1971	3.3	——

Source: World Tables, 3rd ed., vol. 1, Economic Data (Washington, D.C.: World Bank, 1983).

agricultural and industrial sectors as measured around two time points and the change on this measure for the three countries. Turkey ranks highest on this measure in the 1960s with a value almost 10 points higher than that of Costa Rica and 16 points higher than that of India. Although all three countries have reduced the discrepancies in income distribution between the industrial and agricultural sectors, the achievements of Turkey and India in this area have been marginal compared with Costa Rica, which accomplished a major reduction in sectoral inequalities.

Analysis of the three countries' budgets through time finds that the Costa Rican governments spared about 2 to 6 percent of their budget to support agriculture, while the industrial sector did not receive even 1 percent. Moreover, in the 1970s, Costa Rica increased government expenditures on agriculture. Government expenditures in India reflect a relatively more balanced support for the two sectors, although the industrial sector was favored until the 1970s. The agricultural sector started to receive more support in the late 1970s. The budget for research and development in agriculture was increased, and several organizations were founded by the central government and some state governments to create appropriate technology for rural development. Among the projects initiated by the central government, the most important are a chain of agricultural universities and institutions run by the Indian Council of Agricultural Research, and regional research laboratories and other institutions set up by the Council of Scientific and Industrial Research.[29] The Council of Scientific and Industrial Research prepared plans for "rural development," and it is reported that Prime Minister Indira Gandhi, in her 1976 address to the Indian Science Congress,

Table 6.4   Trends in the Extent of Poverty in India

Year	Rural Areas		Urban Areas	
	Percent of Population	Number (millions)	Percent of Population	Number (millions)
1956–1957	54.1	178		
1957–1958	50.2	168		
1958–1959	46.5	159		
1959–1960	44.4	154		
1960–1961	38.9	138	40.0	32
1961–1962	39.4	142	39.4	32
1963–1964	44.5	167	42.5	37
1964–1965	46.8	180	45.7	42
1965–1966	53.9	211	46.4	44
1966–1967	56.6	226	48.4	47
1967–1968	56.5	230	48.3	49
1968–1969	51.0	212	45.5	47
1969–1970	49.2	208	44.4	48
1970–1971	47.5	205	41.5	46
1971–1972	41.2	181		
1972–1973	43.1	192	44.6	53
1973–1974	46.1	208	38.7	48
1977–1978	39.1	186	40.8	59
1977–1978[a]	51.2		38.2	
1983–1984[a]	40.4		28.1	

Source: R. M. Sundrum, *Growth and Income Distribution in India: Policy and Performance Since Independence* (New Delhi: Sage Publications, 1987), pp. 159–160.
Note: a. Figures are estimates from the Seventh Plan.

"exhorted the scientific community to impart a 'rural bias' to science and pleaded that a person who 'takes science to the field' should receive as much importance as one who has published a thesis."[30] Again in the 1970s, as a result of the nationalization of banking and other government efforts, there was a noticeable and steady increase in the number and variety of credit institutions, as well as in the quantum of loans given for agricultural development.

Table 6.5   Gini Coefficients for Income Inequality Between Agricultural and Industrial Sectors

Country	Rank	Circa 1960	Circa 1970	Shift
India	73	23.4	0.5	– 2.9
Turkey	29	39.5	37.4	– 2.1
Costa Rica	77	30.0	19.8	–10.2

Source: Charles Lewis Taylor and David A. Jodice, *World Handbook of Political and Social Indicators*, 3d ed., vol. 1 (New Haven: Yale University Press, 1983), pp. 137–138.

Although the projects have been criticized for "their inadequate coverage of the target groups, neglect of the numerically larger group of marginal farmers and agricultural laborers, and the totally inadequate level of assistance per beneficiary," the Indian government established small farmers development programs (SFDA) and the integrated rural development programs (IRDP). Even though they have not lived up to expectations, these programs were targeted at reducing poverty, sectoral inequalities, and the income gap between the rich and poor within the agricultural sector.

Turkish development policies have been in favor of the industrial sector. Starting in the 1970s particularly, the share of industry in government expenditures has been double or triple that of agriculture. Although some agricultural price support policies have been pursued in Turkey, their overall impact has been inegalitarian because they benefited the wealthy and commercial farmers most and skewed the income distribution within the sector.[31] Moreover, since the price support and subsidies for the agricultural sector have been funded usually through printing money, these strategies were criticized for their inflationary impact on the Turkish economy.[32]

Turkish agricultural support policies have focused on increasing the productivity of land. This can be accomplished by improving agricultural technology as well as by using more labor per unit of land. The types of capital invested in agricultural technology are crucial because their impact on distribution and sectoral imbalance may be drastic. Some forms of capital (e.g., tractors) reduce agricultural employment by substituting capital for labor, whereas other forms (e.g., fertilizers and irrigation) increase the productivity of labor in agriculture without causing unemployment. In Turkey, agricultural policies and credits have been toward capital-intensive farming, which has helped increase agricultural output, at least in some areas, but also has created a flood of immigrants who ended up living in substandard conditions in squatter houses surrounding major cities and working in the informal sector for marginal incomes.

LAND DISTRIBUTION AND REFORM

Contrary to common belief, Costa Rica has not had egalitarian land distribution. Although colonial practices in Costa Rica did not lead to the establishment of haciendas—the large landholdings in Latin America with social and economic relationships resembling those of feudal Europe—the distribution of land has been skewed. Fertile land, especially, has been concentrated in the hands of the few. As reflected by the data from the 1970s, the Gini coefficient for land inequality in Costa Rica was 82.5, the 6th highest among 52 countries analyzed by Taylor and Jodice (Table 6.6).[33] Moreover, the inequalities have increased since the 1960s, when the Gini coefficient was slightly lower at 78.2 percent.

Although not to the same extent as in Costa Rica, land distribution in Turkey and India has also been skewed. On the same scale developed by Taylor and Jodice, India ranked 25th with a Gini coefficient of 64. A study focused on Turkey shows that concentration in land distribution is also high, and it increased between 1963 and 1973 (Table 6.6).

Table 6.6   Gini Coefficients for Inequality in Land Distribution

Country	Rank	Circa 1960	Circa 1970	Shift
India	25	—	—	64.0
Turkey	—	59.1	65.0	5.9
Costa Rica	6	78.2	82.5	4.3

Sources: Charles Lewis Taylor and David A. Jodice, *World Handbook of Political and Social Indicators*, 3d ed., vol. 1 (New Haven: Yale University Press, 1983), pp. 140–141. The information on Turkey is from Aydín Ulusan, "Public Policy Toward Agriculture and Its Redistributive Implications," in Ergun Özbudun and Aydín Ulusan, *The Political Economy of Income Distribution in Turkey* (New York: Holmes and Meier, 1980), pp. 125–168.

Concentration of land ownership is a common feature of developing countries, a condition often argued to be preferable on the basis of economies of scale. However, many economists agree that the redistribution of land would not diminish productivity but would result in increasing returns if land reform is rapidly and efficiently administered—if viable-sized units are set up and the new owners are provided with educational, technological, and financial support.[34] On the other hand, as stated by Russell King, "If there are long delays in reform's implementation, if reform farms are economically too small, if the former landlords' functions in the field of credit, expertise etc. are not replaced, and if the peasants are alienated from working the land, then production is likely to fall."[35] If the favorable conditions are met, then land reforms would not only be a means of social justice but by increasing productivity, they would also slow peasant migration to the cities until industry can absorb labor more rapidly[36] and serve as a catalyst for meaningful and balanced economic development. The positive effects of the Japanese and Taiwanese land reforms on both distribution and economic growth are attributed to their comprehensiveness, rapid implementation, and supplementary agricultural programs.[37]

Data from developing countries also indicate that in these countries the rule of economies of scale does not work. On the contrary, an inverse relationship between farm size and productivity is displayed. Individual studies of Brazil, Colombia, Ecuador, India, Mexico, and the Philippines and the *U.N. Land Reform, Fourth Report,* which includes 52 countries, confirmed this negative correlation. These studies attributed the higher productivity levels of smaller farms to the common practice of labor-intensive cultivation on them as well as the more intensive use of land and other related resources.[38] In addition to its economic and social drawbacks, concentration of land restricts the political participation of the peasant and distorts the democratic process. Even if the peasant has a vote, one can argue, the landlord would tell him "what to do with it."[39]

The economic advantage of egalitarian land distribution, however, is often overlooked. Land reforms have been initiated usually for political purposes. Huntington states that "no social group is more conservative than a landowning peasantry, and none is more revolutionary than a peasantry which owns too little land or pays too high a rental."[40] But governments tend to be more responsive to the propertied classes and are reluctant to undertake land reforms, unless they are revolutionary governments whose ideology calls for reform. Otherwise, they take reformist action only when they encounter organized peasants who present a major threat to the system. It is observed that among the 22 countries whose landless constitute one-quarter or more of their total population, 15 have experienced revolution or protracted civil conflict in the twentieth century.[41] Most of the major land reforms of this century were undertaken by revolutionary governments after a revolution (Russia, China, North Vietnam, Cuba, Ethiopia, Nicaragua, Mexico, Bolivia, and Egypt) or by existing governments that were under a substantial revolutionary threat (Ireland, Taiwan, South Vietnam, and El Salvador).[42]

Land reform has been on party programs and among the goals of the state in the three countries we are concerned with here, though it has not been a top item on the active agendas of many of their governments. Land distribution policies were either left on paper without reaching the stage of implementation or circumscribed at that stage. Redistributive land reforms are also replaced by "agrarian reforms" to achieve the "green revolution," which benefited mostly the large and middle-size holdings and led to a rapid increase in both production and productivity, but stimulated income inequality.[43]

The most comprehensive land reform among these three countries was undertaken by India immediately after independence. It is argued that "since its independence in 1947, India has perhaps enacted more land reform laws than any other country in the world."[44] The Agrarian Reforms Committee of the Congress Party declared that "land must belong to the tiller" and recommended setting an upper limit on individual holdings. The first two five-year plans (1951–1956 and 1956–1961) contained the guidelines for state legislatures on abolishing intermediaries (*zamindars*), instituting tenancy reforms, and imposing ceilings on holdings; these measures began to be implemented by the states in 1948, 1953, and 1956, respectively.[45] The abolition of *zamindars* and other intermediaries, who controlled 40 percent of the farmland in India and 20 million of the tenant farmers, allowed the state governments to acquire all rights of intermediaries on land they had not actually cultivated.

Although 172 million hectares were acquired, 2.6 million intermediaries had their interests abolished, approximately 20 million cultivators benefited, and some tenants gained full ownership of land, the Indian legislation failed to make a genuine redistributive impact and solve the landless peasant problem for a number of reasons.[46] First, the land was acquired by the state on payment of compensation that was as high as eight times the net rental in some places. Second, the *zamindars* were able to keep a large portion of the best land. Third, although some peasants gained full ownership without payment, most had to pay the state for full occupancy rights and remained tenants of the state until the full amount was paid. Finally, due to the inefficiency of the bureaucracy and, where the landed interests and caste and class divisions were firmly ingrained, state administrators' hostility toward redistributive reforms prevented effective administration and implementation of the policies prescribed by the plans.[47]

Thus, the major accomplishment of the reform was the elimination of the parasitic intermediaries and bringing the tenants into direct relationship with the state governments. The state, which replaced the *zamindars* as tax collectors, eliminated the illegal extractions by the former *zamindars* and increased its revenues, but most of its new income was spent as compensation payments. "Land reform in India emanates from the central government, but the flow of national authority in connection with the enforcement of reform programs is channeled through state and local agencies where landowning interests are dominant."[48] The redistributive impact of the *zamindar* abolishment and other agrarian reforms has been limited and varied from one state to another. It has been most visible in Uttar Pradesh, Kerela, and Bengal but highly curtailed in Bihar, Madhya Pradesh, and Rajastan, where the reforms were shaped by the views of the regional elites formed partly of traditional landowners. At the national level, the Gini index of inequality of distribution of operational holdings declined from 69.4 in 1953–1954 to 58.4 in 1961–1962, mainly as a result of abolishing the *zamindar* system. But later, in the 1960s, the trend changed toward inequalities. The Gini coefficient increased to 58.5 in 1971–1972, according to the third government survey, and to 63.9 in 1970–1971, according to the agricultural census.[49]

The land reforms in Turkey and Costa Rica were mostly in the form of colonization of public land. That is, land owned by the state rather than that held by individual families or private companies was distributed. Thus, the scope of land reforms has been limited, and they have fallen short of having an actual redistributive impact.

Land distribution in Turkey was initiated around World War II by an authoritarian populist regime. Although Atatürk called for land reforms that would allow farmers to cultivate their own land and limit the maximum amount of private holdings, the legislation by his Republican People's Party—the 1934 Law of Settlement of Immigrants and the 1945 Law of Providing Land to Farmers—fell short of fulfilling that pledge. The distribution was limited to state-owned land, and its impact was modest both in terms of the amount of land involved and the portion of the population served. The distribution of the state-owned land is estimated to have reached approximately a quarter of the landless population.[50]

The restrictions on the maximum amount of land were gradually relaxed in the face of opposition before the competitive general elections of 1950—the maximum amount was raised from the 50 acres stated in the 1945 law first to 2,000 acres and then to 5,000—and then completely undermined at the stage of implementation.[51] Interestingly, the opposition won the 1950 election and adopted the land reform to enhance its support among the rural population. It is estimated that 312,000 families received land during the rule of the Democrat Party (1950–1960), whereas only 33,000 families were reached by its predecessor that initiated the law.[52] The land distribution under both parties appeared in the form of opening up state land to private ownership, benefiting mostly those who had political connections. Although the extension of peasant property benefited some poorer villages and peasants, especially in the later stages, better-off villages and peasants benefited most. Nevertheless, from 1950 to 1960, the proportion of landless peasant families declined from 16 percent to 10 percent.[53]

Although landlessness continued to exit as an economic and social problem in Turkey and the proportion of landless started to increase in the 1960s, no distributive or redistributive steps were taken by the elected governments after the transition to the multiparty electoral system. An indicator of the persistence of this acute problem is the scope of migration to the major cities, which occurs at a rate beyond their employment and housing capacities. In the early 1960s, the significant number of temporary workers who went to Western Europe reduced the pressure to some extent, but this option ceased to be viable in the 1970s.

In Costa Rica, the draft of an agrarian reform bill, Law to Create the Institute of Lands and Land Colonization, reached the Costa Rican Assembly in 1955, but the legislation did not come into existence until 1961.[54] On October 14, 1961, the Law of Lands and Land Settlement was enacted, and a year later on October 3, the Instituto de Tierras y Colonización (Lands and Colonization Institute), commonly referred as ITCO, was created to administer the law. A student of Costa Rica identifies three stages in ITCO's land reform administration that are not mutually exclusive.[55] During the first phase, the period from 1962 to 1966, inexpensive and unused private lands in remote areas were acquired by ITCO and set up as colonies for mainly landless peasant families. During this time 1,272 families were settled on 11 colonies established over 35,412 hectares.[56] Although this policy was slowed down in the subsequent years, by the end of 1979, the number of families benefited by settlements increased to 5,428, and the amount of land reached 167,134 hectares.[57]

The second phase, 1966–1970, was characterized by the settling of squatter conflicts. Squatting by landless peasants on private lands as well as on state property and Indian reservations has been common in Costa Rica, and resolving squatter conflicts was listed among ITCO's responsibilities by the law. A peasant who could prove legitimate right to the land was granted the title to it. If the landlord was able to make a stronger case, the peasant was offered a small plot on a colony upon the abandonment of the squatted land. Between 1966 and 1969, 2,093 titles were granted.[58]

During the third phase (1970–1978), ITCO concentrated on the formation of agricultural enterprises on economically viable farmland that was located in regions already developed. The land distribution process was similar to that of the colonization, except that cooperatives called "self-run communal enterprises" (*empresas comunitarias de autogestión*) were created in addition to individual parcel ownership. Moreover, a program aimed at granting titles to landowning peasants who do not hold legal title to their property was incorporated into ITCO projects.

Notwithstanding these activities of distributing land and granting title, the impact of the land reform laws in Costa Rica has been minor. Between 1962 and 1979, only 33,665 families received a total of 782,889 hectares of land.[59] Moreover, the largest landowners, the multinationals, have never been seriously threatened by the reform. Although only 14 percent of United Fruit's nearly 500,000 acres (202,500 hectares) was cultivated by the company during the 1950s, only 25,900 acres (10,490 hectares) of the company land was taken for one of the colonies started in the mid-1960s, and the company was paid $549,414 for it.[60] In fact, some scholars consider the distributive (as opposed to the redistributive) nature of the land reform in Costa Rica as fortunate because it did not establish a threat to land owned by US companies. By comparison, the redistributive land reform programs in Guatemala and Honduras included the holdings of US companies and resulted in US intervention and subsequent political instability; the limited and restricted scope of the Costa Rican reforms avoided such conflicts.[61] The land distribution efforts in Costa Rica were much too modest to be a major threat to either the foreign companies or their domestic landlords. Mitchell Seligson describes the limited accomplishments of the reform in Costa Rica:

> If one is willing to include the provision of titles to squatters as a part of land reform, then the 782,889 hectares of land titled and distributed amounts to 15.3 percent of the national land area or 25.1 percent of the total land in farms of the 1973 census (3,122,456 hectares). On the other hand, if the only land to be included in one's estimate of the impact of land reform is the land actually expropriated and redistributed, then the impact is much smaller. Land redistribution amounted to only 167,134 hectares or 3.3 percent of the national territory and 5.4 percent of the land in farms in 1973.[62]

As reported by Seligson, the population increase and continuation of sell-offs as a result of poverty led the size of the landless population to grow at a rate of approximately 900 families a year. By distributing land to only approximately 300 families a year over the 1963–1979 period, ITCO was unable to halt the increasing trend of landlessness let alone reverse it. Moreover, the economic crisis that started in the 1970s and became more evident in the 1980s put the land reform programs in Costa Rica in further jeopardy, though a partial recovery during the mid-1980s resulted partially from US assistance. Some estimated US aid in 1983 to be equal to 10 percent of Costa Rica's gross domestic product, which made the country the second-highest recipient of US aid in the world in per capita measures.[63] Moreover, land reform became a major item for President Luis Monge, whose "return to the land" campaign slogan was partially responsible for his victory in the 1982 election. A new reform law enacted March 29, 1982, changed ITCO's name to the Instituto de Desarrollo Agrario (Agrarian Development Institute), increased its power and income, and established agrarian tribunals that are expected to be more sympathetic to the reforms than the regular court system, which has been criticized for being conservative and biased by ITCO officials.[64]

In all three countries, land reforms failed to make a major redistributive impact, and Turkey fared somewhat poorer than the other two. Nevertheless, despite their limitations, land reforms have led to increases in the income of most of their beneficiaries and served as a relief for some of the poor in India and Costa Rica, where a large portion of the peasantry has been landless.[65] According to some studies focused on land distribution in the late 1960s and early 1970s, the landless constitute 22.0 percent of the economically active peasant population in Costa Rica,[66] 12.3 percent of the rural population in India,[67] and 22.4 percent of rural households in Turkey.[68] Thus, even though they have been limited in scope, land reforms have had some social impact, helped the democratic system, and aided the governments that carried out the reforms in gaining the loyalty of their beneficiaries. A survey of Costa Rican peasants found the beneficiaries of land reforms less cynical and more trusting of state officials and of the political system than the other landless peasants.[69] Furthermore, compared with other Central American countries, the absence of organized peasant uprisings and unrest in Costa Rica is attributed to the presence of agrarian and social reforms there.[70]

UNEMPLOYMENT

The right to work is a major socioeconomic right, and unless there is family wealth to rely upon, one's capacity to enjoy other socioeconomic rights (e.g., to shelter, food, and health care) is largely determined by the recognition of this right. Unemployment and underemployment, however, have been major problems in developing countries. Specific information on these issues is difficult to obtain; Table 6.7 reports the available data.

Because the unemployed measured as a percentage of the labor force is not reported except for Costa Rica (only since 1976), a direct comparison between the three countries is not possible. However, the change in the magnitude of problem throughout the period 1965–1983 can be studied. The data show that unemployment became an acute problem starting in the mid-1970s and increased in severity in the 1980s. The unemployment rate in Costa Rica doubled from the 1970s to the 1980s. The same pattern is observed in the rate of underemployment, which increased from 11 percent in 1977 to 22.4 percent in 1982.[71] Employment-related problems have not been felt at the same severity in all economic sectors. They are observed to be more serious and increasingly so in the rural areas and the agricultural sector. Seligson makes an assessment:

Table 6.7.   Unemployment Data for Selected Years (in thousands)

Year	Costa Rica	India	Turkey
1965		2524	
1966		2610	23.5
1967		2706	26.8
1968		2903	33.0
1969		3204	39.0
1970		3726	43.8
1971		4602	44.9
1972		5928	43.9
1973		7714	44.8
1974		8378	81.7
1975		8917	116.8
1976	30.3 (4.4)	9565	141.3
1977	31.4 (4.6)	10513	142.7
1978	32.7 (4.5)	11837	166.8
1979	36.3 (4.9)	13794	170.7
1980	45.6 (5.9)	15317	256.3
1981	69.6 (8.7)	16854	267.0
1982	78.6 (9.4)	18646	425.7
1983	76.2 (9.0)	20802	549.1

Source: United Nations, *Statistical Yearbook* (New York: United Nations).
Note: The numbers in parentheses refer to the unemployed as a percentage of the total labor force.

Between 1976 and 1981 a total of 13,000 jobs was lost in the agricultural sector, the only economic sector to suffer an absolute net decline in this period. From a longer-term perspective agriculture is rapidly diminishing as a major source of employment. Hence, whereas in 1950, 54.7 percent of the labor force was employed in the agricultural sector, by 1981 this figure dropped to 27.8 percent. . . . This decline reflects the growing urbanization and industrialization of Costa Rica. In absolute terms, however, there were 34 percent more people employed in agriculture in 1981 than there were in 1950 (202,023 vs. 150,317). Hence, despite its declining role the agricultural sector remains an important source of employment for many Costa Ricans.[72]

Recent trends in the policies of foreign employers in this country exacerbate the problem. For nearly a century bananas and coffee have been Costa Rica's main sources of export earnings and constituted the major source of employment in the agricultural sector. Among these employers, the foreign banana companies—United Fruit, Standard Fruit, and Del Monte—have always complained that Costa Rica is a high-cost producer. Citing higher wages, higher disease control, and the $1 export tax per box (agreed to by the Union of Banana Exporting Countries in 1974 but imposed fully only by Costa Rica in 1981) as reasons of high production cost, these companies started to cut back their operations or diversify into crops such as African oil palm that absorb little labor.[73] The continuation of this trend will worsen the unemployment problem of the Costa Rican economy, which needs to create over 27,000 new jobs each year just to keep pace with the rate of increase in the labor force.[74] Moreover, banana companies refuse to hire older workers and systematically fire workers at age forty.[75] This contributes to the pool of unskilled and unemployable labor.

Despite the recent problems, however, compared with the other two countries, Costa Rica has managed its economy more successfully. The average annual percentage change in labor force during the 1965–1985 period is reported as 3.8 for Costa Rica and 1.7 for India and Turkey. When the average annual percentage change in the number of unemployed is calculated for these countries (using the data in Table 6.7), the rate of increase in unemployment is found to be 14 percent for Costa Rica and India and 23 percent for Turkey. Although this is a crude estimate, a lower rate of increase in unemployment in the presence of a higher rate of increase in the labor force identifies Costa Rica as more successful in coping with this problem. This conclusion is even clearer when we considered that data for Costa Rica started in 1976 and the average increase in its unemployment is based on the period when unemployment rates were generally higher. India ranks in the middle; Turkey, which matched India's rate of increase in the labor force but experienced a much higher rate of increase in unemployment (23 percent as opposed to 14 percent), appears to be the least successful.

SOCIAL WELFARE AND HEALTH CARE

Social Security and Welfare Expenditures

Costa Rica has established a comprehensive social security and welfare system, one of the most advanced systems in Latin America.[76] The government disburses a large percent of its budget on social welfare and health care. India and Turkey, however, lag behind Costa Rica; defense expenditures have swallowed a quarter to a third of the government budgets in these two countries. Hofferbert's cross-national analysis of the relationship between democracy and budgetary priorities finds that higher percentages of central government expenditures for education, health care, and welfare are positively related to the level of democracy in developing countries. Defense expenditures demonstrate a negative relationship.[77]

Approximately 60 percent of the government budget in Costa Rica is spent on health, education, social security, and welfare.[78] Education is the major component with 25 to 29 percent; at least one-third of the government budget in Costa Rica goes to health care and social security. Turkish governments have also assigned a high priority to education by reserving 14 to 23 percent of the budget for this category. Total expenditures on social welfare and health care in this country, however, have not exceeded 7 percent of the annual budget.

The Indian national government's support for welfare policies is not as easy to analyze because welfare services and health care in this country are largely provided by the state governments. The Indian national government, however, transfers at least 30 percent of its total budget to the state governments and the emphasis on welfare policies varies from one state to another. National government spending does not exceed 3 percent either for education or for health care.

Trend analysis of the data reported in *The Cost of Social Security*[79] shows that state participation in the social security system is higher in India and Costa Rica than it is in Turkey. Social security contributions from state and other public funds have been 25 to 34 percent of total social security expenditures in India and 26 to 33 percent in Costa Rica. In Turkey, the state contribution has never constituted more than 12 percent (in 1960), and for some years it has been as low as 2.1 percent (in 1971).

A comparative analysis of the distribution of social security benefits in these countries would recognize the Costa Rican program as more comprehensive than the others. The bulk of social security benefits in India and Turkey appears to be in the form of pensions; the Costa Rican system provides a better package, with more medical and cash benefits for sickness, maternity, and employment injuries.[80] However, balance-of-payment problems in the late 1970s forced Costa Rica to cut its welfare expenditures, and major reductions were made in social security. In 1978, the state share of total social security expenditures was as low as 1.8 percent. Although the US government and IMF administrations bailed Costa Rica out of its severe economic crisis in the early 1980s, these aid and loan packages aimed at an economic restructuring (geared toward a liberalized export-oriented economy) have undermined the country's traditional emphasis on social welfare.[81] Nevertheless, despite the difficulties, the social security program continued to cover 78 percent of the population in 1982 (the same as in 1979), even though it failed to reach its original goal of 94 percent coverage by 1980.[82]

Infant Mortality Rate

Infant mortality statistics are reported as a national average; thus they do not reflect the variation among different income groups. However, because infant mortality rates tend to be higher among the rural and low income groups, the scope of reduction in these rates can be used as a proxy indicator of the increases in the availability of sanitary conditions and the accessibility of health care for the lower classes.

Costa Rica has been most successful in reducing the infant mortality rate, cutting it from 74 per 1,000 in 1965 to 18 in 1985, a level comparable to what is maintained by industrial societies. India, despite its large population burden and low national income, managed to reduce the infant mortality rate from 151 to 89 within the two decades from 1965 to 1985. Similarly, Turkey recorded major progress in this area and during the same period reduced its infant mortality rate from 152 to 84. However, it is important to note that as a wealthier country, Turkey's accomplishment is not as impressive as India's. (During this time period GNP per capita in Turkey has been 4 to 6 times that in India.)

The relative success of Costa Rica in this area can be attributed to its quite developed and socialized health care system, which has emphasized preventive health care. The system and its performance have been defined as "impressive" by the World Health Organization.[83] Despite the prevailing inequalities in the distribution (e.g., physician services are concentrated in metropolitan areas), the development of medical care institutions and the community health care systems under the Public Health and Social Security agencies has brought considerable progress in the area of preventive health care.[84] Widespread vaccination programs reduced the polio, diphtheria, and measles cases significantly. Moreover, malaria has been eliminated, and malnutrition has been diminished. On average, 33 percent of Central American children have suffered from second- and third-degree malnutrition, but the ratio in Costa Rica was reduced to 9 percent and .3 percent, respectively, in 1973.[85] In addition to vaccination, access to clean water for more than three-quarters of the population reduced the cases of infectious diseases that used to constitute the major causes of death. Thus, the emphasis on preventive health care—a message carried by rural health care workers, maternal and child care centers sponsored by government agencies, health education through radio, and nutrition programs—established an effective and egalitarian health care model.[86]

SUMMARY OF CASE STUDIES

This comparative analysis of the three countries supports the argument that the distributive impact of economic policies is important for the fate of democracy in developing countries. Turkey, the least stable democracy among the three countries, also has the least egalitarian conditions, which governments failed to gear their efforts toward reversing. Costa Rica and India, in contrast, relatively more stable democracies, have pursued different strategies to recognize social and economic rights and improve the living conditions of their citizens. Indians have enjoyed a relatively more egalitarian distribution of income and land, which their government has tried to maintain through progressive taxation and support for agriculture, the major source of employment. They were also provided with relative economic security as consumer price increases were kept below 10 percent. Costa Rican governments were faced with skewed income and land distributions, and they failed to take corrective steps in these areas. However, they tried to compensate for these inequalities by providing accessible services through comprehensive and viable welfare and health care systems, by controlling prices, and by supporting the agricultural sector, the main source of employment and income.[87]

However, the oil shock in the 1970s and the economic crisis in the 1980s threatened the stability of democracy in these countries, which have highly dependent economies. India has been able to exercise some control over foreign investments and managed to take a more flexible political position during the cold war years by pursuing a policy of nonalliance. But this does not mean that India escaped dependent status in the world system. Indeed, India has been one of the major recipients of development aid from the World Bank and loans from the IMF. As already discussed, capital flows through such means do not come without concessions: suspension of government subsidies, privatization, deregulation, and reductions in government spending, especially on welfare.[88]

Costa Rica and Turkey also have been recipients of loans with strings attached. But these two countries have put themselves in a more fragile position due to their political and military dependency, in addition to economic dependency, on the Western powers, especially the United States. The vulnerability of Costa Rica became most evident in the face of the US-Nicaraguan problem. Costa Rica's assistance to maintain the Nicaraguan counterrevolutionary forces was sought as a condition by the Reagan administration, and the government's decision to close the contra bases at the Costa Rican border caused major friction between the two countries that could have hurt the Costa Rican economy. Although the success of the Aries Plan in easing regional tensions prevented real damage to the country's economy and vulnerable democracy, the 1980s witnessed increasing numbers of strikes and protests.[89] Moreover, production of Costa Rica's major export products, coffee and bananas, remain in the control of foreign companies, and the trust and positive view of government observed among the peasantry in the 1960s and the early 1970s appeared to be fading according to surveys conducted in the late 1970s and the 1980s.[90]

Thus, when economic bottlenecks were reached, the quest for relief was sought in foreign assistance, and the consequential impact of the donors' advice or conditions has been an increasing gap between the haves and have-nots. The trend of borrowing, however, has been at an increasing rate and on unfavorable terms for all three countries. According to World Bank data, public borrowing by India jumped from $959 million to $4,668 million from 1970 to 1985. During the same period, it increased from $491 million to $3,388 million for Turkey and from $58 million to $469 million for Costa Rica. Moreover, the recent borrowings were based on poorer terms: higher average interest rates (from 2.5 to 6.4 percent in India, from 3.6 to 8.7 percent in Turkey, and from 5.7 to 6.7 percent in Costa Rica), shorter maturity dates, and lower grace periods.[91] It is becoming more evident that political autonomy depends on breaking the cycle of borrowing and indebtedness. This would require the revival of the economic policies of self-reliance and adoption of a strategy of cooperation with other developing countries, instead of pursuing competition.

Finally, although not inescapable at the moment, a threat to the stability of democracy in India may come from its military. The military and paramilitary forces have been used to cope with social unrest at an escalating rate, and appointments and promotions within the military have been increasingly politicized.[92]

CONCLUSION

The 1980s is marked as a decade of rising democracies. Military regimes in
Latin America, Pakistan, and Turkey as well as other authoritarian rules in
Spain, Portugal, and the Philippines gave way to democratic politics. Those
nations that gained independence at the turn of the decade, including Papua
New Guinea, Fiji, and Vanuatu, established highly democratic structures. Steps
toward liberalization of political life took place in many African countries, with
Senegal experiencing the most prominent process of democratization. One-
party systems in Eastern Europe collapsed and were replaced by multiparty
regimes. In Asia, Mongolia, Jordan, and Nepal moved in the same direction in
1990, and some other countries tried to improve and institutionalize existing
democratic elements.

Robert Wesson, who had witnessed only part of these transformations at
the time of his writing, indicated that the trend is in the direction of democratization because "democracy is basically nonviolent, rationalistic, and voluntary;
nontraditional absolutist ideologies are more violent, emotional, and revolutionary in purpose."[93] He predicted that this trend "will probably continue unless or
until there is major breakdown of the world economic order or a big new explo-
sion of violence to charge an authoritarian passion or new antidemocratic ideology."[94] Such expectations, shared by many observers, are products of wishful
thinking rather than of historical analysis of conditions that lead to democratization and reinforcement of the stability of democratic processes.

Early developers in the West pursued models of gradual change both in
political and economic realms. Their economic development was the result of a
long and oppressive industrialization process. Steps toward redistribution of
wealth in the form of welfare policies were taken only after their modern industrial economies were established. Similarly, their process of democratization
followed a gradual course. Political rights were incrementally extended to the
lower classes, nonwhites, and women. As the first modernizers and highly independent political entities, these countries were able to set the standards, keep
the expectations low, and hold their impoverished and suppressed masses in
line.

The demonstration effect of the early developers on the late developers,
however, has prevented the late developers from following a gradual course.
Twentieth-century criteria for government legitimacy include equality. As political equality is sought by opening the democratic structures to all citizens, economic equality needs to be attended to through a redistributive development
strategy. Equitable economic growth is treated as necessary also by Donnelly:

The inability of many Third World countries to meet even modest growth goals, plus lack of success with the trickle-down growth and redressing inequality, clearly suggest that the trade-offs may not be justifiable once we take into account the likelihood that present sacrifices may not in fact bring about the predicted future benefits, whether because of bad planning, bad administration, or just plain bad luck.[95]

Carole Pateman, in her critique of the "civic culture," points out that "the main thrust of liberal theory has always been to give a well-defined but minimal role to the citizen," and where it has been put into practice, "only minimal levels of activity and interest, and largely apolitical attitudes, are required from most citizens; anything more would threaten the smooth working of the political system."[96] We can add to this argument that citizens in developing countries, experiencing wider economic and social discrepancies and being aware of other possibilities, are more politicized and less willing to confine their activities to those "well-defined" roles. Thus, the old process, which worked rather smoothly in the West, encounters more strains in its new homes.

The findings presented here confirm the argument that the stability of democratic systems is threatened if the elected government cannot reinforce socioeconomic rights at levels comparable to those of civil-political rights. A conflict arises if socioeconomic rights draw a declining curve or a constant line while civil and political rights expand over time. This observation, unfortunately, does not allow me to share others' optimistic expectations about the future of democracy in developing countries—expectations that seemed to increase after the wave of democratization in the 1980s. As long as social and economic inequalities persist, developing countries that go through a process of democratization today are doomed to return to some form of authoritarianism.[97] In fact, reversal of the democratic trend has already been observed in Pakistan, and many other young democracies are barely holding their own while their current records of economic and social indicators point to decline.

By the same token, those early developers that have sustained highly democratic political structures but relatively weak welfare states are not immune to major social upheavals, which may require coercive measures. Increasing problems of homelessness, poverty, a shrinking middle class, unemployment, and inflation are likely to outweigh the advantages that these countries had over the late developers, and these problems may surface in social unrest in the absence of ample welfare programs and of substantial structural modifications.

NOTES

1. See Offe, p. 226; For a discussion of similar attacks on equality and various nonsocialist advocates of equality, see Glassman.
2. Offe.
3. Laski.
4. Ibid., p. 84.
5. Ibid., p. 77.

6. Sundrum, p. 213.
7. Schatz; Fatton, 1988 and 1990.
8. Chase-Dunn, p. 736.
9. Ibid.; Delacroix and Ragin; Portes; Supple; Kohli, 1987.
10. Delacroix and Ragin.
11. Diamond, Linz, and Lipset, 1989 and 1990; Wiener and Özbudun.
12. Kohli, 1987.
13. Bardhan.
14. *Turkey: The Problems of Transition.*
15. Bianchi, especially pp. 251–274; Arat, 1989.
16. Cohen.
17. Ibid., p. 112.
18. Ibid., p. 119.
19. Needler, 1987, p. 15.
20. Payer, pp. 166–183.
21. International Studies of Values in Politics, p. 79. Among the values considered are commitments to innovative change, action propensity (an individual's personal disposition to act despite risk or uncertainties), economic development, citizen participation in decisionmaking, conflict avoidance, concern for national interests as opposed to local interests, selfishness, honesty, and *concern for economic equality.* The average score of the Indian leaders on these scales (where maximum commitment to a value would yield 4.00 and minimum commitment would yield 1.00) were 3.47, 1.60, 3.64, 2.13, 3.13, 2.57, 3.41, 3.38, and *3.50,* respectively. The average score of commitment to economic equality was 2.74 in Poland, 1.72 in the United States, and 3.03 in Yugoslavia.
22. Mas.
23. Palma.
24. Sundrum, p. 309.
25. Even for absolute poverty, different statistics provide different interpretations regarding the scope of poverty in India. According to a study that used data from the 1970s, India ranked at the top with almost 153 million people living in absolute poverty. If one takes the large population of India into consideration, however, the percent of the population in absolute poverty appears to be 26 percent in India, much below that recorded for some of its neighbors (64 percent in Bangladesh, 58 percent in Pakistan, and 44 percent in Indonesia). See Scandizzo and Knudsen.
26. The Gini coefficients reported for comparison here are calculated by using data on income distribution by quintiles. It should be noted, however, that more detailed information on income distribution would provide a more accurate picture. Thus, an alternative estimate of Gini coefficients that includes the highest 10 percent is calculated. This second Gini coefficient (Gini2 in Table 6.2) has a higher value than the one based on fewer numbers of income groups.
27. Ojha and Bhatt, reprinted by the *World Bank Reprint Series*, no. 18.
28. Charles W. Anderson, p. 94.
29. Maheshwari, p. 165.
30. Ibid., p. 164.
31. Dervis and Robinson. These authors report the Gini coefficient for household income in the agricultural and nonagricultural sectors as 56 and 45 respectively (p. 112).
32. Ergüder, p. 178.
33. Taylor and Jodice, pp. 140–141.
34. King.
35. Ibid., p. 71.
36. Thiesenhusen.
37. King, pp. 187–219; Maheshwari, pp. 19–20, 152, and 224–225.
38. Tai, pp. 111–112.

39. For a brief review of the literature on this, see Tai, pp. 43–46.
40. Huntington, 1968, p. 375.
41. Prosterman and Reidinger, pp. 25–29.
42. Ibid., p. 12.
43. Frankel, 1978 and 1976. On Turkey, see Parvin and Hiç.
44. Tai, p. 289.
45. Maheshwari; and King, pp. 279–302.
46. See Tai, pp. 214–216; and King, p. 286.
47. In addition to the works by King, Sundrum, and Maheshwari, see also Tai. Tai argues (p. 472) that

the implementation of reform programs was seriously hampered by the lack of both a national and state agency exclusively responsible for enforcement. The federal parliament did not enact a law to create a national agency because it regarded land reform as a state responsibility. State legislatures failed to create state agencies because they considered the state revenue administration adequate for assuming reform enforcenemt responsibilities. In reality, however, the revenue administration was too understaffed to be able to carry on effectively the additional work. Some of its personnel, such as the *patwaris* [village officials who keep land records and revenue rolls], who derived income from land or had maintained in the past an intimate relationship with the local gentry, could not be expected to execute reform laws with impartiality and dispatch.

48. Tai, p. 369.
49. Sundrum, p. 291, and also see p. 189.
50. Prosterman and Reidinger, p. 29.
51. For a brief overview of the land reform in Turkey, see Parvin and Hiç.
52. Keyder, p. 126.
53. Ibid., p. 131.
54. For a detailed history of discussions and struggle for a land reform bill in Costa Rica and for the content of drafts and changes in provisions, see Rowles.
55. Seligson, 1980, pp. 125–136.
56. Ibid., p. 127.
57. Seligson, 1984, p. 34.
58. Seligson, 1980, p. 131.
59. Seligson, 1984, p. 34.
60. Brockett, P. 124.
61. Ibid., pp. 197–201.
62. Seligson, 1984, pp. 33–34.
63. Brockett, p. 136.
64. Seligson, 1984, p. 43.
65. Although many beneficiaries were found to be still living in poverty, their income level tends to be higher than the other landless peasants. According to USAID estimates, only 18 percent of the settlers in Costa Rica earned income above the USAID's poverty line of $330 in 1976 (Seligson, 1984, p. 37). Also, whereas 30.5 percent of the landless earned less than the minimum wage in 1973, only 18.9 percent of reform peasants earned less than that amount (Seligson, 1980, p. 138). Moreover, Seligson's survey yields that while 15.5 percent of the landless earned more than double the minimum wage, 21.2 percent of the reform peasants earned that much money; comparison of the top 1 percent of distributions shows that whereas the wealthiest landless peasants earned no more than an average of 4.1 times the minimum wage, their counterparts among the reform peasants earned 14.3 times the minimum wage (Seligson, 1980, p. 138).
66. Seligson, 1979.
67. Sundrum, p. 179.
68. Ulusan, p. 140.

69. See Seligson, 1979 and 1980.

70. Kincaid.

71. Etomba, p. 202.

72. Seligson, 1984, p. 39.

73. Coone.

74. Edelman and Kenen, p. 190.

75. Leslie Anderson.

76. Sloan.

77. Hofferbert.

78. The data on government expenditures are gathered from several volumes of the *World Tables* published by the World Bank.

79. *The Cost of Social Security.*

80. Ibid.

81. See Shallat; Morgan.

82. Lynn M. Morgan, p. 215.

83. Harrison.

84. See Low.

85. Harrison p. 14.

86. Harrison.

87. The increasing trade deficits, however, make it harder for Costa Rica to finance its welfare programs and force the government to cut government expenditures. A viable alternative for Costa Rica would be to undertake a comprehensive land reform and increase tax revenues, especially those from income tax, which has been a neglected source.

88. Payer.

89. Seligson and Gomez.

90. Leslie Anderson.

91. World Bank, *World Development Report 1987*, pp. 240–241.

92. Cohen.

93. Wesson, p. 239.

94. Ibid., p. 241.

95. Donnelly, p. 42.

96. Pateman, quotations at pp. 62 and 65, respectively.

97. My observations are shared by O'Donnell and his coauthors, especially for the Latin American democracies. See O'Donnell, Schmitter, and Whitehead. The same view is presented for Argentina by William C. Smith.

Appendixes

Appendix A   **Estimating Government Coerciveness: Regression of Government Sanctions on Social Unrest Indicators**

Year	N	Constant	X1	X2	X3	X4	X5	R	F-Ratio

Year	N	Constant	X1	X2	X3	X4	X5	R	F-Ratio
1948	65	10.2[a]	3.6[c]	-2.4	-4.1	-10.6	.02	.29	1.12
1949	65	11.2[b]	2.7	4.6	13.8	-4.0	.02	.27	.93
1950	65	9.5[a]	-2.1	6.7	24.6[a]	2.8	-.001	.39	2.09[c]
1951	65	6.6[a]	-.4	3.0	5.1[c]	3.5	.09[a]	.66	9.25[a]
1952	65	8.0[a]	4.5[a]	1.3	2.4	2.4	.01	.68	10.29[a]
1953	79	6.4[a]	9.0[a]	4.1	-2.2	-11.2[b]	-.01	.70	14.14[a]
1954	79	5.0a	3.2a	4.9a	-1.1	9.3b	.01	.68	12.77a
1955	79	1.8	6.9[c]	1.3	27.4[c]	6.6	.09[a]	.68	12.76[a]
1956	79	0.6[a]	1.0	4.9[a]	13.5[a]	8.3	.02[b]	.78	22.20[a]
1957	79	15.9	-9.5	6.2	1.2	6.2	.11	.14	.28
1958	78	9.7[a]	-.8	32.2[a]	0.7	2.5	.01	.59	7.85[a]
1959	78	7.3[a]	4.2	8.6[b]	-0.4	2.6	.06[a]	.49	4.54[a]
1960	106	6.0[b]	4.2[a]	-3.3	-4.9	2.5[b]	.02	.57	9.65[a]
1961	107	5.2[a]	1.3	9.8[a]	-1.9	5.4[a]	.03[b]	.60	11.25[a]
1962	107	5.2[a]	1.9	1.9	7.9[a]	23.0[a]	.05[a]	.68	17.16[a]
1963	107	4.9[a]	.6	4.1[a]	3.8	-.2	.03[a]	.73	22.60[a]
1964	107	4.9[a]	3.2[a]	1.3	4.5	4.0	.01	.63	13.58[a]
1965	107	4.9[a]	1.0	-3.7	7.3[a]	2.2	.04[a]	.79	34.60[a]
1966	107	7.1[a]	1.8	-.7	23.2[a]	2.3	.13[a]	.64	14.04[a]
1967	131	6.2[a]	2.6[a]	5.8	-3.8	.5	.03[a]	.76	35.21[a]
1968	134	4.6[a]	2.4[a]	2.8	-3.8	-2.2[b]	.01	.49	7.67[a]
1969	134	2.4[a]	1.5[a]	-.8	2.2[a]	3.8[a]	.01	.82	52.11[a]
1970	135	2.1[a]	.9[c]	.1	.4	2.4[a]	.01[a]	.71	26.30[a]
1971	135	2.2[b]	1.0	3.0	2.3	22.9[a]	.01	.60	14.78[a]
1972	140	3.2[c]	4.4[c]	-2.3	-3.0	21.5[a]	.03[a]	.40	5.12[a]
1973	141	2.6[c]	-16.3[a]	14.3[a]	.2[a]	18.0	.01	.63	17.33[a]
1974	143	3.0	-1.6	4.5[a]	1.2	9.4[a]	.02	.44	6.57[a]
1975	150	1.1	1.1	23.3[a]	-4.6[a]	11.6[a]	.01	.81	53.47[a]
1976	150	2.3[a]	7.7[a]	19.8[a]	-3.0[a]	-5.1[a]	-.002	.67	23.76[a]
1977	151	1.3[c]	3.8[a]	1.1	0.7	11.0[a]	.001	.78	45.12[a]
1978	147	1.4[a]	-1.1[b]	2.5[a]	2.2[b]	1.2[a]	.04	.72	30.47[a]
1979	147	1.4[b]	3.4[a]	1.5	-1.0[a]	-.9[b]	.01	.66	21.99[a]
1980	147	2.5[a]	.5	2.6	2.1[b]	.2[a]	.003	.47	7.95[a]
1981	147	1.7[a]	2.3[a]	.6[b]	-1.4	2.0	.06	.70	26.59[a]
1982	147	1.8[a]	.0	.7	.7	0.7	1.70[a]	.52	12.92[a]

Notes: N refers to the number of countries included in the analysis. X1-X5: Riots, general strikes, assassinations, antigovernment demonstrations, and deaths from domestic violence. R and F-Ratio are the regression coefficient and its significance level.
a. Significant at .01 level
b. Significant at .05 level
c. Significant at .10 level

Appendix B   Index Scores of Democraticness: By Country and Year

Year	Afghanistan	Albania	Algeria	Angola	Argentina
1948	54	57			81
1949	55	59			72
1950	54	60			65
1951	55	57			65
1952	56	59			69
1953	55	58			70
1954	56	60			69
1955	54	58			32
1956	55	60			36
1957	52	57			38
1958	54	59			70
1959	54	58			73
1960	54	59			77
1961	55	58			78
1962	56	60			43
1963	56	60			78
1964	45	60			76
1965	64	60			80
1966	64	61			43
1967	65	61	46		45
1968	65	62	46		45
1969	66	63	49		48
1970	66	62	47		48
1971	66	63	49		52
1972	67	64	50		51
1973	50	64	50		87
1974	51	64	51		89
1975	51	64	51	51	87
1976	51	64	53	54	52
1977	51	64	67	50	52
1978	47	63	67	48	52
1979	46	62	66	48	48
1980	46	62	65	62	48
1981	47	62	67	62	46
1982	46	61	65	61	47

(continues)

Appendix B *(continued)*

Year	Australia	Austria	Bahamas	Bahrain	Bangladesh
1948	98				
1949	97				
1950	97				
1951	99				
1952	98				
1953	97				
1954	98				
1955	97				
1956	98				
1957	97				
1958	98				
1959	97				
1960	98	99			
1961	98	100			
1962	98	99			
1963	99	100			
1964	100	100			
1965	99	100			
1966	101	99			
1967	100	100			
1968	99	100			
1969	102	101			
1970	103	101			
1971	101	102			
1972	101	102		60	82
1973	102	103	97	61	87
1974	103	103	97	61	67
1975	103	102	96	51	50
1976	106	102	96	51	50
1977	102	101	96	51	50
1978	101	102	95	50	53
1979	100	100	94	48	75
1980	100	100	94	48	75
1981	100	99	94	47	75
1982	100	99	94	46	45

(continues)

Appendix B *(continued)*

Year	Barbados	Belgium	Benin	Bhutan	Bolivia
1948		96			76
1949		98			76
1950		99			75
1951		98			41
1952		98			43
1953		99			41
1954		98			44
1955		101			42
1956		97			77
1957		97			77
1958		98			77
1959		97			77
1960		98	69		79
1961		99	68		78
1962		98	69		78
1963		100	44		85
1964		100	64		44
1965		99	44		42
1966		99	46		74
1967	101	99	47		74
1968	101	100	46		75
1969	102	101	49		49
1970	101	100	48		49
1971	96	101	48		49
1972	97	104	49	57	50
1973	97	102	50	57	52
1974	97	102	51	58	50
1975	96	102	51	58	53
1976	96	102	51	58	53
1977	96	101	51	58	51
1978	95	100	50	57	47
1979	94	101	62	56	97
1980	94	99	66	56	46
1981	100	100	65		48
1982	100	100	65		98

(continues)

Appendix B *(continued)*

Year	Botswana	Brazil	Bulgaria	Burma	Burundi
1948		84	57		
1949		84	57		
1950		83	57		
1951		83	57		
1952		86	59		
1953		85	58	92	
1954		88	60	93	
1955		83	58	93	
1956		89	55	98	
1957		90	57	98	
1958		90	58	67	
1959		91	58	66	
1960		92	59	82	
1961		92	59	87	
1962		94	64	43	
1963		86	64	43	
1964		39	65	43	
1965		44	64	43	
1966		73	64	45	
1967	90	76	65	46	47
1968	90	46	65	46	47
1969	91	51	66	49	49
1970	97	70	66	48	48
1971	98	72	67	49	49
1972	98	73	67	50	52
1973	99	74	68	50	48
1974	93	81	68	69	51
1975	92	80	68	70	51
1976	92	80	68	66	51
1977	91	80	67	67	51
1978	91	80	67	66	50
1979	90	79	66	66	48
1980	90	78	66	66	48
1981	90		65	65	47
1982	89		65	65	64

(continues)

Appendix B *(continued)*

Year	Cameroon	Canada	Cape Verde	Central African Republic	Chad
1948		97			
1949		92			
1950		92			
1951		91			
1952		92			
1953		98			
1954		98			
1955		97			
1956		97			
1957		97			
1958		92			
1959		91			
1960	91	92		72	74
1961	91	92		73	68
1962	90	98		67	63
1963	68	99		68	64
1964	68	99		68	64
1965	68	98		68	64
1966	68	99		45	64
1967	68	100		47	65
1968	68	100		47	65
1969	69	100		49	68
1970	69	95		48	66
1971	70	101		49	66
1972	70	102		50	67
1973	67	103		50	67
1974	67	103		51	67
1975	67	105	67	51	51
1976	68	102	68	51	51
1977	67	100	67	50	51
1978	66	101	66	50	49
1979	65	100	65	47	49
1980	65	100	65	48	48
1981	65	100	65	47	47
1982	64	99	65	46	46

(continues)

Appendix B *(continued)*

Year	Chile	China	Colombia	Comoros	Congo
1948	81	64	82		
1949	88	41	76		
1950	89	41	74		
1951	88	41	72		
1952	90	40	70		
1953	88	43	66		
1954	87	61	51		
1955	89	59	52		
1956	90	62	46		
1957	88	61	46		
1958	89	61	82		
1959	94	59	81		
1960	92	59	83		80
1961	96	59	83		81
1962	95	60	84		81
1963	97	60	83		64
1964	97	60	85		65
1965	97	60	84		62
1966	97	48	84		64
1967	97	51	85		65
1968	97	59	85		47
1969	99	61	86		49
1970	100	62	85		48
1971	102	63	89		49
1972	104	64	87		49
1973	54	64	87		64
1974	51	64	93		64
1975	50	66	93	51	64
1976	51	68	97	51	65
1977	50	64	95	56	50
1978	45	63	92	66	49
1979	50	68	92	66	62
1980	45	63	90	66	62
1981	46	61	90	65	62
1982	48	60	89	65	61

(continues)

Appendix B *(continued)*

Year	Costa Rica	Cuba	Cyprus	Czechoslovakia	Denmark
1948	58	88		48	82
1949	86	90		48	82
1950	86	89		49	82
1951	87	90		54	83
1952	86	40		55	84
1953	91	41		57	97
1954	92	40		58	98
1955	91	73		57	96
1956	92	68		54	97
1957	91	71		56	96
1958	92	62		57	97
1959	91	29		57	96
1960	92	29	89	58	97
1961	93	36	91	58	98
1962	93	42	90	59	98
1963	94	44	83	59	99
1964	94	42	79	60	99
1965	94	42	80	60	100
1966	93	44	79	60	99
1967	94	46	80	60	100
1968	94	45	80	56	99
1969	95	49	81	56	100
1970	94	48	79	55	100
1971	96	49	82	61	101
1972	97	50	83	62	102
1973	97	50	84	64	102
1974	97	51	84	64	103
1975	103	51	84	68	102
1976	102	68	87	67	102
1977	102	68	85	61	101
1978	101	67	85	63	101
1979	100	66	84	63	100
1980	100	66	84	65	100
1981	99	65	84	65	100
1982	99	64	83	64	100

(continues)

Appendix B *(continued)*

Year	Dominican Republic	Ecuador	Egypt	El Salvador	Equatorial Guinea
1948	59	81		42	
1949	59	82		43	
1950	58	82		60	
1951	59	82		61	
1952	60	83		62	
1953	59	77	40	61	
1954	60	79	44	62	
1955	58	76	42	62	
1956	59	76	41	62	
1957	57	75	66	61	
1958	59	76	66	62	
1959	58	78	62	62	
1960	57	89	63	41	
1961	63	89	43	56	
1962	51	90	64	73	
1963	40	43	64	74	
1964	44	44	64	85	
1965	45	45	63	84	
1966	85	48	61	84	
1967	83	49	63	85	
1968	85	65	62	85	75
1969	86	67	65	86	65
1970	92	48	65	85	65
1971	93	50	65	86	51
1972	93	49	66	81	50
1973	93	50	67	81	50
1974	87	51	68	87	51
1975	87	51	67	86	51
1976	87	49	74	87	51
1977	86	53	70	89	51
1978	92	49	68	82	49
1979	92	95	71	50	49
1980	91	96	71	50	48
1981	92	96	66	45	47
1982	90	96	76	84	48

(continues)

Appendix B *(continued)*

Year	Ethiopia	Fiji	Finland	France	Gabon
1948	48		96	97	
1949	49		97	98	
1950	48		98	97	
1951	49		98	98	
1952	51		98	96	
1953	50		98	98	
1954	51		97	98	
1955	48		97	99	
1956	49		97	96	
1957	57		97	97	
1958	58		98	98	
1959	58		97	96	
1960	58		98	97	85
1961	58		98	96	63
1962	59		98	95	63
1963	60		99	98	64
1964	60		99	97	75
1965	60		99	98	64
1966	60		99	99	64
1967	61		100	101	65
1968	61		100	92	65
1969	63		101	92	66
1970	62	100	100	95	65
1971	63	101	101	98	66
1972	63	102	103	95	67
1973	64	102	103	103	67
1974	53	102	103	103	67
1975	52	102	102	104	67
1976	51	102	103	104	67
1977	51	101	102	103	67
1978	50	100	101	101	66
1979	48	99	100	99	65
1980	48	99	100	97	71
1981	47	99	100	99	72
1982	46	99	100	99	70

(continues)

Appendix B *(continued)*

Year	Gambia	Germany, DR	Germany, FR	Ghana	Greece
1948					87
1949					88
1950					90
1951					89
1952					90
1953		48	89		84
1954		53	92		86
1955		57	94		90
1956		55	89		92
1957		57	90		91
1958		57	89		92
1959		56	88		91
1960		60	88	62	92
1961		56	90	61	92
1962		52	89	61	92
1963		60	93	63	93
1964		60	92	62	93
1965		60	92	52	91
1966		61	91	46	93
1967	95	64	92	45	34
1968	95	62	93	64	35
1969	95	63	94	77	38
1970	95	64	95	78	38
1971	96	63	95	79	61
1972	93	63	95	49	61
1973	94	63	96	50	36
1974	94	64	92	51	92
1975	93	64	92	51	96
1976	93	66	94	51	98
1977	92	67	92	51	102
1978	86	64	93	54	104
1979	85	64	91	95	103
1980	85	65	94	96	103
1981	84	65	99	47	104
1982	84	65	94	46	103

(continues)

Appendix B *(continued)*

Year	Grenada	Guatemala	Guinea	Guinea–Bissau	Guyana
1948		94			
1949		89			
1950		82			
1951		89			
1952		91			
1953		84			
1954		42			
1955		71			
1956		71			
1957		62			
1958		83			
1959		82			
1960		84	63		
1961		77	64		
1962		83	64		
1963		42	64		
1964		44	64		
1965		45	64		
1966		83	64		
1967		84	65		101
1968		84	65		101
1969		87	66		102
1970		86	65		101
1971		88	67		102
1972		87	67		103
1973		87	67		97
1974	95	88	68		97
1975	93	87	68	64	96
1976	99	87	68	64	96
1977	98	87	67	67	96
1978	98	89	67	66	95
1979	47	84	54	65	93
1980	49	85	66	48	91
1981	47	87	65	47	90
1982	46	45	65	46	90

(continues)

Appendix B *(continued)*

Year	Haiti	Honduras	Hungary	Iceland	India
1948	66	63	71	97	
1949	66	67	57	98	
1950	64	66	56	99	
1951	72	67	55	98	
1952	73	68	58	98	
1953	72	67	56	98	95
1954	72	56	60	98	96
1955	67	53	56	97	95
1956	59	39	63	98	92
1957	65	65	47	97	92
1958	64	83	47	98	91
1959	63	82	57	97	91
1960	64	83	58	98	93
1961	63	83	63	98	96
1962	62	84	62	98	91
1963	57	43	64	99	93
1964	57	45	63	100	97
1965	60	84	59	99	93
1966	60	84	60	99	93
1967	59	85	61	100	97
1968	60	85	61	100	92
1969	62	87	63	101	92
1970	62	85	62	100	92
1971	63	86	63	101	98
1972	64	50	64	102	102
1973	64	50	64	103	100
1974	64	51	64	103	103
1975	64	52	64	102	96
1976	64	51	65	102	93
1977	64	51	64	101	100
1978	63	49	63	101	100
1979	61	48	62	100	98
1980	61	48	62	100	100
1981	60	47	62	100	96
1982	60	90	61	99	101

(continues)

Appendix B *(continued)*

Year	Indonesia	Iran	Iraq	Ireland	Israel
1948		59	63	97	
1949		58	65	98	
1950		61	58	98	
1951		60	64	98	
1952		61	64	99	
1953	62	54	65	98	92
1954	62	54	52	98	93
1955	85	54	52	97	92
1956	81	54	50	97	92
1957	75	52	51	97	92
1958	73	54	40	98	93
1959	77	54	41	97	92
1960	54	54	41	98	93
1961	55	48	42	98	94
1962	57	43	42	98	93
1963	57	61	40	99	95
1964	54	70	44	100	94
1965	46	75	43	99	95
1966	49	76	44	99	93
1967	49	70	45	100	94
1968	65	70	44	100	91
1969	66	73	46	100	91
1970	67	71	45	100	90
1971	79	73	49	99	94
1972	79	73	50	100	92
1973	80	73	50	102	93
1974	80	74	51	102	94
1975	80	73	51	101	93
1976	80	68	51	100	94
1977	80	71	50	101	95
1978	80	68	50	101	92
1979	78	47	47	100	86
1980	78	69	62	100	83
1981	77	73	62	100	90
1982	75	70	61	99	78

(continues)

Appendix B *(continued)*

Year	Italy	Ivory Coast	Jaimaica	Japan	Jordan
1948	97				54
1949	97				55
1950	97				57
1951	96				58
1952	97				58
1953	96			98	58
1954	96			99	59
1955	97			97	57
1956	98			98	56
1957	97			97	51
1958	97			98	55
1959	97			98	55
1960	100	62		101	56
1961	100	63		100	58
1962	98	63		102	58
1963	99	62		100	59
1964	99	64		100	59
1965	99	64		101	59
1966	99	64		99	44
1967	99	65	100	101	59
1968	100	65	100	99	59
1969	99	66	101	98	61
1970	101	65	100	101	59
1971	104	66	101	103	62
1972	103	67	96	102	62
1973	100	67	96	103	63
1974	105	67	96	104	51
1975	108	67	96	104	51
1976	104	68	96	101	51
1977	101	67	97	101	51
1978	101	66	95	104	50
1979	97	65	95	100	48
1980	98	65	95	100	48
1981	98	65	94	100	47
1982	96	65	94	100	46

(continues)

Appendix B *(continued)*

Year	Kampuchea	Kenya	Korea, PR	Korea, R	Kuwait
1948					
1949					
1950					
1951					
1952					
1953	43		59	66	
1954	45		60	66	
1955	64		58	65	
1956	64		59	59	
1957	62		57	62	
1958	64		59	65	
1959	64		58	65	
1960	64		59	64	
1961	65		59	38	
1962	65		60	40	
1963	65		60	73	
1964	66		61	74	
1965	66		60	74	
1966	66		60	76	
1967	66	74	61	71	60
1968	66	74	62	69	60
1969	68	70	62	73	61
1970	68	69	62	72	61
1971	49	69	63	78	62
1972	74	70	67	51	63
1973	73	70	68	86	63
1974	74	71	68	81	64
1975	50	70	68	80	64
1976	67	72	68	78	50
1977	67	71	67	83	50
1978	61	76			50
1979	48	76			48
1980	48	76			48
1981	65	75			
1982	64	75			

(continues)

Appendix B *(continued)*

Year	Laos	Lebanon	Lesotho	Liberia	Libya
1948		89		65	
1949		86		66	
1950		91		65	
1951		90		65	
1952		90		67	
1953		93		66	55
1954		95		67	58
1955		92		59	54
1956		92		59	52
1957		93		58	53
1958		93		59	55
1959		92		59	54
1960	75	93		59	55
1961	76	81		60	55
1962	78	78		61	56
1963	77	82		61	56
1964	84	84		61	61
1965	86	83		61	60
1966	46	82		61	61
1967	62	84	86	62	61
1968	60	84	87	62	62
1969	62	82	88	63	48
1970	64	84	50	63	45
1971	63	84	51	64	49
1972	65	85	51	64	49
1973	63	86	63	64	50
1974	51	87	64	65	51
1975	58	84	64	65	51
1976	56	80	64	65	64
1977	55	78	64	65	67
1978	54	79	63	64	67
1979	54	76	61	62	66
1980	53	78	61	47	66
1981	53	78	61	46	65
1982	52	75	60	46	64

(continues)

Appendix B *(continued)*

Year	Luxembourg	Madagascar	Malawi	Malaysia	Maldives
1948	97				
1949	98				
1950	98				
1951	98				
1952	98				
1953	98				
1954	98				
1955	97				
1956	98				
1957	97				
1958	98				
1959	97				
1960	98	88		84	
1961	98	88		84	
1962	98	89		83	
1963	99	89		83	
1964	100	90		85	
1965	99	90		88	
1966	99	89		88	
1967	100	90	68	89	68
1968	100	90	68	90	72
1969	101	91	69	75	73
1970	100	91	69	76	72
1971	101	91	63	91	73
1972	103	52	63	92	74
1973	103	64	64	93	74
1974	103	64	64	86	74
1975	103	64	64	86	70
1976	103	59	64	86	71
1977	102	67	64	86	70
1978	101	65	63	84	70
1979	100	65	62	84	69
1980	100	65	62	83	69
1981	100	67	61	83	68
1982	100	65	61	80	68

(continues)

Appendix B *(continued)*

Year	Mali	Malta	Mauritania	Mauritius	Mexico
1948					76
1949					77
1950					77
1951					77
1952					78
1953					77
1954					78
1955					76
1956					77
1957					76
1958					77
1959					75
1960	62		62		78
1961	63		63		79
1962	63		63		77
1963	64		63		78
1964	64		64		79
1965	64		64		78
1966	64		64		78
1967	65	100	64		80
1968	46	100	65	96	80
1969	49	100	66	97	80
1970	48	100	65	97	81
1971	49	101	66	98	80
1972	50	102	67	98	81
1973	50	102	67	99	81
1974	51	103	67	99	81
1975	51	103	67	98	82
1976	51	103	68	99	82
1977	51	102	67	98	80
1978	48	100	49	99	79
1979	51	100	48	97	81
1980	51	100	48	97	79
1981	49	99	46	97	78
1982	68	100	46	96	90

(continues)

Appendix B *(continued)*

Year	Mongolia	Morocco	Mozambique	Nepal	Netherlands
1948	48			42	97
1949	49			43	97
1950	48			41	97
1951	59			43	97
1952	60			44	97
1953	59			43	97
1954	60			45	98
1955	58			42	96
1956	59			42	97
1957	57			39	97
1958	59			42	98
1959	58			63	97
1960	59	41		41	98
1961	59	48		41	98
1962	60	51		42	98
1963	60	70		59	99
1964	61	71		59	100
1965	60	44		59	99
1966	61	44		60	99
1967	62	46		61	99
1968	62	46		61	100
1969	63	47		62	100
1970	62	61		62	101
1971	63	61		63	100
1972	64	49		63	102
1973	64	49		64	103
1974	68	51		64	103
1975	68	51	52	64	102
1976	68	51	51	64	102
1977	67	72	64	63	99
1978	67	84	63	63	101
1979	66	83	62	62	100
1980	66	83	62	65	101
1981	65	82	61	65	100
1982	65	82	61	64	101

(continues)

Appendix B *(continued)*

Year	New Zealand	Nicaragua	Niger	Nigeria	Norway
1948	98	63			97
1949	99	65			97
1950	99	70			98
1951	99	75			98
1952	99	75			98
1953	99	74			98
1954	99	76			97
1955	98	73			97
1956	99	74			98
1957	98	72			97
1958	99	74			98
1959	98	74			97
1960	99	74	62	91	98
1961	99	74	63	91	98
1962	99	75	63	91	98
1963	100	80	63	92	99
1964	101	80	63	79	99
1965	100	80	64	77	99
1966	100	80	64	47	99
1967	101	80	65	44	99
1968	101	81	65	46	100
1969	102	82	66	48	101
1970	102	81	65	44	100
1971	102	78	66	48	101
1972	103	76	67	49	102
1973	103	76	67	50	102
1974	103	81	51	51	102
1975	102	79	51	50	102
1976	105	80	51	50	101
1977	101	79	51	50	101
1978	100	75	50	49	101
1979	100	44	48	94	100
1980	99	51	48	94	100
1981	101	50	47	92	100
1982	99	50	46	94	100

(continues)

Appendix B *(continued)*

Year	Oman	Pakistan	Panama	Papua New Guinea	Paraguay
1948			87		57
1949			88		58
1950			83		57
1951			84		58
1952			88		59
1953		74	82		58
1954		67	77		59
1955		77	75		57
1956		77	75		58
1957		81	75		56
1958		42	76		63
1959		40	82		62
1960		43	82		63
1961		45	83		63
1962		81	83		64
1963		86	83		76
1964		84	82		77
1965		79	83		76
1966		76	84		77
1967		67	84		77
1968		66	67		77
1969		51	47		79
1970		77	48		77
1971		70	49		79
1972		78	63		80
1973		78	64		80
1974	51	80	64		80
1975	51	79	66		80
1976	51	79	64		80
1977	51	48	64	98	80
1978	50	45	68	98	78
1979	48	45	68	96	79
1980	48	47	66	97	77
1981	53	45	65	97	77
1982	52	49	64	96	76

(continues)

Appendix B *(continued)*

Year	Peru	Philippines	Poland	Portugal	Qatar
1948	42	86	60	55	
1949	42	87	65	55	
1950	60	85	64	54	
1951	60	88	65	56	
1952	63	84	58	56	
1953	61	86	57	56	
1954	62	87	57	58	
1955	60	87	57	55	
1956	84	82	57	56	
1957	86	81	57	54	
1958	88	82	55	54	
1959	87	82	56	55	
1960	88	83	57	56	
1961	90	84	58	55	
1962	45	89	59	55	
1963	87	90	59	57	
1964	87	90	58	58	
1965	88	91	60	58	
1966	88	90	58	56	
1967	89	92	59	58	
1968	46	91	53	57	
1969	49	87	62	62	
1970	48	87	59	62	
1971	49	89	67	63	
1972	51	64	64	64	55
1973	52	50	64	63	55
1974	50	53	64	44	56
1975	51	54	64	94	56
1976	50	51	68	101	56
1977	55	52	63	104	56
1978	73	73	63	101	55
1979	47	72	62	100	54
1980	90	69	59	100	53
1981	89	73	59	100	53
1982	89	69	60	100	52

(continues)

Appendix B *(continued)*

Year	Romania	Rwanda	Sao Tome and Principe	Saudi Arabia	Senegal
1948	55			42	
1949	57			43	
1950	55			41	
1951	58			43	
1952	58			45	
1953	59			44	
1954	59			45	
1955	58			42	
1956	57			42	
1957	57			39	
1958	58			42	
1959	58			42	
1960	59			42	62
1961	59			42	62
1962	60			44	63
1963	60			44	63
1964	61			44	63
1965	60			45	64
1966	61			45	64
1967	65	65		46	63
1968	65	65		47	64
1969	67	66		48	65
1970	66	65		47	65
1971	67	66		49	66
1972	67	67		50	67
1973	68	50		50	67
1974	68	51		51	67
1975	71	51	67	51	73
1976	71	51	68	51	73
1977	70	51	67	51	73
1978	70	51	66	49	72
1979	69	50	65	48	71
1980	69	50	65	47	71
1981	69	65	65	47	77
1982	68	65	64	46	76

(continues)

Appendix B *(continued)*

Year	Seychelles	Sierra Leone	Singapore	Somalia	South Africa
1948					75
1949					77
1950					74
1951					76
1952					73
1953					75
1954					75
1955					71
1956					73
1957					74
1958					71
1959					71
1960				89	68
1961				90	68
1962				91	72
1963				90	69
1964				86	66
1965				86	68
1966				91	67
1967		44	90	86	69
1968		95	78	87	69
1969		85	79	49	70
1970		79	79	47	67
1971		86	78	49	70
1972		86	80	50	74
1973		73	80	50	70
1974		74	80	51	72
1975		73	80	51	72
1976	83	74	79	51	73
1977	50	80	79	51	72
1978	49	66	79	49	65
1979	65	65	78	62	69
1980	65	65	78	66	72
1981	65	66	78	65	64
1982	64	66	77	66	66

(continues)

Appendix B *(continued)*

Year	Spain	Sri Lanka	Sudan	Suriname	Swaziland
1948	46				
1949	49				
1950	47				
1951	50				
1952	49				
1953	48	96			
1954	50	97			
1955	47	96			
1956	49	97			
1957	46	97			
1958	47	96			
1959	46	95			
1960	47	98	42		
1961	47	98	42		
1962	47	97	44		
1963	49	99	44		
1964	48	99	41		
1965	48	99	66		
1966	49	97	68		
1967	50	100	68		
1968	47	99	96		71
1969	51	100	46		72
1970	56	101	46		71
1971	53	98	49		72
1972	52	102	70		73
1973	54	103	70		50
1974	51	103	70		51
1975	49	103	70	99	51
1976	49	102	70	99	51
1977	90	96	70	98	51
1978	96	91	73	97	63
1979	95	92	73	97	62
1980	94	90	69	46	62
1981	91	90	64	47	61
1982	95	91	65	45	60

(continues)

Appendix B *(continued)*

Year	Sweden	Switzerland	Syria	Tanzania	Thailand
1948	97	90	77		58
1949	97	90	55		59
1950	98	90	58		58
1951	98	90	42		59
1952	96	91	44		58
1953	98	90	69		57
1954	98	90	70		59
1955	96	88	75		57
1956	97	90	74		55
1957	97	88	77		72
1958	98	90			38
1959	97	89			48
1960	98	90			48
1961	98	90	67		48
1962	98	91	43		49
1963	99	91	41		50
1964	99	92	45		50
1965	99	92	43		50
1966	99	91	48		51
1967	100	93	45	77	52
1968	100	93	46	78	52
1969	100	94	48	78	74
1970	100	100	56	79	73
1971	104	101	56	80	48
1972	102	102	56	80	57
1973	102	103	74	81	50
1974	102	103	74	81	53
1975	102	101	73	81	98
1976	103	101	73	81	48
1977	101	100	73	74	50
1978	101		72	73	50
1979	100		70	73	86
1980	101		73	72	86
1981	100		71	73	85
1982	100		71	72	85

(continues)

Appendix B *(continued)*

Year	Togo	Trinidad and Tobago	Tunisia	Turkey	Uganda
1948				85	
1949				87	
1950				86	
1951				85	
1952				86	
1953				85	
1954				85	
1955				84	
1956				82	
1957				91	
1958				90	
1959				89	
1960	62		67	40	
1961	62		68	84	
1962	63		67	85	
1963	63		67	86	
1964	64		67	86	
1965	64		67	93	
1966	63		67	92	
1967	46	100	68	94	74
1968	47	100	68	94	74
1969	49	101	69	95	74
1970	48	100	68	94	70
1971	49	82	70	82	49
1972	51	83	71	85	51
1973	52	84	70	95	51
1974	53	83	70	95	51
1975	53	83	70	100	52
1976	53	103	71	94	50
1977	53	102	70	98	50
1978	51	101	68	94	50
1979	65	94	69	94	47
1980	65	95	69	43	85
1981	65	94	68	41	86
1982	64	94	67	43	85

(continues)

Appendix B *(continued)*

Year	United Arab Emirates	USSR	United Kingdom	United States	Upper Volta (Burkina Faso)
1948		58	96	96	
1949		58	97	97	
1950		58	97	98	
1951		55	97	97	
1952		56	98	96	
1953		54	98	98	
1954		56	97	96	
1955		57	97	97	
1956		56	98	97	
1957		57	97	95	
1958		58	97	97	
1959		54	97	96	
1960		56	98	97	62
1961		56	100	92	63
1962		56	98	100	63
1963		55	99	98	63
1964		57	100	97	64
1965		58	99	100	64
1966		57	98	99	46
1967		57	98	103	47
1968		57	98	100	47
1969		55	98	103	49
1970		55	96	97	74
1971		57	99	92	75
1972	55	60	87	98	76
1973	55	58	99	107	76
1974	56	59	88	101	51
1975	56	61	92	109	51
1976	56	60	93	100	51
1977	56	55	95	102	51
1978	54	55	98	97	78
1979	54	61	100	86	77
1980	54	61	98	86	47
1981	53	61	101	89	46
1982	52	58	99	88	46

(continues)

Appendix B *(continued)*

Year	Uruguay	Venezuela	Vietnam	Vietnam, PR	Vietnam, S
1948	90	41			
1949	90	42			
1950	91	41			
1951	92	41			
1952	99	58			
1953	99	69			
1954	98	71			
1955	98	69			
1956	98	69			
1957	98	56			
1958	99	60			
1959	98	85			
1960	99	84		63	74
1961	100	87		63	74
1962	100	87		64	76
1963	100	82		64	41
1964	102	85		64	41
1965	99	87		64	44
1966	99	87		60	41
1967	101	88		66	
1968	99	88		65	
1969	101	90		63	
1970	101	89		62	
1971	102	89		63	
1972	104	90		64	
1973	57	91		64	
1974	56	91		64	
1975	56	90		64	52
1976	56	90	64		
1977	56	89	64		
1978		95	63		
1979		94	62		
1980		94	62		
1981		94	62		
1982		94	61		

(continues)

Appendix B *(continued)*

Year	Western Samoa	Yemen, AR	Yemen, PDR	Yugoslavia	Zaire
1948		42		54	
1949		43		57	
1950		41		55	
1951		43		53	
1952		45		53	
1953		43		71	
1954		45		71	
1955		42		70	
1956		43		69	
1957		39		70	
1958		42		70	
1959		42		70	
1960		42		71	75
1961		42		71	72
1962		44		71	78
1963		45		72	55
1964		44		72	44
1965		45		72	46
1966		48		71	43
1967	76	46	48	71	46
1968	76	48	47	73	47
1969	76	51	48	73	49
1970	76	47	47	72	65
1971	77	59	56	72	67
1972	77	60	58	73	67
1973	77	61	57	74	67
1974	77	55	58	74	68
1975	77	56	58	73	67
1976	77	56	58	73	68
1977	77	56	57	73	67
1978	76	57	67	74	65
1979	99	55	66	73	66
1980	99	55	66	72	65
1981	99	56	65	70	65
1982	99	54	65	72	65

(continues)

Appendix B *(continued)*

Year	Zambia	Zimbabwe
1948		
1949		
1950		
1951		
1952		
1953		
1954		
1955		
1956		
1957		
1958		
1959		
1960		
1961		
1962		
1963		
1964		
1965		
1966		
1967	75	66
1968	75	67
1969	76	67
1970	75	69
1971	76	70
1972	77	69
1973	68	71
1974	68	72
1975	68	71
1976	67	72
1977	66	82
1978	66	68
1979	65	47
1980	66	87
1981	65	91
1982	65	89

Appendix C   Regression Analyses of Democracy and Economic Development Levels: By Year

Year	N	Constant	ECO	ECO^2	lnECO	R	F-Ratio
1948			60				
Linear		69.2[a]	.005[a]			.47	16.2[a]
Polynomial		65.9[a]	.01[a]	−.000[b]		.53	11.4[a]
Log-linear		42.5[a]			5.5[a]	.51	19.5[a]
1949	60						
Linear		69.6[a]	.005[a]			.46	15.4[a]
Polynomial		66.3[a]	.01[a]	−.000[b]		.52	10.8[a]
Log-linear		42.3[a]			5.6[a]	.50	19.0[a]
1950	60						
Linear		69.8[a]	.004[a]			.47	16.0[a]
Polynomial		66.6	.01[a]	−.000		.52	10.8[a]
Log-linear		41.5[a]			5.6[a]	.50	19.2[a]
1951	60						
Linear		69.5[a]	.004[a]			.46	15.6[a]
Polynomial		66.1[a]	.01[a]	−.000[b]		.52	10.7[a]
Log-linear		39.9[a]			5.8[a]	.50	18.3[a]
1952	60						
Linear		69.5[a]	.004[a]			.45	15.1[a]
Polynomial		66.5[a]	.01[a]	−.000[b]		.51	10.0[a]
Log-linear		41.2[a]			5.7[a]	.47	15.8[a]
1953	72						
Linear		70.5[a]	.004[a]			.40	13.6[a]
Polynomial		68.1[a]	.01[a]	−.000[c]		.44	8.5[a]
Log-linear		44.1[a]			5.2[a]	.46	18.3[a]
1954	72						
Linear		69.5[a]	.004[a]			.42	15.2[a]
Polynomial		66.9[a]	.01[a]	−.000[c]		.47	9.8[a]
Log-linear		41.1[a]			5.6[a]	.47	20.1[a]
1955	76						
Linear		68.7[a]	.004[a]			.40	14.3[a]
Polynomial		66.4[a]	.01[a]	−.000[c]		.44	8.9[a]
Log-linear		43.2[a]			5.1[a]	.46	20.1[a]

(continues)

Notes: N = number of countries included in the analysis. ECO = energy consumption per capita. ln ECO = natural log of energy consumption per capita. R and F-Ratio are the regression coefficient and its significance level.
a. Significant at .01 level
b. Significant at .05 level
c. Significant at .10 level

Appendix C *(continued)*

Year	N	Constant	ECO	ECO^2	lnECO	R	F-Ratio
1956	76						
Linear		69.3[a]	.004[a]			.39	10.9[a]
Polynomial		67.1[a]	.01[a]	−.000[b]		.42	7.9[a]
Log-linear		43.7[a]			5.0[a]	.46	19.9[a]
1957	76						
Linear		70.0[a]	.003[a]			.35	10.3[a]
Polynomial		68.3[a]	.01[b]	−.000		.38	6.0[a]
Log-linear		46.7[a]			4.5[a]	.41	15.2[a]
1958	75						
Linear		70.4[a]	.003[a]			.35	10.2[a]
Polynomial		68.6[a]	.01[a]	−.000		.38	6.1[a]
Log-linear		43.3[a]			5.1[a]	.47	20.6[a]
1959	75						
Linear		70.1[a]	.003[a]			.35	10.4[a]
Polynomial		67.9[a]	.01[a]	−.000		.39	6.5[a]
Log-linear		40.9[a]			5.4[a]	.47	20.4[a]
1960	102						
Linear		69.8[a]	.004[a]			.37	15.7[a]
Polynomial		68.1[a]	.01[a]	−.000[c]		.41	9.7[a]
Log-linear		50.2[a]			4.2[a]	.41	20.5[a]
1961	104						
Linear		69.8[a]	.004[a]			.36	15.5[a]
Polynomial		67.9[a]	.01[a]	−.000[b]		.41	10.0[a]
Log-linear		49.0[a]			4.4[a]	.43	23.5[a]
1962	104						
Linear		69.9[a]	.004[a]			.38	17.7[a]
Polynomial		67.2[a]	.01[a]	−.000[c]		.42	10.7[a]
Log-linear		49.3[a]			4.2[a]	.41	21.1[a]
1963	104						
Linear		67.7[a]	.004[a]			.44	24.8[a]
Polynomial		65.5[a]	.01[a]	−.000[b]		.49	16.1[a]
Log-linear		43.3[a]			5.1[a]	.49	32.8[a]

(continues)

Appendix C *(continued)*

Year	N	Constant	ECO	ECO^2	lnECO	R	F-Ratio
1964	104						
Linear		67.1[a]	.004[a]			.45	25.7[a]
Polynomial		64.9[a]	.01[a]	−.000[b]		.50	16.5[a]
Log-linear		42.2[a]			5.2[a]	.49	32.2[a]
1965	104						
Linear		67.2[a]	.004[a]			.46	27.5[a]
Polynomial		64.9[a]	.01[a]	−.000[b]		.51	17.4[a]
Log-linear		42.0[a]			5.2[a]	.49	32.6[a]
1966	104						
Linear		66.9[a]	.004[a]			.45	26.5[a]
Polynomial		64.7[a]	.01[a]	−.000[b]		.50	16.4[a]
Log-linear		40.1[a]			5.4[a]	.51	35.9[a]
1967	123						
Linear		68.8[a]	.003[a]			.38	21.0[a]
Polynomial		66.0[a]	.01[a]	−.000[a]		.46	15.9[a]
Log-linear		42.2[a]			5.2[a]	.49	38.9[a]
1968	128						
Linear		68.8[a]	.003[a]			.36	26.5[a]
Polynomial		66.7[a]	.01[a]	−.000[b]		.41	12.7[a]
Log-linear		46.7[a]			4.4[a]	.42	26.5[a]
1969	128						
Linear		68.3[a]	.003[a]			.40	24.2[a]
Polynomial		66.1[a]	.01[a]	−.000[b]		.45	15.9[a]
Log-linear		43.7[a]			4.9[a]	.46	33.5[a]
1970	129						
Linear		68.9[a]	.003[a]			.39	22.2[a]
Polynomial		66.9[a]	.01[a]	−.000[b]		.43	14.3[a]
Log-linear		45.2[a]			4.6[a]	.44	30.4[a]
1971	129						
Linear		69.6[a]	.003[a]			.39	23.3[a]
Polynomial		67.4[a]	.01[a]	−.000[b]		.44	15.4[a]
Log-linear		43.9[a]			4.9[a]	.47	35.4[a]

(continues)

Appendix C *(continued)*

Year	N	Constant	ECO	ECO^2	lnECO	R	F-Ratio
1972	133						
Linear		70.7[a]	.002[a]			.27	10.0[a]
Polynomial		67.3[a]	.01[a]	−.000[a]		.41	13.4[a]
Log-linear		48.3[a]			4.1[a]	.40	25.6[a]
1973	134						
Linear		70.7[a]	.001[a]			.28	11.4[a]
Polynomial		66.9[a]	.01[a]	−.000[a]		.46	17.6[a]
Log-linear		45.3[a]			4.5[a]	.44	32.1[a]
1974	136						
Linear		70.5[a]	.002[a]			.28	11.0[a]
Polynomial		66.8[a]	.01[a]	−.000		.44	15.6[a]
Log-linear		44.2[a]			4.7[a]	.46	35.1[a]
1975	144						
Linear		71.2[a]	.001[a]			.22	7.1[a]
Polynomial		67.4[a]	.01[a]	−.000[a]		.44	16.5[a]
Log-linear		40.2[a]			5.3[a]	.51	50.1[a]
1976	144						
Linear		70.6[a]	.001[a]			.25	9.3[a]
Polynomial		66.8[a]	.01[a]	−.000[a]		.45	17.7[a]
Log-linear		41.4[a]			5.1[a]	.49	45.4[a]
1977	144						
Linear		69.5[a]	.002[a]			.32	16.5[a]
Polynomial		65.6[a]	.01[a]	−.000[a]		.46	18.9[a]
Log-linear		41.2[a]			5.2[a]	.50	47.5[a]
1978	140						
Linear		68.8[a]	.002[a]			.33	16.9[a]
Polynomial		65.6[a]	.01[a]	−.000[a]		.43	15.5[a]
Log-linear		41.1[a]			5.1[a]	.49	43.8[a]
1979	140						
Linear		71.2[a]	.001[a]			.19	5.0[b]
Polynomial		67.6[a]	.01[a]	−.000[a]		.39	12.6[a]
Log-linear		44.5[a]			4.6[a]	.45	35.0[a]
1980	140						
Linear		71.1[a]	.001[b]			.18	4.5[b]
Polynomial		67.5[a]	.01[a]	−.000[a]		.39	12.0[a]
Log-linear		45.6[a]			4.3[a]	.43	31.0[a]

Appendix D **Regression Analyses of Democracy and Economic Development Levels: By Country**

Country	N	Constant	ECO	ECO^2	lnECO	R	F-Ratio
Afghanistan	26						
Linear		58.6[a]	−.09			.23	1.4
Polynomial		48.2[a]	.65[b]	−.01[a]		.55	5.1[b]
Log-linear		58.3[a]			−.8	.08	.2
Albania	33						
Linear		57.7[a]	.01[a]			.83	70.9[a]
Polynomial		55.7[a]	.02[a]	−.00[a]		.90	62.2[a]
Log-linear		43.5[a]			2.9[a]	.85	84.2[a]
Algeria	14						
Linear		40.2[a]	.03[a]			.70	11.5[a]
Polynomial		26.4[c]	.07	−.00		.73	6.4[b]
Log-linear		−52.7[c]			17.1[a]	.73	13.6[a]
Angola	6						
Linear		51.9[a]	.002			.02	.0
Polynomial		21.6	.44	−.001		.47	.4
Log-linear		45.7			1.3	.08	.03
Argentina	33						
Linear		69.6[a]	−.01			.14	.6
Polynomial		133.9[b]	−.11	.00		.26	1.1
Log-linear		128.2[c]			−9.4	.16	.9
Australia	33						
Linear		91.9[a]	.002[a]			.89	119.3[a]
Polynomial		97.6[a]	−.00	.00		.90	64.3[a]
Log-linear		36.8[a]			7.5[a]	.87	100.2[a]
Austria	21						
Linear		96.4[a]	.001[a]			.71	19.7[a]
Polynomial		82.9[a]	.01[a]	−.00[b]		.80	16.2[a]
Log-linear		65.9[a]			4.3[a]	.74	22.6[a]
Bahamas	8						
Linear		88.8[a]	.001[a]			.89	23.7[a]
Polynomial		89.9[a]	.00	.00		.89	10.0[b]
Log-linear		37.5[b]			6.7[a]	.89	23.2[a]

(continues)

Notes: N = number of countries included in the analysis. ECO = energy consumption per capita. 1n ECO = natural log of energy consumption per capita. R and F-ratio are the regression coefficient and its significance level.
a. Significant at .01 level
b. Significant at .05 level
c. Significant at .10 level

Appendix D *(continued)*

Country	N	Constant	ECO	ECO^2	lnECO	R	F-Ratio
Bahrain	9						
Linear		78.4[a]	−.002[b]			.76	9.8[b]
Polynomial		97.8[c]	−.005	.00		.77	4.4[c]
Log-linear		285.2[a]			−24.7[b]	.77	10.2[b]
Bangladesh	9						
Linear		54.5	.32			.12	.1
Polynomial		170.8	−6.19	.09		.22	.2
Log-linear		28.5			14.5	.11	.1
Barbados	14						
Linear		101.8[a]	−.004[b]			.58	6.2[b]
Polynomial		105.5[a]	−.01	.00		.62	3.5[c]
Log-linear		130.0[a]			−4.7[b]	.62	7.6[b]
Belgium	33						
Linear		92.9[a]	.001[a]			.79	50.9[a]
Polynomial		93.1[a]	.001	.00		.79	24.6[a]
Log-linear		44.6[a]			6.5[a]	.78	49.6[a]
Benin	21						
Linear		55.2[a]	−.04			.07	.1
Polynomial		50.7[b]	.18	−.002		.09	.1
Log-linear		59.3[a]			−1.6	.07	.1
Bolivia	33						
Linear		62.7[a]	−.005			.14	.6
Polynomial		66.0[a]	−.02	.00		.16	.4
Log-linear		82.8[a]			−4.1	.17	.9
Brazil	33						
Linear		83.5[a]	−.012			.18	1.0
Polynomial		113.1[a]	−.16[b]	.00[b]		.40	2.8[c]
Log-linear		120.7[a]			−7.2	.24	1.8
Bulgaria	33						
Linear		57.0[a]	.002[a]			.92	180.0[a]
Polynomial		55.3[a]	.004[a]	−.00[a]		.95	136.2[a]
Log-linear		33.6[a]			3.9[a]	.91	146.5[a]

(continues)

Appendix D *(continued)*

Country	N	Constant	ECO	ECO^2	lnECO	R	F-Ratio
Burma	28						
Linear		124.2[a]	−1.18[a]			.60	14.6[a]
Polynomial		261.8[a]	−7.07[a]	.06[b]		.69	11.6[a]
Log-linear		293.0[a]			−58.6	.64	17.6[a]
Burundi	14						
Linear		43.2[a]	.6[c]			.46	3.3[c]
Polynomial		6.1	8.5[b]	−.42[b]		.68	4.8[b]
Log-linear		35.1[a]			6.3[c]	.50	4.0[c]
Cameroon	21						
Linear		95.2[a]	−.28[a]			.56	8.9[a]
Polynomial		146.2[a]	−1.54	.007		.61	5.3[b]
Log-linear		177.0[a]			−24.2[a]	.59	9.9[a]
Canada	33						
Linear		85.5[a]	.002[a]			.79	50.8[a]
Polynomial		63.7[a]	.008[b]	−.00		.82	29.8[a]
Log-linear		−13.4			12.5[a]	.80	55.7[a]
Cape Verde	6						
Linear		68.5[a]	−.01[c]			.75	5.1[c]
Polynomial		81.8[a]	−.17[b]	.00[b]		.95	14.4[b]
Log-linear		79.5[a]			−2.6[c]	.80	6.9[c]
Central Africa	21						
Linear		74.5[a]	−.50[a]			.57	9.0[a]
Polynomial		162.7[a]	−4.77[a]	.05[a]		.76	12.0[a]
Log-linear		139.0[a]			−23.1[a]	.62	12.1[a]
Chad	21						
Linear		76.6[a]	−.84[b]			.53	7.5[b]
Polynomial		91.6[a]	−2.71	.05		.56	4.0[b]
Log-linear		101.5[a]			−14.0[a]	.54	8.0[a]
Chile	33						
Linear		73.8[a]	.009			.10	.3
Polynomial		225.3[a]	−.31[b]	.00[b]		.42	3.3[b]
Log-linear		52.6			4.4	.05	.1

(continues)

Appendix D *(continued)*

Country	N	Constant	ECO	ECO^2	lnECO	R	F-Ratio
China	26						
Linear		55.2[a]	.012[b]			.44	5.7[b]
Polynomial		67.6[a]	−.06[b]	.00[a]		.66	8.8[a]
Log-linear		41.6[a]			3.2	.32	2.7
Colombia	33						
Linear		57.1[a]	.05[a]			.60	17.2[a]
Polynomial		77.5[a]	−.06	.00[c]		.66	11.5[a]
Log-linear		−13.9			15.3[a]	.50	10.5[a]
Comoro Islands	6						
Linear		96.1[a]	−.73[a]			.95	33.9[a]
Polynomial		−28.5	4.47[b]	−.05[b]		.99	98.7[a]
Log-linear		196.0[a]			−35.0[a]	.93	25.9[a]
Congo	21						
Linear		67.4[a]	−.04			.19	.7
Polynomial		26.9[b]	.54[a]	−.002[a]		.67	7.2[a]
Log-linear		65.2[b]			−.8	.03	.02
Costa Rica	33						
Linear		80.3[a]	.04[a]			.63	20.9[a]
Polynomial		65.9[a]	.12[c]	−.00		.66	11.5[a]
Log-linear		13.3			13.7[a]	.66	23.5[a]
Cuba	33						
Linear		65.8[a]	−.01			.14	.6
Polynomial		289.2[a]	−.50[a]	.00[a]		.64	10.2[a]
Log-linear		154.2[c]			−14.4	.20	1.3
Cyprus	21						
Linear		85.2[a]	−.001			.14	.4
Polynomial		106.2[a]	−.04[b]	.00[b]		.48	2.7[c]
Log-linear		100.6[a]			−2.4	.21	.9
Czechoslovakia	33						
Linear		43.0[a]	.003[a]			.86	90.8[a]
Polynomial		45.2[a]	.002	.00		.86	44.2[a]
Log-linear		−60.0[a]			13.9[a]	.86	87.5[a]

(continues)

Appendix D *(continued)*

Country	N	Constant	ECO	ECO^2	lnECO	R	F-Ratio
Denmark	33						
Linear		83.5[a]	.004[a]			.75	39.5[a]
Polynomial		54.9[a]	.02[a]	−.00[a]		.84	37.4[a]
Log-linear		−11.8			13.3[a]	.80	53.3[a]
Dominican Republic	33						
Linear		53.0[a]	.06[a]			.72	33.7[a]
Polynomial		36.9[a]	.19[a]	−.00[b]		.77	22.0[a]
Log-linear		−34.7[c]			19.5a	.74	37.8[a]
Ecuador	33						
Linear		71.0[a]	−.01			.10	.3
Polynomial		145.6[a]	−.51[a]	.00[a]		.63	10.0[a]
Log-linear		118.9[a]			−9.3	.21	1.4
Egypt	28						
Linear		37.9[a]	.08[a]			.62	16.6[a]
Polynomial		−8.0	.36[b]	−.00[c]		.67	10.4[a]
Log-linear		−89.1[b]			26.4[a]	.65	19.2[a]
El Salvador	33						
Linear		42.4[a]	.17[a]			.68	26.6[a]
Polynomial		6.1	.66[a]	−.01[b]		.75	19.4[a]
Log-linear		−65.1[a]			26.9[a]	.72	34.1[a]
Equatorial Guinea	13						
Linear		24.5[a]	.28[a]			.90	46.4[a]
Polynomial		42.8	−.04	.001		.90	22.0[a]
Log-linear		−98.4[a]			32.9[a]	.89	40.3[a]
Ethiopia	33						
Linear		52.4[a]	.17[b]			.35	4.6[b]
Polynomial		50.5[a]	.59[c]	−.01		.42	3.3[c]
Log-linear		52.5[a]			1.4	.16	.7
Fiji	11						
Linear		106.0[a]	−.01			.70	8.8
Polynomial		90.2[a]	.05	−.00		.77	5.9[b]
Log-linear		130.6[a]			−4.7[b]	.68	7.7[b]

(continues)

Appendix D (*continued*)

Country	N	Constant	ECO	ECO^2	lnECO	R	F-Ratio
Finland	33						
Linear		96.2[a]	.001[a]			.90	129.5[a]
Polynomial		96.1[a]	.001[b]	−.00		.90	62.7[a]
Log-linear		79.0[a]			2.6[a]	.86	91.9[a]
France	33						
Linear		94.0[a]	.001[b]			.40	6.0[b]
Polynomial		111.4[a]	−.01[b]	.00[b]		.53	6.0[a]
Log-linear		68.8[a]			3.7[b]	.37	4.8[b]
Gabon	21						
Linear		67.4[a]	−.00			.04	.0
Polynomial		69.0[a]	−.005	.00		.19	.3
Log-linear		71.7[a]			−.7	.12	.3
Gambia	14						
Linear		102.2[a]	−.13[a]			.90	53.2[a]
Polynomial		86.8[a]	.27[b]	−.002[a]		.96	60.3[a]
Log-linear		135.1[a]			−10.0[a]	.86	34.0[a]
Germany, DR	28						
Linear		40.5[a]	.004[a]			.87	79.1[a]
Polynomial		22.9[b]	.01[b]	−.00[c]		.88	43.9[a]
Log-linear		−103.0[a]			19.0[a]	.88	89.1[a]
Germany, FR	28						
Linear		85.3[a]	.001[a]			.68	22.4[a]
Polynomial		79.5[a]	.004	−.00		.69	11.2[a]
Log-linear		37.7[a]			6.5[a]	.68	22.7[a]
Ghana	21						
Linear		63.2[a]	−.01			.02	.0
Polynomial		−106.1	2.63[b]	−.01[b]		.45	2.2
Log-linear		57.1			1.0	.02	.0
Greece	33						
Linear		84.0[a]	−.002			.06	.1
Polynomial		121.5[a]	.11[a]	.00[a]		.68	13.1[a]
Log-linear		114.5[a]			−4.9	.18	1.1

(*continues*)

Appendix D *(continued)*

Country	N	Constant	ECO	ECO^2	lnECO	R	F-Ratio
Grenada	7						
Linear		11.0	.33			.45	1.3
Polynomial		−469.6	4.5	−.009		.58	1.0
Log-linear		−343.4			79.2	.47	1.5
Guatemala	33						
Linear		62.5[a]	.09[c]			.32	3.7[c]
Polynomial		109.5[b]	−.43	.001		.38	2.5[c]
Log-linear		1.2			14.9[c]	.30	3.1[c]
Guinea	21						
Linear		57.1[a]	.08			.15	.4
Polynomial		−227.6	6.23	−.03		.34	1.2
Log-linear		27.3			8.3	.16	.5
Guinea-Bissau	6						
Linear		89.7[b]	−.38			.39	.7
Polynomial		−217.1	8.75	−.07		.57	.7
Log-linear		167.4			−24.7	.37	.6
Guyana	14						
Linear		127.1[a]	−.03[a]			.68	10.6[a]
Polynomial		102.3	.02	−.00		.69	4.9[b]
Log-linear		296.7[a]			−28.7[a]	.68	10.4[a]
Haiti	33						
Linear		69.4[a]	−.18[b]			.41	6.4[b]
Polynomial		78.8[a]	−.79[b]	.01[c]		.50	5.0[b]
Log-linear		83.9[a]			−5.9[a]	.46	8.2[a]
Honduras	33						
Linear		76.2[a]	−.06			.17	.9
Polynomial		−24.7	1.03[c]	−.003[c]		.37	2.3[c]
Log-linear		111.1[c]			−8.8	.14	.6
Hungary	33						
Linear		54.7[a]	.002[b]			.39	5.6[b]
Polynomial		66.0[a]	−.01[c]	.00[b]		.53	5.9[a]
Log-linear		36.3[b]			3.1	.27	2.3

(continues)

Appendix D *(continued)*

Country	N	Constant	ECO	ECO^2	lnECO	R	F-Ratio
Iceland	33						
Linear		92.6[a]	.002[a]			.77	44.5[a]
Polynomial		96.6[a]	−.00	.00		.77	22.3[a]
Log-linear		46.2[a]			6.5[a]	.75	40.7
India	28						
Linear		87.9[a]	.04[b]			.39	4.6[b]
Polynomial		95.9[a]	−.06	.00		.40	2.4
Log-linear		61.4[a]			6.7[b]	.37	4.2[b]
Indonesia	28						
Linear		45.6[a]	.17[a]			.60	14.4[a]
Polynomial		10.6	.66[c]	−.002		.63	8.4[a]
Log-linear		−54.8[c]			25.3[a]	.62	15.9[a]
Iran	33						
Linear		56.6[a]	.01[a]			.52	11.5[a]
Polynomial		50.6[a]	.04[b]	−.00		.57	7.3[a]
Log-linear		24.9[a]			6.3[a]	.55	13.4[a]
Iraq	33						
Linear		68.4	−.03			.67	24.7[a]
Polynomial		98.3[a]	−.20[a]	.00		.85	37.6[a]
Log-linear		140.7[a]			−14.6[a]	.74	38.5[a]
Ireland	33						
Linear		94.9[a]	.002[a]			.82	62.5[a]
Polynomial		94.7[a]	.002	−.00		.82	30.1[a]
Log-linear		69.0[a]			3.9[a]	.80	56.9[a]
Israel	28						
Linear		92.8[a]	−.00			.06	.1
Polynomial		96.0[a]	−.004	.00		.14	.3
Log-linear		95.9[a]			−.5	.07	.1
Italy	33						
Linear		95.4[a]	.002[a]			.71	32.1[a]
Polynomial		94.2[a]	.003	−.00		.72	16.1[a]
Log-linear		74.8[a]			3.3[a]	.71	34.0[a]

(continues)

Appendix D *(continued)*

Country	N	Constant	ECO	ECO^2	lnECO	R	F-Ratio
Ivory Coast	21						
Linear		62.0[a]	.02[a]			.92	107.0[a]
Polynomial		59.8[a]	.04[a]	−.00[a]		.96	93.3[a]
Log-linear		49.2[a]			3.1[a]	.96	200.8[a]
Jamaica	14						
Linear		101.8[a]	−.003			.45	3.0
Polynomial		107.5[a]	−.01	.00		.46	1.5
Log-linear		130.5[a]			−4.6[c]	.46	3.2[c]
Japan	28						
Linear		97.1[a]	.001[a]			.73	29.8[a]
Polynomial		96.9[a]	.002	−.00		.73	14.4[a]
Log-linear		79.3[a]			2.8[a]	.74	31.4[a]
Jordan	33						
Linear		59.0[a]	−.01[b]			.42	6.6[b]
Polynomial		54.4[a]	.03[c]	−.00[a]		.59	8.1[a]
Log-linear		65.5[a]			−1.8	.28	2.7
Kampuchea	28						
Linear		55.4[a]	.24[a]			.48	7.7[a]
Polynomial		53.2[a]	.45	−.003		.49	4.1[b]
Log-linear		49.9[a]			4.1[b]	.47	7.4[b]
Kenya	14						
Linear		92.8[a]	−.14[a]			.71	12.1[a]
Polynomial		72.8	.15	−.001		.71	5.7[b]
Log-linear		167.4[a]			−19.2[a]	.67	11.5[a]
Korea, PR	10						
Linear		47.9[a]	.01[a]			.84	19.5[a]
Polynomial		−19.2	.06[b]	−.00[b]		.93	22.6[a]
Log-linear		−77.6[b]			18.4[a]	.86	23.7[a]
Korea, R	25						
Linear		57.6[a]	.02[a]			.57	11.1[a]
Polynomial		60.7[a]	.005	.00		.58	5.5[b]
Log-linear		20.8			7.9[a]	.50	7.8[a]

(continues)

Appendix D *(continued)*

Country	N	Constant	ECO	ECO^2	lnECO	R	F-Ratio
Kuwait	14						
Linear		32.1[a]	.003[a]			.79	19.3[a]
Polynomial		−19.9	.02[c]	−.00		.82	11.7[a]
Log-linear		−160.7[a]			24.0[a]	.80	21.3[a]
Laos	21						
Linear		76.4[a]	−.23[c]			.41	3.7[c]
Polynomial		107.7[a]	−1.46[b]	.01[c]		.56	4.2[b]
Log-linear		116.2[a]			−13.3[b]	.46	5.2[b]
Lebanon	33						
Linear		95.7[a]	−.01[a]			.50	10.2[a]
Polynomial		122.3[a]	−.10[a]	.00[a]		.66	11.4[a]
Log-linear		156.2[a]			−10.9[a]	.56	13.8[a]
Liberia	33						
Linear		62.0[a]	.00			.05	.1
Polynomial		62.6[a]	−.007	.00		.18	.5
Log-linear		63.3[a]			−.2	.08	.2
Libya	26						
Linear		52.2[a]	.01[a]			.55	10.2[a]
Polynomial		57.7[a]	−.01	.00[b]		.67	9.1[a]
Log-linear		35.1[a]			3.4[b]	.41	4.8[b]
Luxembourg	33						
Linear		89.3	.00			.89	121.5[a]
Polynomial		96.8[a]	−.00	.00		.90	64.9[a]
Log-linear		4.1			10.0[a]	.87	100.2[a]
Madagascar	21						
Linear		110.1[a]	−.55[a]			.61	11.0[a]
Polynomial		85.9[c]	.42	−.01		.62	5.5[b]
Log-linear		190.3[a]			−27.9[a]	.59	10.2[a]
Malawi	14						
Linear		82.3[a]	−.37[a]			.71	12.0[a]
Polynomial		157.5[a]	−3.60[c]	.03		.78	8.7[a]
Log-linear		132.0[a]			−17.4[a]	.72	13.2[a]

(continues)

Appendix D *(continued)*

Country	N	Constant	ECO	ECO^2	lnECO	R	F-Ratio
Malaysia	21						
Linear		84.5[a]	.002			.08	.1
Polynomial		75.6[a]	.04	−.00		.30	.9
Log-linear		77.0[a]			1.4	.13	.3
Mali	21						
Linear		76.3[a]	−.93[a]			.63	12.5[a]
Polynomial		91.1[a]	−2.30	.03		.64	6.2[a]
Log-linear		117.8[a]			−20.2[a]	.63	12.8[a]
Malta	14						
Linear		99.0[a]	.002			.25	.8
Polynomial		81.9[a]	.03	−.00		.39	1.0
Log-linear		85.3[a]			2.3	.27	1.0
Mauritania	21						
Linear		67.6[a]	−.05[b]			.44	4.5[b]
Polynomial		55.8[a]	.29[a]	−.002[a]		.82	18.2[a]
Log-linear		72.7[a]			−2.3	.26	1.4
Mauritius	13						
Linear		96.4[a]	.006			.46	2.9
Polynomial		94.4[a]	.02	−2.79		.48	1.5
Log-linear		88.9[a]			1.6[c]	.48	3.3[c]
Mexico	33						
Linear		74.3[a]	.004[a]			.73	34.8[a]
Polynomial		69.1[a]	.01[a]	−.00[a]		.79	25.4[a]
Log-linear		48.3[a]			4.4[a]	.76	41.9[a]
Mongolia	13						
Linear		59.2[a]	.005[b]			.64	7.5[b]
Polynomial		30.4[a]	.06[a]	−.00[a]		.88	17.9[a]
Log-linear		16.7			6.7[a]	.70	10.3[a]
Morocco	21						
Linear		30.7[a]	.12[a]			.61	11.0[a]
Polynomial		75.5[a]	−.30	.00[c]		.69	8.0[a]
Log-linear		−70.7			24.1[a]	.55	8.1[a]

(continues)

Appendix D *(continued)*

Country	N	Constant	ECO	ECO^2	lnECO	R	F-Ratio
Mozambique	6						
Linear		81.8[a]	−.21[b]			.83	8.8[b]
Polynomial		1.2	1.38	−.008[c]		.95	13.2[b]
Log-linear		157.2[b]			−21.1[c]	.79	6.7[c]
Nepal	20						
Linear		46.8[a]	1.32[a]			.68	15.6[a]
Polynomial		25.6[a]	6.20[a]	−.25[a]		.88	29.4[a]
Log-linear		30.4[a]			13.3[a]	.80	32.3[a]
Netherlands	33						
Linear		94.7[a]	.001[a]			.92	162.4[a]
Polynomial		93.9[a]	.002[b]	−.00		.92	80.0[a]
Log-linear		67.6[a]			4.2[a]	.91	153.5[a]
New Zealand	33						
Linear		94.1[a]	.002[a]			.73	35.7[a]
Polynomial		92.3[a]	.004	−.00		.73	17.4[a]
Log-linear		52.7[a]			6.0[a]	.73	35.9[a]
Nicaragua	33						
Linear		70.8[a]	.013			.23	1.7
Polynomial		70.3[a]	.02	−.00		.23	.8
Log-linear		56.1[a]			3.4	.25	2.1
Niger	21						
Linear		69.9[a]	−.42[a]			.76	26.7[a]
Polynomial		63.7[a]	.15	−.01		.79	15.3[a]
Log-linear		86.5[a]			−8.8[a]	.69	16.8[a]
Nigeria	21						
Linear		65.0[a]	−.02			.04	.0
Polynomial		120.7[a]	−1.78[a]	.01[a]		.59	4.8[b]
Log-linear		86.7[b]			−5.7	.15	.4
Norway	33						
Linear		95.5[a]	.001[a]			.84	76.8[a]
Polynomial		92.4[a]	.003[a]	−.00[b]		.88	49.4[a]
Log-linear		69.4[a]			3.7[a]	.86	86.2[a]

(continues)

Appendix D *(continued)*

Country	N	Constant	ECO	ECO^2	lnECO	R	F-Ratio
Oman	7						
Linear		52.5[a]	−.004			.50	1.7
Polynomial		45.3[a]	.03	−.00		.61	1.2
Log–linear		61.8[a]			−1.9	.47	1.4
Pakistan	28						
Linear		68.6[a]	−.02			.07	.1
Polynomial		53.6[b]	.29	−.001		.17	.4
Log-linear		73.6[a]			−1.6	.05	.1
Panama	33						
Linear		97.0[a]	−.04[a]			.69	28.3[a]
Polynomial		93.5[a]	−.03	−.00		.69	13.7[a]
Log-linear		207.1[a]			−21.2[a]	.67	25.6[a]
Papau New Guinea	4						
Linear		115.9[a]	−.07			.78	3.2
Polynomial		400.4	−2.08	.004		.87	1.6
Log-linear		202.9[c]			18.7	.79	3.3
Paraguay	33						
Linear		54.3[a]	.14[a]			.88	106.4[a]
Polynomial		48.4[a]	.28[a]	−.00[a]		.91	74.5[a]
Log-linear		18.0[a]			11.6[a]	.87	94.1[a]
Peru	33						
Linear		67.5[a]	−.003			.02	.01
Polynomial		−259.3[a]	1.38[a]	−.001[a]		.68	12.3[a]
Log-linear		47.7			2.9	.04	.0
Philippines	33						
Linear		97.3[a]	−.09[a]			.59	10.9[a]
Polynomial		69.8[a]	.23[c]	−.00[b]		.67	12.3[a]
Log-linear		155.1[a]			−14.5[a]	.53	11.9[a]
Poland	33						
Linear		55.7[a]	.001[b]			.39	5.6[b]
Polynomial		70.1[a]	−.01[c]	.00[b]		.54	6.1[a]
Log-linear		31.4[c]			3.6[c]	.31	3.4[c]

(continues)

Appendix D *(continued)*

Country	N	Constant	ECO	ECO^2	lnECO	R	F-Ratio
Portugal	33						
Linear		41.0[a]	.04[a]			.74	36.6[a]
Polynomial		60.5[a]	−.03	.00		.76	20.3[a]
Log-linear		−77.2[a]			22.7[a]	.69	28.7[a]
Qatar	9						
Linear		55.7[a]	−.00			.17	.2
Polynomial		54.7[a]	.00	−.00		.19	.1
Log-linear		59.6[a]			−.4	.15	.2
Romania	33						
Linear		54.1[a]	.004[a]			.97	477.2[a]
Polynomial		53.2[a]	.005[a]	−.00		.97	244.9[a]
Log-linear		11.6[a]			6.8[a]	.92	177.9[a]
Rwanda	14						
Linear		77.2[a]	−1.44[a]			.84	29.4[a]
Polynomial		96.4[a]	−4.42	.10		.86	15.9[a]
Log-linear		107.6[a]			−19.5[a]	.85	32.0[a]
Sao Tome and Principe	6						
Linear		72.1[a]	−.04[c]			.80	7.2[c]
Polynomial		70.1[b]	−.01	−.00		.80	2.7
Log-linear		94.6[a]			−5.7[c]	.80	7.0[c]
Saudi Arabia	26						
Linear		42.1[a]	.01[a]			.87	77.2[a]
Polynomial		39.2[a]	.02[a]	−.00[a]		.94	87.5[a]
Log-linear		21.3[a]			3.9[a]	.94	195.0[a]
Senegal	21						
Linear		56.4[a]	.06[a]			.79	31.0[a]
Polynomial		43.4[a]	.22[b]	−.00		.82	18.3[a]
Log-linear		8.6			11.5[a]	.81	35.3[a]
Seychelles	5						
Linear		66.1	−.005			.04	.0
Polynomial		521.9	−1.38	.001		.44	.2
Log-linear		95.9			−5.2	.06	.0

(continues)

Appendix D *(continued)*

Country	N	Constant	ECO	ECO^2	lnECO	R	F-Ratio
Sierra Leone	14						
Linear		64.2[a]	.11			.22	.6
Polynomial		20.8	1.23	−.006		.40	1.0
Log-linear		22.7			11.5	.29	1.1
Singapore	14						
Linear		22.4[a]	−.001			.42	2.6
Polynomial		89.2[a]	−.007	.00		.54	2.2
Log-linear		103.6[a]			−3.1[c]	.50	3.9[c]
Somalia	21						
Linear		83.3[a]	−.36[b]			.48	5.8[b]
Polynomial		118.1[a]	−1.85[b]	.01[b]		.62	5.6[b]
Log-linear		150.4[a]			−22.7[a]	.58	9.8[a]
South Africa	33						
Linear		81.9[a]	−.004[a]			.51	11.1[a]
Polynomial		136.9[a]	−.05[a]	.00[a]		.68	13.2[a]
Log-linear		157.4[a]			−11.0[a]	.55	13.2[a]
Spain	33						
Linear		34.3[a]	.02[a]			.69	27.7[a]
Polynomial		64.7[a]	−.03[c]	.00[a]		.76	21.4[a]
Log-linear		−77.2[b]			19.7[a]	.62	19.6[a]
Sri Lanka	28						
Linear		88.2[a]	.08[b]			.39	4.7[b]
Polynomial		60.0[b]	.54	−.002		.43	2.9[c]
Log-linear		47.1[b]			10.7[b]	.40	5.1[b]
Sudan	21						
Linear		46.5[a]	.15[c]			.38	3.2[c]
Polynomial		10.5	.94	−.004		.48	2.7[c]
Log-linear		−14.5			16.9[c]	.44	4.5[c]
Suriname	6						
Linear		93.2	−.001			.01	.0
Polynomial		7419.9	−5.75	.001		.52	.6
Log-linear		152.3			−8.0	.02	.0

(continues)

Appendix D *(continued)*

Country	N	Constant	ECO	ECO^2	lnECO	R	F-Ratio
Sweden	33						
Linear		92.5[a]	.002[a]			.89	123.1[a]
Polynomial		97.1[a]	−.00	.00		.90	66.0[a]
Log-linear		46.8[a]			6.3[a]	.87	99.8[a]
Switzerland	30						
Linear		82.7[a]	.005[a]			.87	86.1[a]
Polynomial		97.8[a]	−.01[a]	.00[a]		.96	177.0[a]
Log-linear		24.1[b]			9.0[a]	.79	46.4[a]
Syria	30						
Linear		54.6[a]	.01			.30	2.8
Polynomial		63.2[a]	−.03	.00		.40	2.6[c]
Log-linear		44.3[b]			3.0	.16	.8
Tanzania	14						
Linear		66.7[a]	.17[a]			.66	9.3[a]
Polynomial		52.0[a]	.61	−.003		.69	5.0[b]
Log-linear		29.2[c]			11.7[a]	.67	10.0[a]
Thailand	33						
Linear		52.4[a]	.03[c]			.32	3.5[c]
Polynomial		59.1[a]	−.11	.00[c]		.43	3.3[c]
Log-linear		47.0[a]			2.3	.20	1.2
Togo	21						
Linear		62.7[a]	−.10			.36	2.8
Polynomial		90.0[a]	−1.15[a]	.008[a]		.71	9.2[a]
Log-linear		84.9[a]			−7.1[b]	.45	4.8[b]
Trinidad and Tobago	14						
Linear		96.1[a]	−.00			.03	.0
Polynomial		−68.5	.07	−.00		.13	.1
Log-linear		111.3			−2.1	.02	.0
Tunisia	21						
Linear		66.8[a]	.01[a]			.61	11.1[a]
Polynomial		60.3[a]	.05[a]	−.00[a]		.88	30.5[a]
Log-linear		56.3[a]			2.2[a]	.69	17.2[a]

(continues)

Appendix D *(continued)*

Country	N	Constant	ECO	ECO^2	lnECO	R	F-Ratio
Turkey	33						
Linear		82.0[a]	.01			.17	.9
Polynomial		51.8[a]	.16[c]	−.00[c]		.35	2.1
Log-linear		49.1			6.3	.21	1.5
Uganda	14						
Linear		58.8[a]	.01			.01	.0
Polynomial		59.1	−.009	.00		.01	.0
Log-linear		59.1			−.01	.00	.0
USSR	33						
Linear		55.2[a]	.00[b]			.39	5.4[b]
Polynomial		59.6[a]	−.002[c]	.00[b]		.51	5.2[b]
Log-linear		45.7[a]			1.4[c]	.33	3.7[c]
United Kingdom	33						
Linear		108.2[a]	−.002			.26	2.2
Polynomial		−10.5	.05	−.00		.35	2.1
Log-linear		187.8[a]			−10.7	.25	2.0
United States	33						
Linear		91.5[a]	.00			.23	1.8
Polynomial		96.7[b]	−.00	.00		.23	.9
Log-linear		41.0			6.2	.23	1.8
Upper Volta	21						
Linear		56.9[a]	.25			.14	.4
Polynomial		53.5[b]	.70	−.01		.15	.2
Log-linear		49.0[b]			4.5	.15	.4
Uruguay	30						
Linear		135.1[a]	−.05[b]			.41	5.6[b]
Polynomial		−154.4	.69[b]	−.00[a]		.60	7.7[a]
Log-linear		348.3[a]			−38.5[b]	.37	4.5[b]
Venezuela	33						
Linear		26.5[a]	.02[a]			.83	70.1[a]
Polynomial		−4.1	.05[a]	−.00[c]		.85	40.5[a]
Log-linear		−254.0[a]			43.0[a]	.85	83.9[a]

(continues)

Appendix D *(continued)*

Country	N	Constant	ECO	ECO^2	lnECO	R	F-Ratio
Vietnam, PR	8						
Linear		65.1[a]	−.01			.39	1.1
Polynomial		67.7[a]	−.06	.00		.44	.6
Log-linear		69.5[a]			−1.2	.41	1.2
Vietnam, S	8						
Linear		66.8[a]	−.10			.49	1.9
Polynomial		83.0[b]	−.42	−.00		.55	1.1
Log-linear		117.8[b]			−13.8	.55	2.5
Vietnam	5						
Linear		66.1	−.03			.30	.3
Polynomial		78.6	−.21	.00		.31	.1
Log-linear		79.8[c]			−3.5	.30	.3
Western Samoa	14						
Linear		65.4[a]	.09[a]			.73	13.5[a]
Polynomial		102.5[a]	−.38[c]	.001[b]		.83	11.9[a]
Log-linear		6.5			14.7[a]	.69	10.6[a]
Yemen, AR	33						
Linear		44.2[a]	.22[a]			.75	39.7[a]
Polynomial		41.2[a]	.75[a]	−.008[a]		.90	65.7[a]
Log-linear		35.8[a]			5.4[a]	.86	69.5[a]
Yemen, PDR	10						
Linear		51.5[a]	.005			.06	.0
Polynomial		49.8	.01	−.00		.06	.0
Log-linear		41.2			2.1	.07	.0
Yugoslavia	33						
Linear		60.8[a]	.01[a]			.68	25.9[a]
Polynomial		49.0[a]	.03[a]	−.00[a]		.82	30.4[a]
Log-linear		11.6			8.4[a]	.78	48.4[a]
Zaire	21						
Linear		80.3[a]	−.26			.17	.6
Polynomial		321.4	−6.86	.04		.25	.6
Log-linear		145.4			−19.5	.18	.6

(continues)

Appendixes 189

Appendix D *(continued)*

Country	N	Constant	ECO	ECO^2	lnECO	R	F-Ratio
Zambia	14						
Linear		55.1[a]	.03			.29	1.1
Polynomial		−156.3	.87	−.00		.41	1.1
Log-linear		−28.1			15.9	.30	1.2
Zimbabwe	14						
Linear		67.1[a]	.004			.04	.0
Polynomial		17.5	.17	−.00		.09	.0
Log-linear		49.3			3.2	.04	.0

Appendix E Gini Coefficient

The Gini coefficient is a common measure for the concentration of income. It is calculated by using information on the frequency distribution of income-recipient units ranked according to the size of their personal income. It is based on a Lorenz curve, which is built with pairs of cumulative percentages measuring units of income and units of recipients. A Lorenz curve can be obtained by plotting the cumulative percentages of households (or other income-recipient units), arrayed in order from smallest incomes to the largest, along the horizontal axis, and cumulative percentages of income along the vertical axis (Figure E.1). With perfect equality of incomes, the Lorenz curve would coincide with the diagonal (or 45° line); here the lowest 20 percent of total households receives 20 percent of total income, 40 percent of total households receives 40 percent of total income, and so on. The closer the curve is to the 45° line, the greater the equality of income distribution. In Figure E.1, Country A has a more egalitarian income distribution than Country B.

The Gini coefficient is the ratio of the area between the Lorenz curve and the 45° line. It is calculated through estimating the area between the Lorenz curve and the 45° line. In the case of perfect equality, the Lorenz curve would coincide with the 45° line, and the

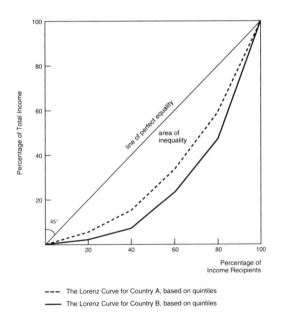

--- The Lorenz Curve for Country A, based on quintiles
— The Lorenz Curve for Country B, based on quintiles

Figure E.1   The Lorenz Curve

value of the Gini coefficient would be 0. In the case of perfect inequality, the coefficient would be unity. Thus, the Gini coefficient ranges from 0 to 1 (or from 0 to 100 in percentage measures); the higher the value, the higher the level of inequality.

As an estimate of income inequality, the Gini coefficient is not free from problems. Generally based on pretax income distribution, this measure oversees the impact of tax policies or other redistributive policies. Moreover, because it is an estimate of the area under the Lorenz curve, the Gini coefficient does not make any distinction between different income distributions that may be represented by different Lorenz curves but yield the same total area. Finally, it is insensitive to marginal utilities.

A formula for the Gini coefficient is provided by James Morgan ("The Anatomy of Income Distribution," *Review of Economics and Statistics* 44:3 (August 1962), pp. 270–283):

$$\text{Gini} \quad = \quad \frac{\text{area between the curve and the diagonal}}{\text{area under the diagonal}}$$

$$= \quad \frac{.5 - \text{area under the curve}}{\text{area under the diagonal}}$$

$$= 1 - (\text{area under the curve} \times 2)$$
$$= 1 - \Sigma[(B - A) \times ((C + D) / 2)] \times 2$$
$$= 1 - \Sigma(B - A) \times (C + D)$$

As illustrated by Figure E.2, A and B refer to the cumulative percentages of income-recipient units, and C and D are the percentages of income received by those recipient groups.

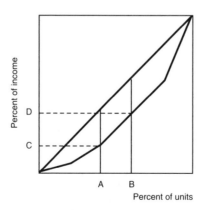

Figure E.2   Illustration for the Gini Coefficient Formula

Bibliography

Abinales, P.N. "Militarization in the Philippines." *The Rise and Fall of Democracies in Third World Societies*. Studies in Third World Societies, No. 27. Williamsburg, Virginia: Department of Anthropology, College of William and Mary, 1986:129–174.

Adelman, Irma, and Cynthia Taft Morris. "A Conceptualization and Analysis of Political Participation in Underdeveloped Countries." Part 2 of the Final Report to the Agency for International Development, February 12, 1971.

Adreski, Stanislav. *Parasitism and Subversion: The Case of Latin America*. New York: Schocken, 1969.

Agbese, Pita Ogaba. "The Impending Demise of Nigeria's Forthcoming Third Republic." *Africa Today* 37,3 (1990, 3d quarter):23–44.

Ahluwalia, Montek S. "Inequality, Poverty and Development." *Journal of Development Economics* 3 (1976):307–342.

Ahmad, Feroz. *The Turkish Experiment in Democracy: 1950–1975*. Boulder, Colorado: Westview Press, 1987.

Ake, Claude. "Modernization and Political Instability: A Theoretical Explanation," in Ikuo Kabashima and Lynn T. White III, eds., *Political System and Change*. Princeton: Princeton University Press, 1986:205–220.

Almond, Gabriel A., and J.S. Coleman, eds. *The Politics of Developing Areas*. Princeton, Princeton University Press, 1960.

Almond, Gabriel, A., and Sidney Verba. *The Civic Culture*. Boston: Little, Brown & Co., 1963.

————, eds. *The Civic Culture Revisited*. Boston: Little, Brown & Co., 1980.

Amin, Samir. *Unequal Development: An Essay on the Social Formations of Peripheral Capitalism*. New York: Monthly Review Press, 1976.

————. *Accumulation on a World Scale: A Critique of the Theory of Underdevelopment*. New York: Monthly Review Press, 1974.

Anderson, Charles W. "Honduras: Problems of an Apprentice Democracy," in Martin C. Needler, ed., *Political Systems of Latin America*. 2nd ed. Princeton: Van Nostrand, 1970:75–88.

Anderson, Leslie. "Alternative Action in Costa Rica: Peasants as Positive Participants." *Journal of Latin American Studies* 22,1 (February 1990):89–114.

Anderson, Martin E. "The Military Obstacle to Latin American Democracy." *Foreign Policy* 73 (Winter 1988–1989):94–113.

Apter, David E. "Machiavelli's Question: Thoughts on Positive and Negative Pluralism," in Ian Shapiro and Grant Reeher, eds., *Power, Inequality and Democratic Politics: Essays in Honor of Robert Dahl*. Boulder, Colorado: Westview Press, 1988:203–218.

Arat, Zehra F. "Democracy and Economic Development: Modernization Theory Revisited." *Comparative Politics* (October 1988): 21–36.

————. "Business Interests and Authoritarianism in Developing Countries: The Case of Turkey." Paper presented at the Annual Meeting of the American Political Science Association, Atlanta, August 31–September 3, 1989.

————. "The Viability of Political Democracy in Developing Countries."

of Turkey." Paper presented at the Annual Meeting of the American Political Science Association, Atlanta, August 31–September 3, 1989.

———. "The Viability of Political Democracy in Developing Countries." Unpublished Ph.D. thesis. Binghamton: State University of New York at Binghamton, 1984.

Arendt, Hannah. *The Origins of Totalitarianism.* 3d ed. New York: Harcourt, Brace and World, 1966.

Ayoade, John A.A. "The African Search for Democracy: Hopes and Reality," in Dov Ronen, ed., *Democracy and Pluralism in Africa.* Boulder, Colorado: Lynne Rienner Publishers, 1986:19–34.

Bachrach, Peter. *The Theory of Democratic Elitism: A Critique.* Boston: Little, Brown Co., 1967.

———, ed. *Political Elites in a Democracy.* New York: Atherton Press, 1971.

Baker, Pauline H. "Reflections on the Economic Correlates of African Democracy," in Dov Ronen, ed., *Democracy and Pluralism in Africa.* Boulder, Colorado: Lynne Rienner Publishers, 1986:53–60.

Banks, Arthur S. "An Index of Socio-Economic Development 1869–1975." *Journal of Politics* 43 (1981):390–411.

———. *Cross-National Time-Series Data Archive.* Binghamton: Center for Social Analysis (CSA), State University of New York at Binghamton, 1979.

———. "Correlation of Democratic Performance." *Comparative Politics* 4 (January 1972): 217–231

———. *Political Handbook of the World.* Binghamton: CSA Publications, State University of New York.

Baran, Paul. *The Political Economy of Growth.* New York: Monthly Review Press, 1957.

Barber, Willard F., and C. Neale Ronning. *International Security and Military Power: Counter-Insurgency and Civic Action in Latin America.* Columbus: Ohio State University Press, 1966.

Bardhan, Pranab. "Dominant Proprietary Classes and India's Democracy," in Atul Kohli, ed., *India's Democracy: An Analysis of Changing State-Society Relations.* Princeton: Princeton University Press, 1988:214–224.

Baumann, Fred E., ed. *Human Rights and American Foreign Policy.* Gambier, Ohio: Public Affairs Conference Center, Kenyon College, 1982.

Bendix, Reinhard. *Nation-Building and Citizenship: Studies of Our Changing Social Order.* New York: John Wiley and Sons, 1964.

Bergmann, Frithjof. "Two Critiques of the Traditional Theory of Human Rights," in J.R. Pennock and J.W. Chapman, eds., *Human Rights.* New York: New York University Press, 1981: 52–57.

Bianchi, Robert. *Interest Groups and Political Development in Turkey.* Princeton: Princeton University Press, 1984.

Binder, Leonard. "The Natural History of Development Theory." *Comparative Studies in Society and History* 28,1 (January 1986):3–33.

Binder, Leonard, James S. Coleman, Joeseph LaPalombara, Lucian Pye, Sidney Verba, and Myron Weiner, eds. *Crises and Sequences in Political Development.* Princeton: Princeton University Press, 1971.

Black, George. *The Good Neighbor.* New York: Pantheon Books, 1988.

Blaustein, Albert, ed. *Constitutions of the Countries of the World.* Dobbs Ferry, New York: Oceana Publications.

Bollen, Kenneth. "World System Position, Dependency and Democracy: The Cross-National Evidence." *American Sociological Review* 48,4 (August 1983):468–479.

———. "Issues in the Comparative Measurement of Political Democracy." *American*

Sociology Review 45 (June 1980):370–390.

———. "Political Democracy and the Timing of Development." *American Sociological Review* 44 (August 1979):572–587.

Boorstein, Edward. *Allende's Chile*. New York: International Publishers, 1977.

Booth, John A., and Mitchell A. Seligson, eds. *Elections and Democracy in Central America*. Chapel Hill: University of North Carolina Press, 1989.

Boratav, Korkut. *100 Soruda Türkiye'de Devletçilik* [Statism in Turkey in 100 questions]. Istanbul, Turkey: Gerçek Yayínlarí, 1974.

Boswell, Terry, and William J. Dixon. "Dependency and Rebellion: A Cross-National Analysis." *American Sociological Review* 55,4 (August 1990):540–559.

Bratton, Michael. "Beyond the State: Civil Society and Associational Life in Africa." *World Politics* 41,3 (April 1989):407–430.

Brinton, Crane. *The Anatomy of Revolution*. New York: Vintage Press, 1965.

Brockett, Charles D. *Land, Power, and Poverty: Agrarian Transformation and Political Conflict in Central America*. Boston: Unwin Hyman, 1988.

Bryce, James. *Modern Democracy*. Vol. 1. New York: John Day Co., 1921.

Burnham, James. *The Machiavellians: Defenders of Freedom*. New York: John Day Co., 1943.

Buultjens, Ralph. *The Decline of Democracy: Essays on an Endangered Political Species*. Maryknoll, New York: Orbis Books, 1978.

Cameron, David R. "Politics, Public Policy, and Distributional Inequality: A Comparative Analysis," in Ian Shapiro and Grant Reeher, eds., *Power, Inequality and Democratic Politics: Essays in Honor of Robert Dahl*. Boulder, Colorado: Westview Press, 1988:219–259.

Campbell, Angus, Philip E. Converse, Warren E. Miller, and Donald E. Stokes. *The American Voter*. New York: John Wiley & Sons, 1960.

Cardoso, Fernando H. "The Consumption of Dependency Theory in the U.S." *Latin American Research Review* 12,3 (1977):7–24.

———. "The Industrial Elite," in Seymour Lipset and Also Solari, eds., *Elites in Latin America*. New York: Oxford University Press, 1967:94–114.

Carr, Edward H. *The New Society*. Boston: Beacon Press, 1956.

Chaffee, Wilber A. "Political Economy of Revolution and Democracy: Toward a Theory of Latin American Politics." *American Journal of Economics and Sociology* 43,4 (October 1984):385–398.

Charvet, John. "A Critique of Human Rights," in J.R. Pennock and J.W. Chapman, eds., *Human Rights*. New York: New York University Press, 1981:31–51.

Chase–Dunn, Christopher. "The Effects of International Economic Dependence on Development and Inequality." *American Sociological Review* 40 (December 1975):720–739.

Chenery, Hollis, ed. *Redistribution with Growth*. London: Oxford University Press, 1974.

Chilcote, Ronald. "Toward the Democratic Opening in Latin America: The Case of Brazil." *Monthly Review* 35,9 (February 1984):15–24.

Chiro, Daniel. *Social Change in the Twentieth Century*. New York: Harcourt, Brace, and Jovanovich, 1977.

Chomsky, Noam, and Ed Herman. *The Pentagon-CIA Archipelago: The Washington Connection and Third World Fascism*. Boston: South End Press, 1978.

Cipolla, C.M., ed. *Industrial Revolution 1700–1914*. Bringhton: Harvester, 1976.

Cnudde, C.F., and D.E. Neubauer, eds. *Empirical Democratic Theory*. Chicago: Markham Publishing Co., 1969.

———. "New Trends in Democratic Theory," in C.F. Cnudde and D.E. Neubauer, eds., *Empirical Democratic Theory*. Chicago: Markham Publishing Co., 1969:511–534.

Cohen, Stephen P. "The Military and Indian Democracy," in Atul Kohli, ed., *India's Democracy: An Analysis of Changing State-Society Relations*. Princeton: Princeton University Press, 1988:99–143.

Coleman, James S., ed. *Education and Political Development*. Princeton: Princeton University Press, 1968.

———. "Conclusion: The Political Systems of the Developing Area," in G.A. Almond and J.S. Coleman, eds., *The Politics of Developing Areas*. Princeton: Princeton University Press, 1960:532–581.

Collier, David, ed. *The New Authoritarianism in Latin America*. Princeton: Princeton University Press, 1979:331–359.

———. "Timing of Economic Growth and Regime Characteristics in Latin America." *Comparative Politics* 7,3 (April 1975).

Coone, Tim. "The Declining Banana Industry," in Marc Edelman and Joanne Kenen, eds., *The Costa Rica Reader*. New York: Grove Weidenfeld, 1989:209–212.

Cornelius, Wayne A., Jr. "Urbanization as an Agent in Latin American Political Instability: The Case of Mexico." *American Political Science Review* 63,3 (September 1969):833–857.

The Cost of Social Security. Triennial reports by the International Labor Organization. Geneva: International Labor Organization.

Coulter, Philip. *Social Mobilization and Liberal Democracy*. Lexington Massachusetts: Lexington Books, 1975.

Cranston, Maurice. "Human Rights, Real and Supposed," in D.D. Raphael, ed., *Political Theory and the Rights of Man*. Bloomington: Indiana University Press, 1967:43–53.

———."Human Rights: A Reply to Professor Raphael," in D.D. Raphael, ed., pp. 95–100.

Cutright, Phillips. "National Political Development: Its Measures and Analysis." *American Sociological Review* 28 (April 1963):253–264.

Cutright, Phillips, and James A. Wiley. "Modernization and Political Representation, 1927–1966." *Studies in Comparative International Development* 5 (1969):23–41.

Dahl, Robert A. *Democracy and Its Critics*. New Haven: Yale University Press, 1989.

———. *Polyarchy, Participation, and Opposition*. New Haven: Yale University Press, 1971.

———. *A Preface to Democratic Theory*. Chicago: University of Chicago Press, 1956.

Das Gupta, Jyotirindra. "India: Democratic Becoming and Combined Development," in Larry Diamond, Juan Linz, and Seymour Martin Lipset, eds., *Democracy in Developing Countries*. Vol. 3. Boulder, Colorado: Lynne Rienner Publishers, 1989:53–104.

———. "Ethnicity, Democracy and Development in India: Assam in a General Perspective," in Atul Kohli, ed., *India's Democracy: An Analysis of Changing State-Society Relations*. Princeton: Princeton University Press, 1988:144–168.

Delacroix, Jacques, and Charles C. Ragin. "Structural Blockage: A Cross-National Study of Economic Dependency, State Efficiency and Underdevelopment." *American Journal of Sociology* 86,6 (May 1981):1311–1347.

Derviş, Kemal, and Sherman Robinson. "The Structure of Income Inequality in Turkey: 1950–1973," in Ergun Özbudun and Aydín Ulusan, eds., *The Political Economy of Income Distribution in Turkey*. New York: Holmes and Meier, 1980:83–121.

Deutsch, Karl W. "Social Mobilization and Political Development." *American Political Science Review* 55 (September 1961): 493–514.

———. *Nationalism and Social Communication: An Inquiry into the Foundations of Nationality*. 2d ed. Cambridge: MIT Press, 1966.

Diamond, Larry, Juan J. Linz, and Seymour Martin Lipset, eds. *Democracy in Developing Countries*. Vols. 2–4. Boulder, Colorado: Lynne Rienner Publishers, 1989.

————, eds. *Politics in Developing Countries: Comparing Experience with Democracy*. Boulder, Colorado: Lynne Rienner Publishers, 1990.

Dodd, C.H. *The Crisis of Turkish Democracy*. Walkington, England: Eothen Press, 1983.

Dominguez, Jorge I., Nigel S. Rodley, Bryce Wood, and Richard Falk. *Enhancing Global Human Rights*. New York: McGraw-Hill, 1979.

Doner, P., ed. *Land Reform in Latin America: Issues and Cases*. Madison: University of Wisconsin Press, Land Economics Monographs 3, 1971.

Donnelly, Jack. "Human Rights and Development: Complementary or Competing Concerns?" in George W. Shepherd, Jr., and Ved P. Nanda, eds., *Human Rights and Third World Development*. Westport, Connecticut: Greenwood Press, 1985:27–55.

Downie, R.S. "Social Equality," in A.S. Rosenbaum, ed., *The Philosophy of Human Rights: International Perspectives*. Westport, Connecticut: Greenwood Press, 1980:127–176.

Downs, Anthony. *An Economic Theory of Democracy*. New York: Harper and Row, 1957.

Duvall, Raymond, and Michal Shamirs. "Indicators from Errors: Cross-National, Time Series Measures of the Repressive Disposition of Governments," in Charles L. Taylor, ed., *Indicator Systems for Political, Economic and Social Analysis*. Cambridge, Massachusetts: Oelgeshlanger, Gunn, and Hain Publishers, 1980:105–182.

Duverger, Maurice. *Political Parties*. New York: John Wiley & Sons, 1954.

Ebel, Ronald H. "Governing the City-State: Notes on the Politics of the Small Latin American Countries." *Journal of Inter-American Studies and World Affairs* 14 (August 1972):325–346.

Eckstein, Harry. *A Theory of Stable Democracy*. Princeton: Princeton University Center for International Studies, 1961.

Edelman, Marc, and Joanne Kenen, eds. *The Costa Rica Reader*. New York: Grove Weidenfeld, 1989.

Ergüder, Üstün. "Politics of Agricultural Price Policy in Turkey," in Ergun Özbudun and Aydín Ulusan, eds., *The Political Economy of Income Distribution in Turkey*. New York: Holmes and Meier, 1980:169–196.

Etomba, Juan Manuel Villasuso. "The Impact of the Economic Crisis on Income Distribution," in Marc Edelman and Joanne Kenen, eds., *The Costa Rica Reader*. New York: Grove Weidenfeld, 1989:197–204.

The Europa World Year Book. London: Europa Publications.

Evans, Peter, and Michael Timberlake. "Dependence, Inequality and the Growth of the Tertiary: A Comparative Analysis of Less Developed Countries." *American Sociological Review* 54,4 (August 1980):531–552.

Eveland, Wilbur Crane. *Ropes of Sand: America's Failure in the Middle East*. New York: W.W. Norton, 1980.

Falk, Richard. "Responding to Severe Violations," in Jorge I. Dominguez, Nigel S. Rodley, Bryce Wood, and Richard Falk, *Enhancing Global Human Rights*. New York: McGraw-Hill, 1979:206–257.

————. "Theoretical Foundations of Human Rights," in Paula R. Newberg, ed. *The Politics of Human Rights*. New York: New York University Press, 1980:65–109.

Farer, Tom J. *Toward a Humanitarian Diplomacy*. New York: New York University Press, 1980.

Fatton, Robert, Jr. "Bringing the Ruling Class Back In: Class, State, and Hegemony in

Africa." *Comparative Politics* 20 (April 1988):253–264.

———. "Liberal Democracy in Africa." *Political Science Quarterly* 105,3 (Fall 1990):455–473.

Feierabend, Ivo, Rosalind L. Feierabend, and Betty Nesvold. "Social Change and Political Violence: Cross-National Patterns," in H.D. Graham and T.R. Gurr, eds., *Violence in America: A Staff Report*. Washington, D.C.: U.S. Government Printing Office, 1969:497–535.

Field, John O. *Consolidating Democracy: Politicization and Partnership in India.* New Delhi: Manohar, 1980.

Finely, M.I. *Politics in the Ancient World.* Cambridge: Cambridge University Press, 1983.

———. *The Ancient Greeks.* Harmondsworth: Penguin Books, 1963.

Finkle, Jason L., and Robert W. Gable, eds. *Political Development and Social Change.* 2d ed. New York: John Wiley & Sons, 1971.

Frank, Andre Gunder. *Latin America: Underdevelopment or Revolution.* New York: Monthly Review Press, 1969.

Frankel, Francine R. "Middle Classes and Castes in India's Politics: Prospects for Political Accommodation," in Atul Kohli, ed., *India's Democracy: An Analysis of Changing State-Society Relations.* Princeton: Princeton University Press, 1988:225–263.

———. *India's Political Economy, 1947–1977: The Gradual Revolution.* Princeton: Princeton University Press, 1978.

———. *India's Green Revolution: Economic Gains and Political Costs.* Princeton: Princeton University Press, 1971.

Furtado, Celso. "The Brazilian 'Model' of Development," in Charles K. Wilber, ed., *The Political Economy of Development and Underdevelopment.* New York: Random House, 1973:297–306.

Galtung, Johan. "Structural Theory of Imperialism." *Journal of Peace Research* 8,2 (1971):81–117.

Garwood, Darrell. *Under Cover: Thirty-Five Years of CIA Deception.* New York: Grove Press, 1985.

Glassman, Ronald M. *Democracy and Equality: Theories and Programs for the Modern World.* New York: Praeger, 1989.

Gorvin, Ian, ed. *Elections Since 1945.* Chicago: St. James Press, 1989.

Graham, H.D., and T.R. Gurr, eds. *Violence in America: A Staff Report.* Washington, D.C.: U.S. Government Printing Office, 1969.

———, eds. *The History of Violence in America: Historical and Comparative Perspectives.* New York: Praeger, 1969.

Gude, Edward W. "Batista and Betancourt: Alternative Responses to Violence," in H.D. Graham and T.R. Gurr, eds., *Violence in America: A Staff Report.* Washington, D.C.: U.S. Government Printing Office, 1969:731–748.

Gurr, Ted R. "A Comparative Study of Civil Strife," in H.D. Graham and T.R. Gurr, eds., *Violence in America: A Staff Report.* Washington, D.C.: U.S. Government Printing Office, 1969:572–687.

Hale, William. *The Political and Economic Development of Modern Turkey.* London: Croom Helm, 1981.

Harrison, Paul. "Success Story." *World Health* (February–March 1981):14–19.

Heard, Kenneth. *General Elections in South Africa.* London: Oxford University Press, 1974.

Hearn, Frank. "The Rationalization of Democracy: Liberal, Elitist and Corporatist Conceptions of Democracy." *New Political Science* 14 (Winter 1985–1986):95–114.

Held, David. *Models of Democracy.* Stanford, California: Stanford University Press,

1987.
Heper, Metin, and Ahmet Evin, eds. *State, Democracy and the Military: Turkey in the 1980s.* Berlin: Walter de Gruyter & Co., 1988.
Hibbs, Douglas A. *Mass Political Violence: A Cross-National Analysis.* New York: John Wiley & Sons, 1973.
Hicks, Norman. "Growth vs. Basic Needs: Is There a Trade-Off?" *World Development* 7 (1979):985–994.
Hofferbert, Richard I. "The Impact of Policy Choice on Democratic Development in Poorer Countries." Paper delivered at the 24th World Congress of the International Political Science Association, Washington, D.C., August 28–September 1, 1988.
Hofferbert, Richard I., and Üstün, Ergüder. "The Penetrability of Policy Systems in a Developing Context." Paper prepared for delivery to the workshop on "Society and Political Economy of the Welfare State," European Consortium for Political Research, Aarhus, Denmark, March 29–April 3, 1982.
Hoselitz, Bert F. "Investment in Education and Its Political Impact," in James S. Coleman, ed., *Education and Political Development.* Princeton: Princeton University Press, 1968:541–565.
Huntington, Samuel P. *The Soldier and the State: The Theory and Politics of Civilian-Military Relations.* Cambridge: The Belknap Press of Harvard University Press, 1985.
————."Will More Countries Become Democratic?" *Political Science Quarterly* 99,2 (Summer 1984):193–218.
————. *Political Order in Changing Societies.* New Haven: Yale University Press, 1968.
Huntington, Samuel P., and Joan M. Nelson. *No Easy Choice: Political Participation in Developing Countries.* Cambridge: Harvard University Press, 1976.
Huntington, Samuel P., and Jorge Dominguez. "Political Development," in Fred I. Greenstein and Nelson W. Polsby, eds., *Handbook of Political Science.* Vol. 3. Reading, Massachusetts: Addison-Wesley, 1975:1–114.
Hyter, Teresa. *Aid as Imperialism.* Baltimore: Penguin Books, 1971.
Immerman, R.H. *The Foreign Policy of Intervention: The CIA in Guatemala.* Austin: University of Texas Press, 1983.
The International Studies of Values in Politics. *Values and the Active Community: A Cross-National Study of the Influence on Local Leadership.* New York: Free Press, 1971.
Jackman, Robert W. "The Predictability of Coups D'état: A Model with African Data." *American Political Science Review* 72,4 (December 1978):1262–1275.
————. "On the Relation of Economic Development to Democratic Performance." *American Journal of Sociology* 17,3 (August 1973):611–621.
Jackson, Steven, Bruce Russett, Duncan Snidal, and David Sylvan. "Conflict and Coercion in Dependent States." *Journal of Conflict Resolution* 22,24 (December 1978):627–657.
Johnson, Thomas H., Robert O. Slater, and Pat McGowan. "Explaining African Military Coups d'État, 1960–1982." *American Political Science Review* 78,3 (September 1984):622–640.
Kabashima, Ikuo, and Lynn T. White III, eds. *Political System and Change.* Princeton: Princeton University Press, 1986.
Karl, Terry Lynn. "Dilemmas of Democratization in Latin America." *Comparative Politics* 23,1 (October 1990):1–22.
Kaufman, Robert R., Harry I. Chernotsky, and Daniel S. Geller. "A Preliminary Test of the Theory of Dependency." *Comparative Politics* 7,3 (April 1975):303–330.
Kavanagh, Dennis A. "Western Europe," in Robert Wesson, ed., *Democracy: A*

World Survey. New York: Praeger, 1987:11–27.

Keyder, Çağlar. *State and Class in Turkey: A Study in Capitalist Development.* London: Verso, 1987.

———."The Political Economy of Turkish Democracy," in Irvin Cemil Schick and Ertuğrul Ahmet Tonak, eds., *Turkey in Transition.* New York: Oxford University Press, 1987:27–65.

Kincaid, A. Douglas. "Costa Rican Peasants and the Politics of Quiescence," in Marc Edelman and Joanne Kenen, eds., *The Costa Rica Reader.* New York: Grove Weidenfeld, 1989:178–186.

King, Russell. *Land Reform: A World Survey.* Boulder, Colorado: Westview Press, 1977.

Klarén, Peter F., and Thomas J. Bossert, eds. *Promise of Development: Theories of Change in Latin America.* Boulder, Colorado: Westview Press, 1986.

Kohli, Atul, ed. *India's Democracy: An Analysis of Changing State-Society Relations.* Princeton: Princeton University Press, 1988.

———. "Interpreting India's Democracy: A State-Society Framework," in Atul Kohli, ed., *India's Democracy: An Analysis of Changing State-Society Relations.* Princeton: Princeton University Press, 1988:3–17.

———. *The State and Poverty in India: The Politics of Reform.* New York: Cambridge University Press, 1987.

Kravis, Irving B. "International Differences in the Distribution of Income." *Review of Economics and Statistics* (November 1960):408–416.

Krippendorff, Klaus. *Content Analysis: An Introduction to Its Methodology.* The Sage CommText Series, Vol. 5. Beverly Hills, California: Sage Publications, 1980.

Kuznets, Simon. "Economic Growth and Income Inequality." *American Economic Review* 45 (1955):1–28.

LaPalombara, Joseph. *Democracy Italian Style.* New Haven: Yale University Press, 1987.

Laski, Harold J. "Democracy." *The Encyclopedia of the Social Sciences.* Vol. 3. New York: Macmillan, 1937:76–84.

Lauterbach, Albert. "Government and Development: Managerial Attitudes in Latin America." *Journal of Inter-American Studies* 7 (1965):201–225.

———. "Managerial Attitudes and Economic Growth." *Kyklos* 15:2 (1962):374–398.

Leichter, Howard. "Comparative Public Policy: Problems and Prospects." *Policy Studies Journal,* Special Issue (1977):583–596.

Lenski, Gerhard. *Power and Privilege.* New York: McGraw-Hill, 1966.

Lerner, Daniel. *The Passing of Traditional Society.* New York: Free Press, 1958.

Library of Congress. Area Handbook Series. (Washington, D.C.: Foreign Area Studies, The American University).

Lijphart, Arend. *Democracies: Patterns of Majoritarian and Consensus Government in Twenty-One Countries.* New Haven: Yale University Press, 1984.

Lineberry, Robert L. *Government in America: People, Politics and Policy.* Boston: Little, Brown & Co., 1980.

Linz, Juan J. "Crisis, Breakdown and Reequilibration," in Linz and Stephan, eds. *The Breakdown of Democratic Regimes.* Baltimore:Johns Hopkins University Press, 1978:1–124.

Linz, Juan J., and Alfred Stepan, eds. *The Breakdown of Democratic Regimes.* Baltimore: Johns Hopkins University Press, 1978.

Lipset, Seymour Martin. *Political Man: The Social Bases of Politics.* Expanded and updated ed. Baltimore: Johns Hopkins University Press, 1981.

———. "Values, Education, and Entrepreneurship," in Seymour Martin Lipset and Also Solari, eds., *Elites in Latin America.* New York: Oxford University Press, 1967:3–60.

————. *Political Man: The Social Bases of Politics*. Garden City, New York: Doubleday & Co., 1960.

————. "Some Social Requisites of Democracy: Economic Development and Political Legitimacy." *American Political Science Review* 53 (March 1959):69–105.

Lipset, Seymour Martin, and S. Rokkan, eds. *Party Systems and Voter Alignments*. New York: Free Press, 1967.

Lipset, Semour Martin, and Also Solari, eds. *Elites in Latin America*. New York: Oxford University Press, 1967.

Lopez, George A., and Michael Stohl. *Dependence, Development and State Repression*. New York: Greenwood Press, 1989.

Low, Setha M. *Culture, Politics and Medicine in Costa Rica: An Anthropological Study of Medical Change*. Bedford Hills, New York: Redgrave Publishing, 1985.

Lowenthal, Abraham F., and Samuel J. Fitch, eds. *Armies and Politics in Latin America*. Rev. ed. New York: Holmes and Meier, 1986.

Lubeck, Paul M., ed. *The African Bourgeoisie: Capitalist Development in Nigeria, Kenya, and the Ivory Coast*. Boulder, Colorado: Lynne Rienner Publishers, 1987.

Lyon, Peter, and James Manor, eds. *Transfer and Transformation: Political Institutions in the New Commonwealth*. Leicester: Leicester University Press, 1983.

MacIver, Robert M. *The Web of Government*. New York: Macmillan, 1947.

Mackie, Thomas. *The International Almanac of Electoral History*. London: Macmillan, 1974.

MacMillan, Michael C. "Social Versus Political Rights." *Canadian Journal of Political Science* 19,2 (June 1986):283–304.

MacPhearson, C.B. *The Real World of Democracy*. New York: Oxford University Press, 1966.

Magnarella, Paul J. "Turkey's Experience with Political Democracy." *The Rise and Fall of Democracies in Third World Societies*. Studies in Third World Societies No:27. Williamsburg, Virginia: Department of Anthropology, College of William and Mary, 1986:43–60.

Maheshwari, Shriram. *Rural Development in India: A Public Policy Approach*. New Delhi: Sage Publications, 1985.

Malloy, James M., and Mitchell A. Seligson, eds. *Authoritarians and Democrats: Regime Transition in Latin America*. Pittsburgh: University of Pittsburgh Press, 1987.

Manor, James. "Parties and Party Systems," in Atul Kohli, ed., *India's Democracy: An Analysis of Changing State-Society Relations*. Princeton: Princeton University Press, 1988:62–98.

Marshall, T.H. *Class, Citizenship and Social Development*. Garden City, New York: Doubleday & Co., 1964.

Mas, Jorge Rovira. "The Social Democrats and the 1948–1949 Junta," in Marc Edelman and Joanne Kenen, eds., *The Costa Rica Reader*. New York: Grove Weidenfeld, 1989:128–132.

Mayo, Bernard. "What Are Human Rights?" in D.D. Raphael, ed., *Political Theory and the Rights of Man*. Bloomington: Indiana University Press, 1967:68–80.

Mayo, Henry B. *An Introduction to Democratic Theory*. New York: Oxford University Press, 1960.

McDonald, Ronald. *Party Politics and Elections in Latin America*. Chicago: Markham Series, 1989.

————. *Party Systems and Elections in Latin America*. Chicago: Markham Series, 1971.

McIver, John P., and Edward G. Carmines. *Undimensional Scaling*. Beverly Hills,

California: Sage Publications, 1981.

McKeon, Richard, ed. *Democracy in a World of Tensions: A Symposium Prepared by UNESCO*. Chicago: University of Chicago Press, 1951.

Michels, Robert. *Political Parties*. New York: Collier Books, 1962.

Mills, C. Wright. *The Power Elite*. New York: Oxford University Press, 1959.

Moore, Barrington, Jr. *Injustice: The Social Bases of Obedience and Revolt*. White Plains, New York: M.E. Sharpe, 1978.

———. "Revolution in America?" *New York Review of Books* (January 30, 1969):6–12.

———. *Social Origins of Dictatorship and Democracy*. Boston: Beacon Press, 1967.

Mosca, Gaetano. *The Ruling Class*. New York: McGraw-Hill, 1939.

Morgan, James. "The Anatomy of Income Distribution," *Review of Economics and Statistics* 44,3 (August 1962): 270–283.

Morgan, Lynn M. "Health Effects of the Costa Rican Economic Crisis," in Marc Edelman and Joanne Kenen, eds., *The Costa Rica Reader*. New York: Grove Weidenfeld, 1989:213–218.

Muller, Edward N., and Mitchell A. Seligson. "Inequality and Insurgency." *American Political Science Review* 81,2 (June 1987):425–451.

Munro, William B. *The Governments of Europe*. New York: Macmillan, 1925.

Nafziger, Wayne E. *Inequality in Africa: Political Elites, Proletariat, Peasants and the Poor*. Cambridge: Cambridge University Press, 1988.

Nagel, Stuart. *Public Policy: Goals, Measures and Methods*. New York: St. Martin's Press, 1984.

Needler, Martin C. *The Problem of Democracy in Latin America*. Lexington, Massachusetts: Lexington Books, 1987.

———, ed. *Political Systems of Latin America*. 2d ed. Princeton: Van Nostrand, 1970.

Neubauer, Deane E. "Some Social Conditions of Democracy." *American Political Science Review* 61 (December 1967):1002–1009.

Newberg, Paula R., ed. *The Politics of Human Rights*. New York: New York University Press, 1980.

Niebuhr, Reinhold, and Paul E. Sigmund. *The Democratic Experience: Past and Prospects*. New York: Praeger, 1969.

Nordlinger, E.A. *Soldiers in Politics: Military Coups and Governments*. Englewood Cliffs, New Jersey: Prentice-Hall, 1977.

———. "Political Development, Time Sequence and Rates of Change," in Jason L. Finkle and Robert W. Gable, eds., *Political Development and Social Change*. 2d ed. New York: John Wiley & Sons, 1971:455–471.

Nyang'oro, Julius E. *The State and Capitalist Development in Africa: Declining Political Economies*. New York: Praeger, 1989.

O'Donnell, Guillermo A. *Modernization and Bureaucratic Authoritarianism: Studies in South American Politics*. 2d ed. Berkeley, California: Institute of International Studies, 1979.

O'Donnell, Guillermo A., Philippe C. Schmitter, and Laurence Whitehead, eds. *Transitions from Authoritarian Rule*. Baltimore: Johns Hopkins University Press, 1986.

Offe, Claus. "Competitive Party Democracy and the Keynesian Welfare State: Factors of Stability and Disorganization." *Policy Studies* 15 (1983): 225–246.

Ojha, P.D., and V.V. Bhatt. "Pattern of Income Distribution in India: 1953–55 to 1963–65." *Sankhya: The Indian Journal of Statistics* 36 (1974):163–166.

Okin, Susan M. "Liberty and Welfare: Some Issues in Human Rights Theory," in J.R. Pennoc and J.W. Chapman, eds., *Human Rights*. New York: New York University Pr

Morgan, Lynn M. "Health Effects of the Costa Rican Economic Crisis," in Marc

Ed*History* 23,4 (December 1963):529–553.

Omang, Joanne. "A Historical Background to the CIA's Nicaragua Manual," in *Psychological Operations in Guerrilla Warfare.* New York: Vintage Books, 1985:1–30.

Özbudun, Ergun, and Aydín Ulusan, eds. *The Political Economy of Income Distribution in Turkey.* New York: Holmes and Meier, 1980.

Palma, Diego. "The State and Social Co-optation in Costa Rica," in Marc Edelman and Joanne Kenen, eds., *The Costa Rica Reader.* New York: Grove Weidenfeld, 1989:132–137.

Parenti, Michael. *Democracy for the Few.* New York: St. Martin's Press, 1974.

Pareto, Vilfredo. *The Mind and Society.* Vol. I–IV. New York: Harcourt Brace, 1935.

Parvin, Manoucher, and Mükerrem Hiç. "Land Reform Versus Agricultural Reform: Turkish Miracle or Catastrophe Delayed?" *International Journal of Middle East Studies* 16 (1984):207–232.

Pateman, Carole. "The Civic Culture: A Philosophical Critique," in Gabriel Almond and Sidney Verba, eds., *The Civic Culture Revisited.* Boston: Little, Brown & Co., 1980:57–102.

Paukert, Felix. "Income Distribution at Different Levels of Development: A Survey of Evidence." *International Labour Review* 108 (July 1973):97–125.

Payer, Cheryl. *The Debt Trap: The International Monetary Fund and the Third World.* New York: Monthly Review Press, 1974.

Peaslee, Amos Jenkins. *Constitutions of Nations.* Netherlands: Martinus Nijoff, 1965–1970.

Peeler, John A. *Latin American Democracies: Colombia, Costa Rica, Venezuela.* Chapel Hill: University of North Carolina Press, 1985.

Peffer, Rodney. "A Defense of Rights to Well-Being." *Philosophy and Public Affairs* 8,1 (Fall 1978):63–87.

Pennock, J.R., and J.W. Chapman, eds. *Human Rights.* New York: New York University Press, 1981.

Pereira, Bresser. "The Rise of Middle Class and Middle Management in Brazil." *Journal of Inter-American Studies* 4 (1962):313–326.

Piven, Frances F., and Richard A. Cloward. *Poor People's Movements: Why They Succeed; How They Fail.* New York: Pantheon Books, 1977.

Polanyi, Karl. *The Great Transformation.* Introduction by R.M. MacIver. Boston: Beacon Press, 1967.

Portes, Alejandro. "On the Sociology of National Development: Theories and Issues." *American Journal of Sociology* 82,1 (July 1976):55–85.

Powell, Bingham G. *Contemporary Democracies: Participation, Stability, and Violence.* Cambridge: Harvard University Press, 1982.

Powers, Thomas. *The Man who Kept Secrets—Richard Helmes and the CIA.* New York: Knopf, 1979.

Prosterman, Roy L., and Jeffery M. Reidinger. *Land Reform and Democratic Development.* Baltimore: Johns Hopkins University Press, 1987.

Pye, Lucian W. *Aspects of Political Development.* Boston: Little, Brown & Co., 1966.

Rae, Douglas W. *The Political Consequences of Electoral Laws.* New Haven: Yale University Press, 1967.

Ranney, Austin. *The Doctrine of Responsible Party Government: Its Origins and Present State.* Urbana: University of Illinois Press, 1954.

Raphael, D.D., ed. *Political Theory and the Rights of Man.* Bloomington: Indiana University Press, 1967.

Roberts, Kenneth. "Democracy and the Dependent Capitalist State in Latin America." *Monthly Review* 37,5 (October 1985):12–26.

Robinson, Richard. "Authoritarian States, Capital-Owning Classes, and the Politics of

204 Democracy & Human Rights in Developing Countries

Newly Industrializing Countries: The Case of Indonesia." *World Politics* 41,1 (October 1988):52–74.

Ronen, Dov, ed. *Democracy and Pluralism in Africa.* Boulder, Colorado: Lynne Rienner Publishers, 1986.

———. "The State and Democracy in Africa," in Dov Ronen, ed., *Democracy and Pluralism in Africa.* Boulder, Colorado: Lynne Rienner Publishers, 1986:189–203.

Rose, Richard, ed. *The Dynamics of Public Policy: A Comparative Analysis.* London: Sage Publications, 1976.

Rose, Thomas, ed. *Violence in America.* New York: Random House, 1969.

———. "How Violence Occurs: A Theory and Review of the Literature," in Thomas Rose, ed., *Violence in America.* New York: Random House, 1969:26–53.

Rosenbaum, A.S., ed. *The Philosophy of Human Rights: International Perspectives.* Westport, Connecticut: Greenwood Press, 1980.

Rowles, James P. *Law and Agrarian Reform in Costa Rica.* Boulder, Colorado: Westview Press, 1985.

Rustow, Dankwart A. "Transition to Democracy: A Global Revolution?" *Foreign Affairs* 69,4 (Fall 1990):75–91.

———. "Transition to Democracy: Toward a Dynamic Model." *Comparative Politics* 2 (April 1970):337–363.

Safranko, Andrew J., Michael F. Nolan, and Robert C. Bealer. "Energy Use and Alternative Measures of Societal Modernity." *Sociology and Social Research* 59 (July 1975):301–317.

Sartori, Giovanni. *Democratic Theory.* Detroit, Michigan: Wayne State University Press, 1965.

———. "Democracy." *International Encyclopedia of the Social Sciences.* Vol. 4. New York: Macmillan and Free Press, 1968:112–121.

Scandizzo, Pasquale, and Odin K. Knudsen. "The Evaluation of the Benefits of Basic Needs Policies." *American Journal of Agricultural Economics* 62,1 (February 1980):46–57.

Schattschneider, E.E. *The Semi-Sovereign People.* Hindsdale, Illinois: Dryden Press, 1960.

Schatz, Sayre P. "Laissez-Faireism for Africa?" *Journal of Modern African Studies* 25 (March 1987):129–138.

Schick, Irvin Cemil, and Ertugrul Ahmet Tonak, eds. *Turkey in Transition.* New York: Oxford University Press, 1987.

Schmitter, Phillipe C. "Still the Century of Corporatism?" *Review of Politics* 36 (1974):85–131.

Schneider, Peter. "Social Rights and the Concept of Human Rights," in D.D. Raphael, ed., *Political Theory and the Rights of Man.* Bloomington: Indiana University Press, 1967:81–94.

Schumpeter, Joseph A. *Capitalism, Socialism, and Democracy.* New York: Harper and Brothers Publishers, 1950.

Seligson, Mitchell A. "Implementing Land Reform: The Case of Costa Rica." *Managing International Development* 1,2 (1984):29–46.

———. *Peasants of Costa Rica and the Development of Agrarian Capitalism.* Madison: University of Wisconsin Press, 1980.

———. "The Impact of Agrarian Reform: A Study of Costa Rica." *Journal of Developing Areas* 13 (January 1979):161–174.

Seligson, Mitchell A., and Miguel B. Gomez. "Ordinary Elections in Extraordinary Times: The Political Economy of Voting in Costa Rica," in John A. Booth and Mitchell A. Seligson, eds., *Elections and Democracy in Central America.* Chapel Hill: University of North Carolina Press, 1989:158–184.

Shah, Ghanshyam. "Grass-Roots Mobilization in Indian Politics," in Atul Kohli, ed.,

India's Democracy: An Analysis of Changing State-Society Relations. Princeton: Princeton University Press, 1988:262–304.

Shallat, Lezak. "Aid and the Secret Parallel State," in Marc Edelman and Joanne Kenen, eds., *The Costa Rica Reader.* New York: Grove Weidenfeld, 1989:221–227.

Shapiro, Ian, and Grant Reeher, eds. *Power, Inequality and Democratic Politics: Essays in Honor of Robert Dahl.* Boulder, Colorado: Westview Press, 1988.

Shepherd, George W., Jr., and Ved Nanda, eds. *Human Rights and Third World Development.* Westport, Connecticut: Greenwood Press, 1985.

Shue, Henry. *Basic Rights: Subsistence, Affluence, and U.S. Foreign Policy.* Princeton: Princeton University Press, 1980.

Sloan, John W. *Public Policy in Latin America: A Comparative Survey.* Pittsburgh: University of Pittsburgh Press, 1984.

Smith, Arthur K., Jr. "Socioeconomic Development and Political Democracy: A Causal Analysis." *Midwest Journal of Political Science* 13,1 (February, 1969):95–125.

Smith, Tony. "Requiem or New Agenda for Third World Studies?" *World Politics* 37,4 (July 1985):532–562.

Smith, William C. "Democracy, Distributional Conflicts and Macroeconomic Policymaking in Argentina, 1983–1989." *Journal of Inter-American Studies* 32,2 (Summer 1990):1–42.

Snyder, David, and Edward Kick. "Structural Position in the World System and Economic Growth, 1955–1970: Multiple-Network Analysis of Transnational Interactions." *American Journal of Sociology* 84 (1979):1096–1126.

Soubol, Albert. *The French Revolution 1789–1799.* New York: Vintage, 1975.*The Statesman's Year-Book.* New York: St. Martin's Press.

Stepan, Alfred. *The Military in Politics: Changing Patterns in Brazil.* Princeton: Princeton University Press, 1971.

Strom, Kaare. "Minority Governments in Parliamentary Democracies: The Rationality of Non-Winning Cabinet Solutions." *Comparative Politics* 17 (July 1984):199–226.

Sundrum, R.M. *Growth and Income Distribution in India: Policy and Performance Since Independence.* New Delhi: Sage Publications, 1987.

Sunkel, Osvaldo. "Transitional Capitalism and National Disintegration in Latin America." *Social and Economic Studies* 22,1 (1973):132–176.

Supple, Barry. "The State and Industrial Revolution, 1700–1914," in C.N. Cipolla, ed., *Industrial Revolution 1700–1914.* Bringhton: Harvester, 1976:301–357.

Swaison, Nicola. "The Rise of National Bourgeoisie in Kenya." *Review of African Political Economy* 8 (January–April 1977):39–55.

Tachau, Frank. *Turkey: The Politics of Authority, Democracy and Development.* New York: Praeger, 1984.

Tai, Hung-Chao. *Land Reform and Politics: Comparative Analysis.* Berkeley: University of California Press, 1974.

Taylor, Charles L., ed. *Indicator Systems for Political, Economic and Social Analysis.* Cambridge, Massachusetts: Oelgeshlanger, Gunn, and Hain Publishers, 1980:105–182.

Taylor, Charles L., and David A. Jodice. *World Handbook of Political and Social Indicators.* 3d ed. New Haven: Yale University Press, 1983.

Taylor, Charles L., and Michael C. Hudson. *World Handbook of Political and Social Indicators.* 2d ed. New Haven: Yale University Press, 1972.

Tekeli, Ilhan and Selim Ilkin. *Uygulmaya Geçerken Türkiye' de Devleçiligin Olusumu* [Formation of the concept of statism prior to Its implementation] Ankara, Turkey: Orta Dogu Teknik Üniversitesi, 1982.

Therborn, Goran. "The Rule of Capital and the Rise of Democracy." *New Left Review* 103 (May–June 1977):3–41.

Thiesenhusen, W.C. "Employment and Latin American Development," in P. Doner, ed., *Land Reform in Latin America: Issues and Cases.* Madison: University of Wisconsin Press, Land Economics Monographs 3, 1971:57–76.

Turkey: The Problems of Transition. A Euromoney Special Study. London: Euromoney Publications Limited, 1982.

Ullman, Richard H. "Human Rights and Economic Power: The United States Versus Idi Amin." *Foreign Affairs* (April 1978):529–543.

Ulusan, Aydín. "Public Policy Toward Agriculture and Its Redistributive Implications," in Ergun Özbudun and Aydín Ulusan, eds., *The Political Economy of Income Distribution in Turkey.* New York: Holmes and Meier, 1980:125–168.

United Nations. *Statistical Yearbook.* New York: United Nations.

Varas, Augusto, ed. *Democracy Under Siege: New Military Power in Latin America.* New York: Greenwood Press, 1989.

———. "Military Autonomy and Democracy in Latin America," in Augusto Varas, ed., *Democracy Under Siege: New Military Power in Latin America.* New York: Greenwood Press, 1989:1–16.

Vega, Mylena. "CODESA, Autonomous Institutions, and the Growth of the Public Sector," in Marc Edelman and Joanne Kenen, eds., *The Costa Rica Reader.* New York: Grove Weidenfeld, 1989:140–144.

Veliz, Claudio. *The Centralist Tradition of Latin America.* Princeton: Princeton University Press, 1980.

Wallerstein, Immanuel. *The Modern World System.* New York: Academic Press, 1974.

———."Semi-Peripheral Countries and the Contemporary World Crisis." *Theory and Society* 3,3 (Fall 1976):461–484.

Walton, John, and Charles Ragin. "Global and National Sources of Political Protest: Third World Responsiveness to the Debt Crisis." *American Sociological Review* 55,6 (December 1990):876–890.

Weede, Erich. "Beyond Misspecification in Sociological Analysis of Income Inequality." *American Sociological Review* 45 (June 1980):497–501.

———. "Political Democracy, State Strength and Economic Growth in LDCs: A Cross-National Analysis." Paper presented at the annual meeting of the American Political Science Association, September 1983.

Weede, Erich, and Horst Tiefenbach. "Some Recent Explanations of Income Inequality." *International Studies Quarterly* 25,2 (June 1981):255–282.

Weiner, Myron. "Empirical Democratic Theory and the Transition from Authoritarianism to Democracy." *PS* 20,4 (Fall 1987):861–866.

———. "Empirical Democratic Theory," in Myron Weiner and Ergun Özbudun, eds., *Competitive Elections in Developing Countries.* Durham, North Carolina: American Enterprise Institute for Public Policy Research; Duke University Press, 1987:3–34.

Weiner, Myron, and Ergun Özbudun, eds. *Competitive Elections in Developing Countries.* Durham, North Carolina: American Enterprise Institute for Public Policy Research; Duke University Press, 1987.

Wesson, Robert, ed. *Democracy: A World Survey.* New York: Praeger, 1987.

Wiarda, Howard J., ed. *Human Rights and U.S. Human Rights Policy.* Washington, D.C.: American Enterprise Institute for Public Policy Research, 1982.

———, ed. *The Continuing Struggle for Democracy in Latin America.* Boulder, Colorado: Westview Press, 1980.

Wiarda, Howard J., and Harvey F. Kline, eds. *Latin American Politics and Development.* Boston: Houghton Mifflin, 1979.

Wiatr, Jerzy J. "The Civic Culture from a Marxist Sociological Perspective," in

Gabriel Almond and Sidney Verba, eds., *The Civic Culture Revisited*. Boston: Little, Brown & Co., 1980:57–102.

Wilber, Charles K., ed. *The Political Economy of Development and Underdevelopment*. New York: Random House, 1973.

Wilkie, James W., and Stephen Haber, eds. *Statistical Abstract of Latin America*. Vol. 21. Los Angeles: UCLA Latin American Center Publications, 1981.

Wilkie, J.W., and K. Ruddle, eds. *Quantitative Latin American Studies: Methods and Findings*. Statistical Abstract of Latin America. Supplement 6. Los Angeles: UCLA, 1977.

Williamson, R.B., N.P. Glade, and K.M. Schmitt, eds. *Latin American-U.S. Economic Interactions*. Washington, D.C.: American Enterprise Institute for Public Policy Research, 1974.

Wood, Bryce. "Human Rights Issues in Latin America," in Jorge I. Dominguez, Nigel S. Rodley, Bryce Wood, and Richard Falk, eds., *Enhancing Global Human Rights*. New York: McGraw-Hill, 1979:155–204.

The World Bank. *World Development Report 1987*. New York: Oxford University Press, 1987.

World Tables. Washington, D.C.: World Bank.

Wright, Charles L. "Income Inequality and Economic Growth: Examining the Evidence." *Journal of Developing Areas* 13,1 (October 1978): 49-66.

Zolberg, Aristide R. "Origins of the Modern World System: A Missing Link." *World Politics* 33,2 (January 1981):253–281.

Index

About the Book
and the Author

The 1980s were exciting years, with a wave of democratization sweeping the globe. Similar transformations were evident in the early 1950s, when modernization theorists were optimistic about the future of democracy in newly emerging states, perceiving it as the form of government that would evolve ultimately from the process of economic development and modernization. These new democracies, however, failed to maintain stability and vacillated between democratic and authoritarian regimes. Through a synthesis of the theories of modernization, dependency, and bureaucratic authoritarianism, Professor Arat explains this instability in terms of the imbalance between two groups of human rights: civil-political and socioeconomic.

Arguing against those who believe that socioeconomic rights are group rights that can be maintained only at the expense of individual, civil-political rights, or vice versa—and that a trade-off between liberty and equality is inevitable—Arat demonstrates that the stability of democracy requires a balance between the two groups of human rights. A historical review, an empirical analysis of the annual scores of "democraticness" for more than 150 countries, and case studies of Costa Rica, India, and Turkey support her thesis that developing countries that recognize civil-political rights and establish democratic systems fail to maintain them if they neglect socioeconomic rights.

Zehra F. Arat is assistant professor of political science in the Division of Social Science at SUNY, Purchase.